Mastering Wireshark

Analyze data network like a professional by mastering Wireshark - From 0 to 1337

Charit Mishra

[PACKT] PUBLISHING | open source*
community experience distilled

BIRMINGHAM - MUMBAI

Mastering Wireshark

First published: March 2016

Production reference: 1210316

Published by Packt Publishing Ltd.
Livery Place
35 Livery Street
Birmingham B3 2PB, UK.

ISBN 978-1-78398-952-2

www.packtpub.com

Credits

Author
Charit Mishra

Copy Editor
Neha Vyas

Reviewer
Anish Nath

Project Coordinator
Bijal Patel

Commissioning Editor
Kunal Parikh

Proofreader
Safis Editing

Acquisition Editor
Kevin Colaco

Indexer
Rekha Nair

Content Development Editor
Onkar Wani

Production Coordinator
Manu Joseph

Technical Editor
Pranjali Mistry

Cover Work
Manu Joseph

About the Author

Charit Mishra works as a consultant and pentester at Protiviti, one of the top global consulting firms. He enjoys his job, which involves helping clients identify security vulnerabilities, more than anything. With real hands-on experience in security, he has obtained leading industry certifications such as OSCP, CEH, CompTIA Security+, and CCNA R&S. He also holds a master's degree in computer science. He has delivered professional talks at various institutions and private organizations on information security and penetration testing. You can reach him at LinkedIn at `https://ae.linkedin.com/in/charitmishra`, and on Twitter at `@charit0819`.

First of all, I would like to express my deepest gratitude to my beloved parents and my lovely sister, Ayushi, for their full support, expert guidance, understanding, and encouragement throughout my journey of making this possible. Without their incredible wisdom and counsel, this would have been an overwhelming pursuit.

I would like to also thank my good friend and mentor Mr. Piyush Verma for believing in me and guiding me whenever I needed direction. I am also thankful to all my friends and well wishers, especially Mr. Siddarth Pandey, Mr. Arham Husain, Mr. Bharath Methari, Mr. Dileep Mishra, and a great friend from Pakistan, Mr. Haider Ali Chughtai, who all helped me in every possible aspects and always motivated me to achieve the best. My apologies if I've missed anyone out.

Last but not least, I am grateful to the amazing team at Packt Publishing for their constant and incredible support for making this happen, and thanks to all the reviewers who helped bring this book into the best shape possible.

As the great influential Swami Vivekananda said, "In a day, when you don't come across any problems, you can be sure that you are traveling on the wrong path".

About the Reviewer

Anish Nath has a YouTube channel that you can visit at `http://youtube.com/zarigatongy`, where he loves to post videos on security, hacking, and other cloud-related technologies.

www.PacktPub.com

eBooks, discount offers, and more

Did you know that Packt offers eBook versions of every book published, with PDF and ePub files available? You can upgrade to the eBook version at www.PacktPub.com and as a print book customer, you are entitled to a discount on the eBook copy. Get in touch with us at customercare@packtpub.com for more details.

At www.PacktPub.com, you can also read a collection of free technical articles, sign up for a range of free newsletters and receive exclusive discounts and offers on Packt books and eBooks.

https://www2.packtpub.com/books/subscription/packtlib

Do you need instant solutions to your IT questions? PacktLib is Packt's online digital book library. Here, you can search, access, and read Packt's entire library of books.

Why subscribe?

- Fully searchable across every book published by Packt
- Copy and paste, print, and bookmark content
- On demand and accessible via a web browser

Table of Contents

Preface   **v**

**Chapter 1: Welcome to the World of Packet Analysis
with Wireshark**   **1**

  Introduction to Wireshark   **1**

  A brief overview of the TCP/IP model   **2**

  The layers in the TCP/IP model   **2**

  An introduction to packet analysis with Wireshark   **5**

    How to do packet analysis   7

    What is Wireshark?   7

    How it works   8

  Capturing methodologies   **10**

    Hub-based networks   10

    The switched environment   10

    ARP poisoning   12

    Passing through routers   14

    Why use Wireshark?   15

    The Wireshark GUI   16

      The installation process   16

    Starting our first capture   20

  Summary   **24**

  Practice questions   **25**

Chapter 2: Filtering Our Way in Wireshark   **27**

  An introduction to filters   **28**

  Capture filters   **28**

    Why use capture filters   33

    How to use capture filters   33

    An example capture filter   35

    Capture filters that use protocol header values   36

Display filters	**38**
Retaining filters for later use	41
Searching for packets using the Find dialog	**42**
Colorize traffic	44
Create new Wireshark profiles	**48**
Summary	**50**
Practice questions	**50**
Chapter 3: Mastering the Advanced Features of Wireshark	**53**
The Statistics menu	54
Using the Statistics menu	54
Protocol Hierarchy	57
Conversations	58
Endpoints	60
Working with IO, Flow, and TCP stream graphs	63
IO graphs	64
Flow graphs	66
TCP stream graphs	68
Round-trip time graphs	68
Throughput graphs	69
The Time-sequence graph (tcptrace)	70
Follow TCP streams	72
Expert Infos	74
Command Line-fu	80
Summary	87
Exercise	88
Chapter 4: Inspecting Application Layer Protocols	**91**
Domain name system	**92**
Dissecting a DNS packet	92
Dissecting DNS query/response	94
Unusual DNS traffic	96
File transfer protocol	**97**
Dissecting FTP communications	98
Passive mode	98
Active mode	99
Dissecting FTP packets	100
Unusual FTP	103
Hyper Text Transfer Protocol	**104**
How it works – request/response	105
Request	105
Response	108
Unusual HTTP traffic	109

Simple Mail Transfer Protocol	**112**
Usual versus unusual SMTP traffic	112
Session Initiation Protocol and Voice Over Internet Protocol	116
Analyzing VOIP traffic	118
Reassembling packets for playback	120
Unusual traffic patterns	121
Decrypting encrypted traffic (SSL/TLS)	122
Summary	**124**
Practice questions	**124**
Chapter 5: Analyzing Transport Layer Protocols	**127**
The transmission control protocol	**128**
Understanding the TCP header and its various flags	128
How TCP communicates	130
How it works	131
Graceful termination	133
RST (reset) packets	134
Relative verses Absolute numbers	135
Unusual TCP traffic	140
How to check for different analysis flags in Wireshark	142
The User Datagram Protocol	**143**
A UDP header	144
How it works	144
The DHCP	145
The TFTP	146
Unusual UDP traffic	148
Summary	**150**
Practice questions	**151**
Chapter 6: Analyzing Traffic in Thin Air	**153**
Understanding IEEE 802.11	**154**
Various modes in wireless communications	155
Wireless interference and strength	158
The IEEE 802.11 packet structure	161
RTS/CTS	166
Usual and unusual WEP – open/shared key communication	**167**
WEP-open key	169
The shared key	170
WPA-Personal	172
WPA-Enterprise	177
Decrypting WEP and WPA traffic	**179**
Summary	**182**
Practice questions	**183**

Chapter 7: Network Security Analysis — 187
Information gathering — 188
PING sweep — 189
Half-open scan (SYN) — 190
OS fingerprinting — 192
ARP poisoning — 194
Analyzing brute force attacks — 199
Inspecting malicious traffic — 208
Solving real-world CTF challenges — 216
Summary — 228
Practice questions — 229

Chapter 8: Troubleshooting — 231
Recovery features — 232
The flow control mechanism — 236
Troubleshooting slow Internet and network latencies — 239
Client- and server-side latencies — 243
Troubleshooting bottleneck issues — 250
Troubleshooting application-based issues — 253
Summary — 260
Practice questions — 260

Chapter 9: Introduction to Wireshark v2 — 263
The intelligent scroll bar — 268
Translation — 270
Graph improvements — 272
TCP streams — 279
USBPcap — 282
Summary — 285
Practice questions — 285

Index — 287

Preface

Almost every device around you is connected to some other device over a network with the motive of sharing information or supporting other devices. With this small picture in your mind, what do you think is the most critical part of a network? Obviously, the channel isn't.

This book is written from a standpoint of using Wireshark to understand and troubleshoot commonly seen network anomalies. It can be the start of your journey into the world of networks/traffic/packet analysis. You can be the savior of your generation or the superhero of your team who helps people with connectivity issues, network administration, computer forensics, and so on. If your routine job requires dealing with computer networks, then this book can give you a strong head start. As the tagline says "From 0 to 1337",that is we will start from the basics gradually moving on to the advanced concepts too.

I have tried to cover the most common scenarios that you could come across while troubleshooting, along with hands-on practical cases that can make you understand the concepts better. By mastering packet analysis, you will learn how to troubleshoot all the way down to the bare wires. This will teach you to make sense of the data flowing around. You will find very interesting sections, such as troubleshooting slow networks, analyzing packets over Wi-Fi, malware analysis, and not to forget, the latest features introduced in Wireshark 2.0 in this book. Happy troubleshooting!

What this book covers

Chapter 1, *Welcome to the World of Packet Analysis with Wireshark*, provides you an introduction to the basics of the TCP/IP model and familiarizes you with the GUI of Wireshark along with a sample packet capture. Here, you will learn how to set up network sniffers for analysis purpose.

Chapter 2, *Filtering Our Way in Wireshark*, talks about different filtering options available in Wireshark, namely capture and display filters, and how to create and use different profiles. Make yourself comfortable with the rich interface of Wireshark and start capturing what you exactly want to.

Chapter 3, *Mastering the Advanced Features in Wireshark*, helps you look under the hood of the statistics menu in Wireshark and work with the different command-line utilities that come prepackaged with Wireshark. You will also learn how to prepare graphs, charts, packet flow diagrams, and most important of all, how to become a command-line fu master.

Chapter 4, *Inspecting Application Layer Protocols*, helps you understand and analyze the normal and unusual behavior of application-layer protocols. Here, we will briefly discuss the techniques you can use to understand the cause. We all are aware of the basics, but have you ever thought how common application-layer protocol traffic can go crazy? In this chapter, you will learn how to deal with them.

Chapter 5, *Analyzing Transport Layer Protocols*, shows how TCP and UDP protocols work, how they communicate, what problems they face, and how Wireshark can be used to analyze them. Make yourself a transport-layer doctor who can easily figure out common anomalies and prove themselves worthy.

Chapter 6, *Analyzing Traffic in Thin Air*, shows you how to analyze wireless traffic and pinpoint any problems that may follow. We will dive into the new world of wireless protocol analysis, where you can become a Wi-Fi ninja.

Chapter 7, *Network Security Analysis*, shows you how to use Wireshark to analyze network security issues, such as malware traffic, intrusion, and footprinting attempts. In this chapter, you will learn how to figure out security anomalies, catch the hackers red handed and make them cry like a baby, and experience how to solve CTF challenges.

Chapter 8, *Troubleshooting*, teaches you how to configure and use Wireshark to perform network troubleshooting. Here, you will master the art of troubleshooting network issues such as slow networks. You will also learn how to troubleshoot networking problems with the most common daily-life examples.

Chapter 9, *Introduction to Wireshark v2*, shows you the amazing features launched in the latest release of Wireshark with practical examples, such as USBpcap, intelligent scrollbar, new graphs, and much more.

What you need for this book

You just need a working installation of Wireshark and a basic understanding of networking protocols. Basic familiarity with network protocols would be beneficial, but it isn't mandatory.

Who this book is for

Are you curious to know what's going on in a network? Do you get frustrated when you are unable to detect the cause of problems in your networks? If your answer to these questions is yes, then this book is for you.

Mastering Wireshark is for Security and network enthusiasts who are interested in understanding the internal workings of networks and have prior knowledge of using Wireshark, but are not aware about all of its functionalities.

Conventions

In this book, you will find a number of text styles that distinguish between different kinds of information. Here are some examples of these styles and an explanation of their meaning.

Code words in text, database table names, folder names, filenames, file extensions, pathnames, dummy URLs, user input, and Twitter handles are shown as follows: "Wireshark with an empty checksum field that generates the `checksum offloading` error."

New terms and **important words** are shown in bold. Words that you see on the screen, for example, in menus or dialog boxes, appear in the text like this: "Navigate to **Edit** | **Preferences** in the menu bar."

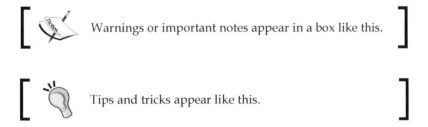

Warnings or important notes appear in a box like this.

Tips and tricks appear like this.

Reader feedback

Feedback from our readers is always welcome. Let us know what you think about this book—what you liked or disliked. Reader feedback is important for us as it helps us develop titles that you will really get the most out of.

To send us general feedback, simply e-mail `feedback@packtpub.com`, and mention the book's title in the subject of your message.

If there is a topic that you have expertise in and you are interested in either writing or contributing to a book, see our author guide at `www.packtpub.com/authors`.

Customer support

Now that you are the proud owner of a Packt book, we have a number of things to help you to get the most from your purchase.

Downloading the color images of this book

We also provide you with a PDF file that has color images of the screenshots/diagrams used in this book. The color images will help you better understand the changes in the output. You can download this file from `https://www.packtpub.com/sites/default/files/downloads/MasteringWireshark_ColoredImages.pdf`.

Errata

Although we have taken every care to ensure the accuracy of our content, mistakes do happen. If you find a mistake in one of our books—maybe a mistake in the text or the code—we would be grateful if you could report this to us. By doing so, you can save other readers from frustration and help us improve subsequent versions of this book. If you find any errata, please report them by visiting `http://www.packtpub.com/submit-errata`, selecting your book, clicking on the **Errata Submission Form** link, and entering the details of your errata. Once your errata are verified, your submission will be accepted and the errata will be uploaded to our website or added to any list of existing errata under the Errata section of that title.

To view the previously submitted errata, go to `https://www.packtpub.com/books/content/support` and enter the name of the book in the search field. The required information will appear under the **Errata** section.

Piracy

Piracy of copyrighted material on the Internet is an ongoing problem across all media. At Packt, we take the protection of our copyright and licenses very seriously. If you come across any illegal copies of our works in any form on the Internet, please provide us with the location address or website name immediately so that we can pursue a remedy.

Please contact us at copyright@packtpub.com with a link to the suspected pirated material.

We appreciate your help in protecting our authors and our ability to bring you valuable content.

Questions

If you have a problem with any aspect of this book, you can contact us at questions@packtpub.com, and we will do our best to address the problem.

1

Welcome to the World of Packet Analysis with Wireshark

This chapter provides you an introduction to the basics of the TCP/IP model and familiarizes you with the GUI of Wireshark along with a sample packet capture. You will be introduced to the following topics:

- What is Wireshark?
- How does it work?
- A brief overview of the TCP/IP model
- An introduction to packet analysis
- Why use Wireshark?
- Understanding the GUI of Wireshark
- The first packet capture

Introduction to Wireshark

Wireshark is one of the most advanced packet capturing software, which makes the life of system/network administrators easy and proves its usefulness among the groups of security evangelists. Wireshark is also called a protocol analyzer, which helps IT professionals in debugging network-level problems. This tool can be of great use to optimize network performance.

Wireshark runs around dissecting network-level packets and showing packet details to concerned users as per their requirement. If you are one of those who deals with packet-level networking everyday, then Wireshark is for you and can be used for multiple troubleshooting purposes.

A brief overview of the TCP/IP model

Next, it's time to discuss the most important topic in the world of networking. In order to understand how all these things stick together, we need to understand the basics of the TCP/IP model. Even the world of computers needs a set of rules and regulations to communicate, and this is taken care by the networking protocols, which govern the transmission of packets/segments/frames over a dedicated channel between hosts.

The TCP/IP model was originally known as the DoD model, and the project was regulated by United States Department of Defense. The TCP/IP model takes care of every aspect of every packet's life cycle, namely, how a packet is generated, how a single packet gets attached with a required set of information (PDU), how a packet is transmitted, how it comes to life, how it is routed through to intermediary nodes to the destination, how it is integrated back with other packets to get the whole information out, and so on.

If you have any confusion regarding the basics of networking protocols, I would recommend that you do a quick revision before proceeding ahead, as this book requires familiarity with the TCP/UDP protocols. By the time you come back, you will be able to visualize and answer all of these questions on your own.

The layers in the TCP/IP model

The TCP/IP model comprises four layers, as shown in the following diagram. Each layer uses a different set of protocols allocated to it. Every protocol has specific designated roles, and all of them are designed in such a way that they comply with industry standards.

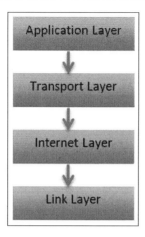

The first layer is the **Application Layer** that directly interacts with users and other network-level protocols; it is primarily concerned with the representation of the data in an understandable format to the user. The Application layer also keeps track of user web sessions, which users are connected, and uses a set of protocols, which helps the application layer interface to the other layers in the TCP/IP model. Some popular protocols that we will cover in this book are as follows:

- **The Hyper Text Transfer Protocol (HTTP)**
- **The File Transfer Protocol (FTP)**
- **The Simple Network Management Protocol (SNMP)**
- **The Simple Mail Transfer Protocol (SMTP)**

The second layer is the **Transport Layer**. The sole purpose of this layer is to create sockets over which the two hosts can communicate (you might already know about the importance of network sockets) which is essential to create an individual connection between two devices.

There can be more than one connection between two hosts at the same instance. IP addresses and port numbers together make this possible. An IP address is required when we talk about WAN-based communication (in LAN-based communication, the actual data transfer happens over MAC addresses), and these days, a single system can communicate with more than one device over multiple channels which is possible with the help of port numbers. Apart from the restricted range of port numbers, every system is free to designate a random port for their communication.

This layer also serves as a backbone to the communication between two hosts. The most common protocols that work in this layer are TCP and UDP, which are explained as follows:

- **TCP**: This is a connection-oriented protocol, often called a reliable protocol. Here, firstly, a dedicated channel is created between two hosts and then data is transferred. Then, the sender sends equally partitioned chunks, over the dedicated channel, and then, the receiver sends the acknowledgement for every chunk received. Most commonly, the sender waits for a particular time after which it sends the same chunk again for assurance. For example, if you are downloading something, TCP is the one that takes care and makes sure that every bit is transferred successfully.

- **UDP**: This is a connection-less protocol and is often termed an unreliable form of communication. It is simple though because there is no dedicated channel created, and the sender is just concerned with sending chunks of data to the destination, whether it is received or not. This form of communication actually does not hamper the communication quality; the sole purpose of transferring the bits from a sender to receiver is fulfilled. For example, if you are playing a LAN-based game, the loss of a few bytes is not going to disrupt your gaming experience, and as a result, the user experience is not harmed.

The third layer is the **Internet Layer**, which is concerned with the back and forth movement of data. The primary protocol that works is the **IP** (**Internet Protocol**) protocol, and it is the most important protocol of this layer. The IP provides the routing functionality due to which a certain packet can get to it's destination. Other protocols included in this layer are ICMP and IGMP.

The last layer is the **Link Layer** (often termed as the Network Interface Layer) that is close to the network hardware. There are no protocols specified in this layer by TCP/IP; however, several protocols are implemented, such as **Address Resolution Protocol** (**ARP**) and **Point to Point** (**PPP**). This layer is concerned with how a bit of information travels inside the real wires. It establishes and terminates the connection and also converts signals from analog to digital and vice versa. Devices such as bridges and switches operate in this layer.

The combination of an IP address and a MAC address for both the client and server is the core of the communication process, where the IP address is assigned to the device by the gateway or assigned statically, and the MAC address comes from the **Network Interface Card** (**NIC**), which should be present in every device that communicates with other hosts. As data progresses from the Application layer to the Link Layer, several bits of information are attached to the data bits in the form of headers or footers, which allow different layers of the TCP/IP model to coordinate with each other. The process of adding these extra bits is called data encapsulation, and in this process, a **Protocol data unit** (**PDU**) is created at the end of the networking model.

It consists of the information being sent along with the different protocol information that gets attached as part of the header or footer. By the time PDU reaches the bottom-most layer, it is embedded with all the required information required for the real transfer. Once it reaches the destination, the embedded header and footer PDU elements are ripped off one by one as it passes through each and every layer of the TCP/IP model as it progresses upward in the model.

The following figure depicts the process of encapsulation:

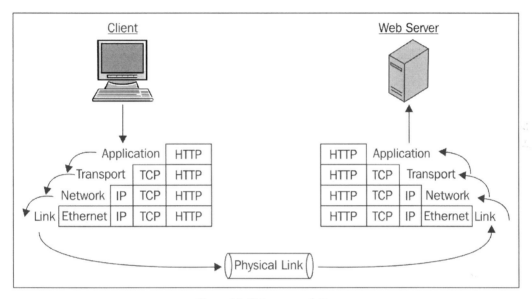

Figure 1.1: Data encapsulation

An introduction to packet analysis with Wireshark

Packet analysis (also known as packet sniffing or protocol analyzing) is used to intercept and capture live data as it travels over the network (Ethernet or Wi-Fi) in order to understand what is happening in the network. Packet analysis is done by protocol analyzers such as Wireshark available on the Internet. Some of these are free and some are paid for commercial use. In this book, we will use Wireshark to perform network analysis, which is an open source software and the best free-network analyzer available on the Internet.

Numerous problems can happen in today's world of networking; for this, we need to be geared up all the time with the latest set of tools that can avail us of the ease of troubleshooting in any situation. Each of these problems will start from the packet level and can gradually grow up to a high network downtime. Even the best of protocols and services running on a system can go bad and behave maliciously. To get to the root of the problem, we need to look into the packet level to understand it better. If you need to maintain your network, then you definitely need to look into the packet level. Packet analysis can be used for the following aspects:

- To analyze network problems by looking into the packets and their specific details so that you can get a better hold over your network.

- To detect network intrusion attempts and whether there are any malicious users who are trying to get into your network, or they have already got access to something in your network.

- To detect network misuse by internal or external users by establishing firewall rules in your security appliance and then monitoring each of these rules through Wireshark.

- To isolate exploited systems so that the affected system doesn't become a pivot point for your network for malicious users.

- To monitor data in motion once it travels live in your network to have better control over the allowed and restricted categories of data. For instance, say you want to create a rule for your firewall that will block the access to Bit Torrent sites. Blocking access to them can be done from your manageable router, but knowing from where the request was originated can be easily audited through Wireshark.

- To gather and report network statistics by filtering the most specific packets as per your requirements and then creating specific capture filters for your perusal that can help you in the long run.

- Learning who is on the network and what they are doing, is there something they are not allowed to do, and is there anyone who is trying to bypass the network restrictions. All of these simple day-to-day tasks can be achieved easily through Wireshark.

- To debug client/server communications so that all the request and replies communicated between the peers on our network can be audited to maintain the integrity of your network.

- To look for applications that are sitting in the corner of your own network and eating the bandwidth. They might be making your network insecure or making it visible to the public network. Through this unnoticed application, different forms of network traffic can enter without any restrictions.

- To debug network protocol implementations and any kind of anomalies present due to various misconfigurations in the current running devices.

To identify possible or malicious attacks that your network can be a victim of, to analyze them, control/supervise them, and make yourself ready for any possible malicious activity.

When performing a packet analysis, you should take care of things such as which protocols can be interpreted, which is the best software you can use according to your expertise, which protocol analyzer will best suit your network requirement. Experience does count in this field; once you start working with Wireshark, gradually you will come up with new ideas to troubleshoot and analyze your packets in a much more advanced way.

Packet sniffers can interpret common network protocols (such as IP and ICMP), transport layers (such as TCP and UDP), and application protocols (such as DNS and HTTP).

Due to the overwhelming amount of information presented by Wireshark's GUI, it might seem complex to some users and might be considered as one of its demerits. There are a few CUI/GUI tools that can solve this purpose. They are pretty simple to use and also present a simpler interface, for example, TShark, tcpdump, Fiddler, and so on.

How to do packet analysis

When traffic is captured, either all raw data is captured or only the header data is captured without capturing the total content of the packet. Captured information is decoded from raw data to a human-readable form, which allows users to understand the exchanged data between the networks in a much more precise manner.

What is Wireshark?

Wireshark is a packet-sniffing software that is used by IT professionals all around the world for analysis purpose. You can download it for free from `https://www.wireshark.org/download.html`.

Wireshark can be installed on a variety of platforms, including Linux, MAC, and Windows (most of the versions). This is open source software, which means that the code of the software and its required libraries can be downloaded from the same website we mentioned earlier.

One of the important key aspects of packet sniffing is where to place the packet sniffer in the physical network to achieve the maximum utilization out of it; packet sniffing is often referred to as tapping into the wire.

Tapping into the wire is not just about starting Wireshark on your system; there are a couple of things a person should know about before starting the sniffer. For instance, placing the sniffer at a proper place in the organization's infrastructure, having working knowledge of different networking devices because each of the networking devices (hubs, switches, routers, and firewalls) behave differently. It is also important to know how each of them work and how network devices handle network traffic. Placing the sniffer in the right place can impact your packet analyzing experience in a detailed manner, which in the end can lead to drastic results if done correctly.

After you have placed your sniffer, you should confirm that your NIC supports promiscuous working. By enabling this, your interface card will start learning about even those packets that are not destined or routed through your machine. A network's broadcasted traffic can be captured and analyzed by every client, which is part of the same network. Network devices broadcast multiple types of traffic that can be listened to by an interface, which supports the promiscuous mode.

The ARP protocol's traffic is broadcasted. The address resolution protocol is responsible for resolving MAC to IP addresses and vice versa. Devices such as switches send an ARP packet to all devices asking for the correct device to respond with it's MAC address. Gradually, the switch will maintain a list of MAC addresses and their corresponding IP addresses, which is even termed as the CAM table (content addressable memory). Now, whenever any host wants to communicate with its other corresponding peers over the LAN, information required for the transfer is communicated to the sender from the switch. Information such as IP and MAC addresses for different devices can be easily captured and recorded through ARP traffic.

How it works

Wireshark comes with the libcap/Winpcap driver, which lets you switch your NIC to the promiscuous mode; the only time you don't want to sniff in the promiscuous mode is when the packets are directly, intentionally destined to your device. On a Windows-based system, you should have elevated administrator privileges to sniff and analyze the packets. There are three common step processes that every protocol analyzer follows: collect, convert, and analyze. These are described as follows:

- **Collect**: This is the first step where you choose a certain interface to listen on, and through this, you can acquire a certain amount of raw data from the network, which can be achieved by switching your interface into a promiscuous mode so that, after capturing what ever traffic is being broadcasted in your network, it can be displayed in your Wireshark GUI.

- **Convert**: This is to increase the readability of the collected binary form. Network packets can be converted by the protocol analyzer, such as Wireshark, to simple and easier formats so that people like us can have a better understanding of packets and solve our day-to-day problems easily.

- **Analyze**: In this final step, after the collection and conversion of the network packets, a step-by-step process of analyzing the data starts where we look into the specific details about the protocols and their specific configuration details. Then, we move on to host and destination addresses and the kind of information they are sharing. Rest of the analysis is left to the user's consent and how they filter and review the collected data.

If you want to get a foothold on understanding the process of packet capturing and analysis, you really need to be well versed with networking protocols and how they work because the whole communication that happens over a network is governed by various protocols, such as ARP, **Dynamic Host Control Protocol (DHCP)**, **Domain Name Service (DNS)**, **Transmission Control Protocol (TCP)**, **Internet Protocol (IP)**, HTTP, and many others.

Protocols are the rules and regulations that govern the process of communication between two network devices and control the environment under which they operate. Each of these protocols has different complexity levels depending on how and where they are being implemented. Majorly, all protocols work in the same fashion, where they send a request and wait for the confirmation, and as they receive an acknowledgement, they let the devices communicate.

After the data has been successfully transferred between them, the connections should be terminated gracefully in order to mark a communication as successful without loss of even a single bit. While the data is transferred, protocols need to maintain the integrity of the communication as well, that is, if abc information is sent from the sender's side, it should be received in the same order and manner. If the bits are being tampered during the transition, this means that the protocol used isn't reliable. Analyzing all of these tasks is the basic work responsibility of any network protocol analyzer.

Capturing methodologies

Network packets can be captured through various techniques. Depending on the requirement, a protocol analyzer is placed at a certain place in network with a particular type of configuration.

Hub-based networks

Hub-based networks are the easiest ones to sniff out because you've the freedom to place the sniffer at any place you want, as hubs broadcast each and every packet to the entire network they are a part of. So, we don't have to worry about the placement. However, hubs have one weakness that can drastically decrease network performance due to the collision of packets. Because hubs do not have any priority-based system for device that send packets, whoever wants to send them can just initiate the connection with the **HUB** (central device) and start transmitting the packets. Often, more than one devices start sending packets at the same instance. Now, as a result, the collision of the packets will happen, and the sending side will be informed to resend the previous packet. As a consequence, things such as traffic congestion and improper bandwidth utilization can be experienced.

The switched environment

Due to some restrictions present in switched-based infrastructures, packet analysis becomes a bit complex. To bypass these restrictions and make the life of administrators easy, we will talk about a couple of solutions such as port mirroring and hubbing out.

In **port mirroring**, once you have the command-line configuration console or web-based interface to mage you're the access point (router/switch), then we can easily configure port mirroring.

Let's make it simpler for you with a logical illustration. For instance, let's assume that we have a 24-ports switch and 8 PCs which (PC-1 to PC-8) are connected. We are still left with more than 15 ports. Place your sniffer in any of those free ports and then configure port mirroring, which will copy all the traffic from whatever device we want to the port of our choice, where our protocol analyzer sits, which can see the whole bunch of data traveling through the mirrored port.

Once this is completely configured, we will be able to easily analyze each and every piece of information going back and forth from the mirrored port. This technique is one of the easiest among others to configure; the only thing you should know beforehand is how to configure switches with command-line interfaces. These days, admins are provided with a GUI for configuration purposes if it is the case for you to just go for it. The following figure depicts a simple demonstration of port mirroring:

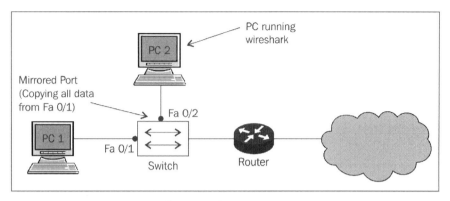

Figure 1.2: Port mirroring

Hubbing out is feasible when your switch doesn't support port mirroring. To use the technique, you have to actually plug the target PC out of the switched network, then plug your hub to the switch, and then connect you analyzer and target device to the switch so that becomes the part of the same network.

Now, the protocol analyzer and the target are part of the same broadcast domain. Your analyzer will easily capture every packet destined to target or originated from the target. But make sure that the target is aware about the data loss that can happen while you try to create hubbing out for analysis. The following figure will make it easier for us to understand the concept precisely:

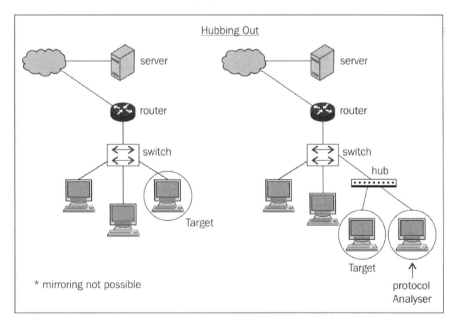

Figure 1.3: Hubbing out

ARP poisoning

This is an unethical way to capture network traffic where we try to imitate another device between two parties. Let's say, for example, we have our default gateway at `192.168.1.1` and our client is located at `192.168.1.2`. Both of these devices must have maintained a local ARP cache that facilitates them to send packets without any extra overhead over the LAN. Now, the question is what kind information does the ARP cache hold, and in which form. Let me tell you, the command to view the ARP cache, which displays MAC addresses associated for a particular IP address is `arp -a`. Issuing the `arp -a` command (the same works for most of the platforms) populates a table that holds a device's IP address and its MAC address. Have a look at the following diagram which shows a normal scenario of ARP poisoning:

```
Before ARP Cache


192.68.1.1 - (Server)
192.68.1.2 - AA:BB:EE
192.68.1.3 - AA:BB:DD


192.68.1.2 - (Client)
192.68.1.1 - AA:BB:CC
192.68.1.3 - AA:BB:DD


192.68.1.3 - (Attacker)
192.68.1.1 - AA:BB:CC
192.68.1.2 - AA:BB:EE
```

Now that we've understood what is stored inside an ARP cache, let's try to poison it.

```
After ARP Cache


192.68.1.1 - (Server)
192.68.1.2 - AA:BB:DD
192.68.1.3 - AA:BB:DD


192.68.1.2 - (Client)
192.68.1.1 - AA:BB:DD
192.68.1.3 - AA:BB:DD
```

```
192.68.1.3 - (Attacker)
192.68.1.1 - AA:BB:CC
192.68.1.2 - AA:BB:EE
```

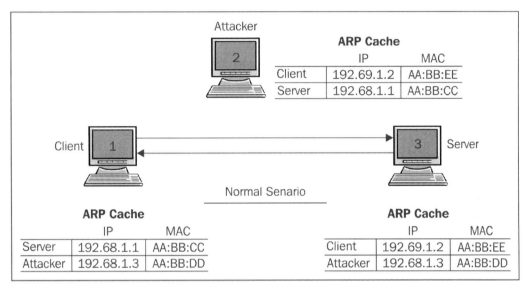

Figure 1.4: ARP poisoning (the normal scenario)

Now that you've understood what is the importance of the ARP protocol and how it works, we can try to poison the `arp` cache of both the default gateway and the client with the attacker's MAC address. In simple terms, we will replace the client's MAC address in the default gateway's ARP cache with the attacker's MAC address. We will do the same in the client's MAC address, replacing the default gateway's MAC address with the attacker's MAC address. As a result, every packet destined to the client from the default gateway and vice versa will be sent to the attacker's machine.

If port forwarding is already configured on the attacker's side, the received packet will be forwarded to the real intended destination, without giving any hints to the client and the default gateway that the packet is being sniffed.

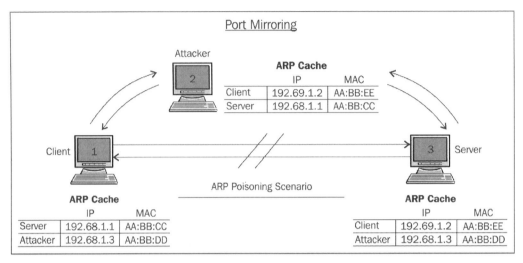

Figure 1.5: ARP poisoning (the poisoned scenario)

Other than these two techniques, there is a variety of hardware available on the market, which are popularly known as taps and can be placed between any two devices to sniff and analyze the traffic. Though this technique is effective to capture network traffic in some scenarios, it should be practised or deployed in a controlled environment because it can prove to be malicious to the internal corporate network.

Passing through routers

When dealing with routed environments, the main aspect of packet analyses is to place your sniffer at the right place from where we can gather the required information. Dealing with routed structures demands more skills, as sometimes you need to rethink about the placement of your sniffer. Consider a routed environment with three routers:

Router 1, router 2, and router 3 are working together; each of them owns 2-3 PCs. Router 1 is the acting like a root node while controlling its child networked nodes (router 2 and router 3). Router 3 clients are not able to connect to router 1 clients. To resolve this issue, the admin of the organization has placed the sniffer inside the router 3 area.

After a while, the admin has collected quite a good amount of packets; the admin is still not able to detect the anomaly within the network. So, he/she decides to move the sniffer to another area in the network. After placing the sniffer in the router 1 area, the admin can see quite a useful stream of packets that he/she was looking for earlier. This is quite a simple illustration of moving the sniffer around, which can be helpful in certain situations. The moral is that placing the sniffer in your networked infrastructure is quite an important task.

After reading this, I hope you would now like to see how Wireshark actually looks like, so let's take a look at the GUI of the software and how we have to initialize the process of capturing network packets.

If you do not have Wireshark installed, you can get a free copy from `https://www.wireshark.org/download.html`. To go through the illustrations in this book, you also need to be familiar with the interface.

Why use Wireshark?

I hope I am not the only one who is obsessed with the simplicity of the packet capturing scenario, which Wireshark facilitates for us. I will just quickly point out the reasons why most people prefer Wireshark to other packet sniffers:

- **User friendly**: It does count for every GUI we have ever seen or worked with, how easily the options are presented, and how convenient it is to use (I guess, even the ones who don't know about packet analysis can start capturing packets in Wireshark without any prior specialized knowledge).

- **Robustness**: The amount of information Wireshark can handle is outstanding; what I actually mean by this is software of this kind may hang or crash (because of thousands of packets that are captured and displayed every second) when trying to display the packets traveling all over the network. However, Wireshark doesn't—a big hand to Wireshark creators for how well they have structured it.

- **Platform independent**: Yeah, this one is definitely on the list. This free software can be installed on any platform that is used for computing purposes by administrators these days, whether Linux-based, Windows-based, or Macintosh-based platforms.

- **Filters**: There are two kinds of filtering options present in Wireshark:
    - You choose what to capture (capture filters)
    - You choose what to display after you've captured (display filters)

- **Cost**: Wireshark comes free, and is developed and maintained by a dedicated community. Wireshark offers some paid professional tools also. For more details refer to Wireshark's official website.

- **Support**: Wireshark is being developed very actively by a group of contributors scattered around the globe . We can sign up to the Wireshark's mailing list or we can get help from the online documentations, which can be accessed through the GUI itself; and various online forums are available to get the most effective; go to Google *paid Wireshark support* to know more about it.

The Wireshark GUI

Before we discuss its awesome features, let me take this opportunity to explain the history of Wireshark and how it came into existence.

Wireshark was built during the late '90s. Combs, a young college graduate from Kansas city developed Ethereal (the basic version of Wireshark), and by the time Combs developed this awesome piece of invention, he had landed himself a job where he signed a formal contract. After a few years of service, Combs decided to quit his job and to pursue his dreams by developing Ethereal further. Unfortunately, as per the legal terms, the Combs invention was part of the company's proprietary software. Despite this, Combs left the job and started working on the new version of Ethereal, which he titled Wireshark. Since 2006, Wireshark has been in active development and is being used worldwide. It supports a majority of protocols (more than 800), which are implemented in the wild today.

The installation process

Follow these steps to install Wireshark on your system:

1. In this book, I am going to you use a Mac PC; for other platforms, the installation is the same. Some OSes, such as Kali Linux, come with a preinstalled version of Wireshark.

2. So, if you are using Macintosh, then first and foremost, you need to download X11 Quartz (XQuartz-2.7.7), which will simulate an environment to run Wireshark (for Windows just download the respective executable compatible with your processor).

3. Now, you can install Wireshark (Wireshark 1.12.6 Intel 64), which we downloaded earlier in this book.

4. Once both of these are successfully installed, we need to restart our computer.

5. After the PC has been restarted, start Wireshark. As soon as the packet analyzer opens, you will see that the X11 server starts on its own. You don't need to worry about it; just leave it in the background.

6. Once it is opened completely, it will look as shown in the following screenshot:

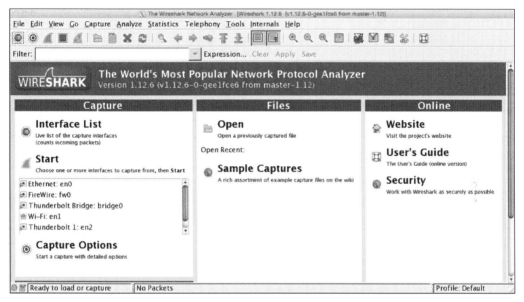

Figure 1.6: The Wireshark screen

Before we go ahead and start the first capture, we need to get a bit familiar with the options and menus available.

There are six main parts in the Wireshark GUI, which are explained as follows:

- **Menu Bar**: This represents tools in a generalized form that are organized in the **Applications** menu.

- **Main Tool Bar**: This consists of the frequently used tools that can offer efficient utilization of the software.

- **Packet List Pane**: This window area displays all the various packets getting captured by Wireshark.

- **Packet Details Pane**: This window gives us details pertaining to the selected packet in the packet list pane are shown. For example, we can view source and destination IP addresses and different protocols used for communication arranged in the bottom-top approach (Link Layer to Application Layer). Information regarding the packets is listed in different categories of protocols that can be expanded to get more details for the selected packet.

- **Bytes Pane**: This shows the data in the packets in the form of hex bytes and their corresponding ASCII values; it shows the values in the form in which they travel in the wires.

- **Status Bar**: This displays details such as total packets captured.

The following screenshot will help you to identify different sections in the application, please make sure you get yourself acquainted with all of them before proceeding to further chapters.

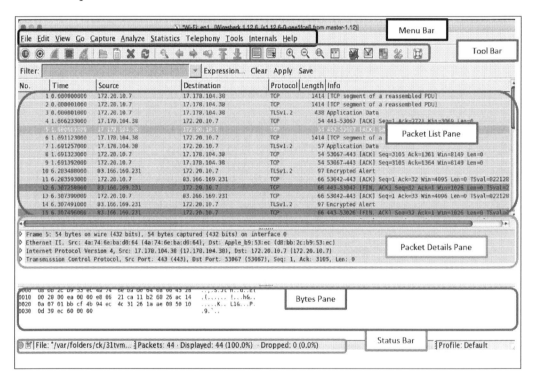

Within the toolbar area, we have a few useful tools. I would like to give you a brief overview of some of them:

- : This gives you the option to choose an interface for listening

- : Through this, you can customize the capturing process

- : These are to start/stop/restart the capturing process

- : This is to open a saved capture file

- :This is to save the current capture in a file

- : This is to reload the current capture file

- : This is to close the current capture file

- : This is to go back to the recent most visited packet

- : This icon is to go forward to the most recently visited packet

- : This is used to go to a specific packet number

- : Toggle Color coding for the packets On/Off

- : This is used to toggle the autoscroll on/off

- : This is to zoom in, zoom out, and reset zoom to the default

- : This is used to change the color coding as per requirements

- : This is used to narrow down the window in order to capture packets

- : This is used to configure display filters to only see what is required

Even after selecting a working interface, sometimes, you won't be able to see any packets in your packet list pane. There can be multiple reasons for this, some of which are listed as follows:

- You do not have any network traffic
- The packets traveling in the network are not destined to your device
- You do not have the promiscuous mode activated or do not have an option for the promiscuous mode

After launching the Wireshark application, you will see something like the following screenshot on our screens. Although it doesn't look so interesting at first glance, what makes it interesting are the packets that are flowing around. Yeah, I am talking about capturing packets.

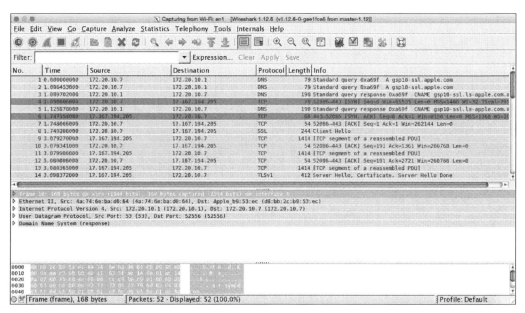

Figure 1.7: The Wireshark capture screen

Starting our first capture

As you've been introduced to the basics of Wireshark and since you have learned how to install Wireshark, I feel you are ready to initiate your first capture. I will be guiding you through the following series of steps to start/stop/save you first Wireshark capture:

1. Open the Wireshark application.
2. Choose an interface to listen to.

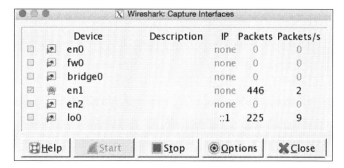

Figure 1.8: The interface window

3. Before you click on **Start**, we have the **Options** button, which gives us the advantage of customizing the capture process; but as of now, we will be using the default configuration.

 Make sure that the **Promiscuous** mode is activated so that we can capture the traffic that is not destined to our machine.

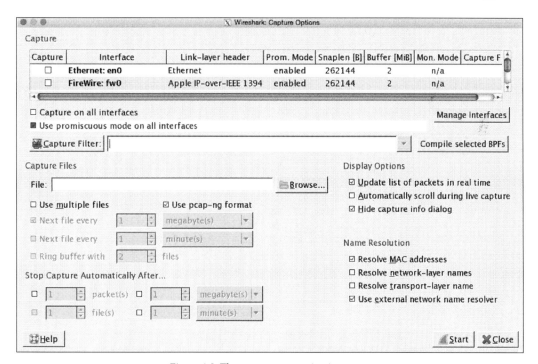

Figure 1.9: The capture customization screen

4. Click on the **Start** button to initiate the capturing process.

5. Open your browser.

6. Visit any website you want to.

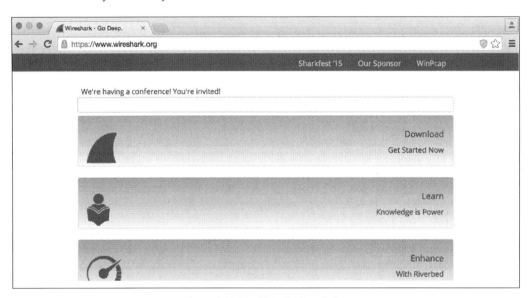

Figure 1.10: The Wireshark website

7. Switch back to the Wireshark screen; if everything goes well, you should be able to see a numerous packets getting captured in your Wireshark GUI inside the packet list pane.

To stop the capture, you can just click on the **stop capture** button in the toolbar area or you can click on **Stop** under the **Capture** menu bar.

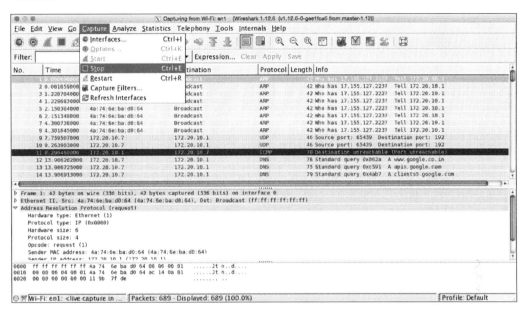

Figure 1.11: Stopping capture

8. I know there is an overwhelming amount of information you will see by now, but don't worry about it. I am here to make it simple for you.

9. The real process of packet analysis starts when you have captured packets— I mean packet filtering. We will be discussing packet filtering in detail in the upcoming chapters.

10. Now, the last step is to save the capture file for later use:

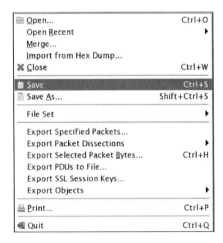

11. Save your file with the default `.pcapng` extension in you folder.

If you have read all the steps all the way up to this point, I would encourage you to create your first capture file.

Summary

This chapter lays the foundation of basic networking concepts along with an introduction of the Wireshark GUI. Wireshark is a protocol analyzer that is used worldwide by IT professionals to capture and analyze network-level packets.

The TCP/IP model has four layers: the Application Layer, Transport Layer, Network Layer, and Link Layer. Data gets encapsulated as it passes on from one layer to another; the resulting packet at the bottom is called a complete PDU, which actually travels over the channel.

To install Wireshark, you just need to visit `http://www.wireshark.org` and then download the appropriate version of this open source software. The Wireshark community is governed by real-world geeks; this can be a good source of learning and for troubleshooting purposes.

The Wireshark GUI is user friendly, robust, and platform independent; even new IT professionals can easily adapt the tool.

One important aspect of protocol analyzing is to place the sniffer at the right place; every organization's infrastructure is different from another, where we might need to apply different techniques in order to get the right packets to use.

Hubbing out, port mirroring, ARP poisoning, and tapping are some of those useful techniques that can be used to monitor and analyze traffic in different situations.

There are six main parts in the Wireshark tool window: **Menu Bar**, **Main Tool Bar**, **Packet List Pane**, **Packet Details Pane**, **Bytes Pane**, and **Status Bar**.

Using the back/forward key during a packet analysis scenario can be really useful. One should know about all the tools that are displayed in the main toolbar area.

In the next chapter, you will learn how to work with different kinds of filters available in Wireshark.

Practice questions

Q.1 How many layers are there in the TCP/IP? Name them.

Q.2 Which layer in the TCP/IP model handles Layer 2 addresses?

Q.3 The Link Layer is also called?

Q.4 The HTTP protocol uses TCP or UDP?

Q.5 IP, ICMP, and _____ are the protocols in the Internet Layer

Q.6 How many parts of the Wireshark window do you know?

Q.7 ARP is a Layer 3 protocol—true/false?

Q.8 Does the TCP protocol follow a three-way handshake?

Q.9 The Port Mirroring technique is possible through switches only—True/False?

Q.10 The Hubbing out technique uses a router to isolate a PC from it peers—true/false?

Q.11 TCP is an unreliable protocol—true/false?

Q.12 Install Wireshark and start a sample capture using your wireless interface. Save your capture file on the desktop with the name `first.pcap`, and close Wireshark.

Q.13 Open your `first.pcap` capture file in Wireshark and check how many packets you captured in total.

Q.14 Which pane displays information in the HEX and ASCII form for each packet we've captured?

Q.15 Switch off the promiscuous mode from the capture options window and observe whether you are still able to receive packets from other devices or not.

2
Filtering Our Way
in Wireshark

This chapter will talk about different filtering options available in Wireshark, namely, capture and display filters. We will also look at how to create and use different profiles. The following are the topics we will cover in this chapter:

- An introduction to capture filters
- Why and how to use capture filters
- Lab up—capture filters
- An introduction to display filters
- Why and how to use display filters
- Lab up—display filters
- Colorizing traffic
- Creating a new Wireshark profile(s)
- Lab up—profiles

I hope you are ready to start analyzing packets using different filtering options present in Wireshark and to reuse the filters that we previously created in a user-defined profile. I will be guiding you with a technique to filter packets based on certain expressions, which we will create using different primitives that are available.

Before we go ahead and start creating awesome filters, I want to mention one more interesting tool that is used to find packets: the find utility.

An introduction to filters

In the world of Wireshark, there are two kinds of filters that can be used over live traffic, and on saved capture files. Filters enhance the flexibility of packet analysis, where a certain user is given the privilege of seeing what he/she wants to see to capture what they want to capture.

The two types of filters are capture filter and display filter. Now, let's have look at each one of them in detail.

Capture filters

This gives you the facility to capture what you want to capture—others will be discarded. Capturing packets is a processor-intensive task, and Wireshark will acquire a quite good amount of primary memory as well. So, sometimes, we will have to save the resources for other processes, which can be utilized to analyze packets, and in some cases, we would like to capture only that data which meets our expression—rest of it will be dropped.

Wireshark offers some interesting options to configure an interface, which will be capturing traffic that meets only a certain expression, and this is achievable through the **Capture Options** window, as shown in the following screenshot:

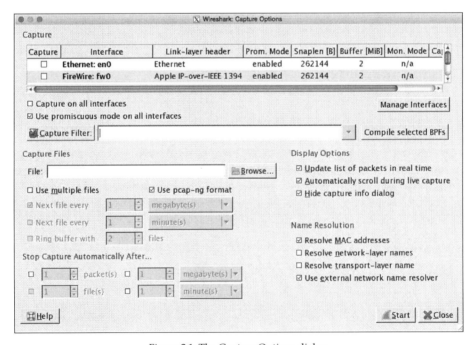

Figure 2.1: The Capture Options dialog

Here, points list various capture options dialog related details

- **Capture**: In this window, you can choose the interface you want to capture packets from, and you can even select multiple interfaces at once to listen on all of them. The details for every interface are listed under separate columns such as **Capture**, **Interface**, the name of the interface, whether the promiscuous mode is enabled or not, and so on. Under the **Capture** dialog, you will see a checkbox to toggle the promiscuous mode, and you can even choose the **promiscuous on all interfaces** option to activate what you require in just one click.

- **Manage Interfaces**: This button facilitates addition or removal of a new interface for listening purposes you intend to. You can add even remote machine interfaces, where you would be required to have root level privileges.

  - **Capture Filter**: By clicking on this **Capture Filter** button, you will be able to see a dialog similar to what is shown here. The already configured capture filters are listed by default, and here, we can create and save our custom capture filters as well.

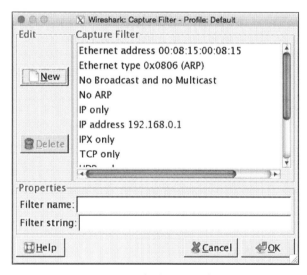

Figure 2.2 :Default Capture filters

To start off, users can use these default filtering profiles and get an idea about how to create custom filtering strings. Once you are well versed with the basics, you can go ahead and use the same window to create your own custom filters, but make sure that you have followed the **Berkley Packet Filtering** (**BPF**) syntax. The BPF syntax is an industry standard and is used by multiple protocol analyzers, which make your filter's configuration file portable.

Let's create one together to get a better hold over it; consider a scenario where we have to capture packets originating from a web server that is located at 192.168.1.1 (change the IP address to the web server's address that you are monitoring), and follow the next steps:

1. Open the **Capture Options** dialog.

2. Click on **Capture Filter**.

3. Click on **New**.

4. Write Web server 192.168.1.1 inside the **Filter name** textbox.

5. Write host 192.168.1.1 and port 80 inside the Filter String text-box

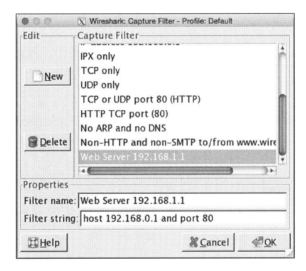

6. Once you've done this, click on **OK**; if you've entered everything correctly, the textbox followed by the **Capture Filter** button will be displayed with a green background, as shown in the following screenshot:

Figure 2.4 :Creating a sample capture filter

- **Capture Files**: This option gives you the flexibility to save your captured packets into the file(s) that already exists on your system. The captured packets will be added to the file of your choice if you don't choose any. A temporary file will be created, and data will be written to it, which can be saved to a user-specified location. To achieve this, write the name of the file that uses absolute path referencing or click on **Browse** followed by the **File** textbox to choose a location.

If you select the multiple files option, then you can save your packets in multiple files, where we can customize more options, which are stated as follows:

- ° **Next File Every**: After capturing a certain amount of data, Wireshark will create a new file and your data will be added to it. For instance, I want to create a new file after Wireshark captures 2 MBs of data.

- ° **Next File Every**: After a certain amount of time, Wireshark will create a new file and your packets will be added to it. For instance, I want to create a new file after every 5 minutes of the capturing process.

- ° **Ring buffer**: Using this option, you can restrict the creation of a new file. Wireshark uses the **First in First Out (FIFO)** option to write data to multiple filesets. For example, you have selected the **Ring buffer** option and increased the number of files to 5, and you have configured that after every 5 MBs, a new file should be created.

Now, according to this configuration, once you start capturing packets, after every 5 MBs of data, a new file will be created and the packets will be written to it. Once the limit that you specified in the **Ring Buffer** area is exceeded, Wireshark will not create a new file; instead, it will roll back to the first file and append data to it. The following screenshot shows a similar kind of configuration:

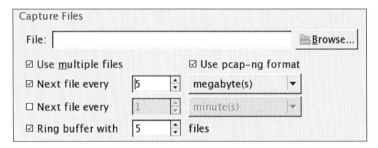

Figure 2.5 : The Capture Files option

- **Stop Capture Settings**: This option lets you stop the capturing process after a certain condition is triggered; we have four different kinds of triggers. Activating these can stop Wireshark from capturing new packets, and they are stated as follows:

  - ° **Packet(s)**: Stop capturing after a certain count of packets is reached

  - ° **File(s)**: Stop capturing after the creation of a certain number of files

  - ° **Megabyte(s)**: Stop capturing after capturing a certain amount of data

  - ° **Minute(s)**: Stop capturing after running for a certain period of time

There might be one question that you may want to ask: what if we select more than one option at a time? For instance, as shown in the following figure.

You can activate more than one option at a time; Wireshark will stop capturing whichever condition is met first.

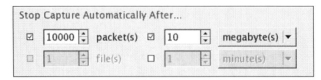

Figure 2.6 : The Stop Capture options

- **Display Options**: There are a few options available in this section that can be configured to restrict how the packets and their corresponding information will be displayed in the **Packet List Pane** option and the **Protocol hierarchy** window. Refer to the following figure to see this.

  If you select **Update list of packets in real-time**, you will observe that **Packet List Pane** is updated as soon as Wireshark captures a new packet, and the pane will be scrolled upwards automatically. Choose these options if needed; otherwise, the resources acquired by these two tasks can be used for other processes.

  If you check the **Hide capture info dialog** box, the **Protocol Hierarchy** window, that shows the statistics (in percentage) , will be hidden. If you don't have any specific purpose, I would recommend that you uncheck all these options.

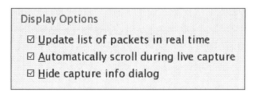

Figure 2.7: Display Options

- **Name Resolution**: If selected, this feature can resolve the Layer 2, Layer 3, and Layer 4 addresses to their corresponding names; for better understanding, refer to the following screenshot:

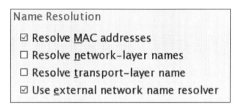

Figure 2.8: Name Resolution

Why use capture filters

Capturing only traffic that meets your requirement is really useful when you have a large volume of packets flowing around. Creating your own custom capture filters can come in really handy while you analyze a production environment. Capture filters are applied before you initiate the actual capture process. In general, every packet captured by Wireshark is passed to the capturing engine so that it gets translated to a human-understandable format, but if you have applied a capture filter, Wireshark will drop the packets that don't meet your expression. All these dropped packets won't be passed to the capturing engine, . In comparison, display filters are much more specific and powerful; while using capture filters, you should be careful, because there is no way of recovering dropped packets that do not meet the expression that you created.

The **Berkley Packet Filter (BPF)** syntax is used to create capture filters, and several protocol analyzers use it as well, thus maintaining industry standards. It is significantly easy to learn and practice, just use the basic format to structure an expression.

How to use capture filters

Using the BPF syntax earlier, we created a simple capture filter through the capture filter dialog; let's discuss it in detail because it is really crucial to know about BPF, as it is used by a variety of analyzers.

If you're using the BPF syntax, you have to follow a certain format structure, which is a combination of two arguments: identifiers and qualifiers, which are explained as follows:

- **Identifiers**: This is the value that you are looking for in your packets. For example, if you are filtering the packets for a certain IP address, then your capture filter will look something like `host 192.168.1.1`, where the value `192.168.1.1` is an identifier.

- **Qualifiers**: These are categorized into three different sections:

  ○ **Type**: There are three types of type qualifiers: `host`, `port`, and `net`. In short, a type qualifier refers to the name or the number that your identifier refers to. For example, in your `host 192.168.1.1` filter, `host` is the type qualifier.

  ○ **Direction**: Sometimes, when you need to capture packets from a particular destination or source, we can specify direction qualifiers as well. For example, in the `src host 192.168.1.1` capture filter, `src` specifies that we've to capture packets originating from a specific host only. Likewise, if you specify `dst host 192.168.1.1`, would capture packets only destined to `host 192.168.1.1`.

  ○ **Proto**: This refers to protocol qualifiers that give us the feature where we can mention the specific protocol that we want to add in our expression for capture purposes. For example, if you want to capture `http` traffic coming from your host `192.168.1.1`, then your expression will look something like `src host 192.168.1.1 and tcp port 80`.

In the previous example, we combined two expressions together using the concatenation operator (&/and). Similarly, we've the alteration operator (|/or) and the negation operator (!/not), which can be used to combine and create complex filters.

For example, as per our previously created filter `src host 192.168.1.1 and tcp port 80`, all the packets originating from `192.168.1.1` and going to port `80` will be captured.

If you add the `or` operator between `src host 192.168.1.1 or tcp port 80`, then when an expression in your filter matches, then the packet will be captured. This means that every packet originating from `192.168.1.1` or any packet associated with port `80` will be captured regardless of the second condition.

In the case of the `not` operator, a capture filter such as `not port 80` states that any packet associated with port `80` should not be captured.

Once you start working in a production environment, you will see how common it is to combine filters using the AND, OR, and NOT operators.

An example capture filter

Though you have a variety of filters available in Wireshark itself, which can give you an overview of the BPF syntax, to access the present filters by default, go to **Capture | Capture Filers** or click on the **Capture Options** button in the main toolbar and then click on **Capture Filter**. From the same window, we have an option to create new filters that we already discussed.

Refer to the following table for sample capture filters:

Filters	Description
host 192.168.1.1	All traffic associated with host 192.168.1.1
port 8080	All traffic associated with port 8080
src host 192.168.1.1	All traffic originating from host 192.168.1.1
dst host 192.168.1.1	All traffic destined to host 192.168.1.1
src port 53	All traffic originating from port 53
dst port 21	All traffic destined to port 21
src 192.168.1.1 and tcp port 21	All traffic originating from 192.168.1.1 and associated with port 21
dst 192.168.1.1 or dst 192.168.1.2	All traffic destined to 192.168.1.1 or destined to host 192.168.1.2
not port 80	All traffic not associated with port 80
not src host 192.168.1.1	All traffic not originating from host 192.168.1.1
not port 21 and not port 22	All traffic not associated with port 21 or port 22
tcp	All tcp traffic
Ipv6	All ipv6 traffic
tcp or udp	All TCP or UDP traffic
host www.google.com	All traffic to and from Google's IP address
ether host 07:34:aa:b6:78:89	All traffic associated with the specified MAC address

 It is essential to know about the BPF syntax. As and when you get into Wireshark in more detail, you will feel its importance. I would suggest that you practice it once when you are comfortable with the syntax.

Capture filters that use protocol header values

Capture filters can be created on the basis of offset values present in protocol header fields. The syntax to create such filters looks like `proto[offset:size(optional)]=value`. Here, `proto` is any protocol that you want to filter, `offset` is the position of the corresponding value in the header, `size` is the length of the data you are looking for, and `value` is the data you want to find.

Say, for instance, we want to capture only ICMP reply packets; now, if you observe the following figure, you will note that the ICMP header type is located at the first place and the offset counting starts from `0`. So, the offset value will be `0` in this case, and the size of the field is 1 bytes. We have all the required information to create a capture filter, so now, the resulting expression will look like `icmp[0:1]=0`.

```
▷ Internet Protocol Version 4, Src: 74.125.130.104 (74
▽ Internet Control Message Protocol
    Type: 0 (Echo (ping) reply)                              → Offset value
    Code: 0
    Checksum: 0x2623 [correct]
    Identifier (BE): 29962 (0x750a)
    Identifier (LE): 2677 (0x0a75)
    Sequence number (BE): 0 (0x0000)
    Sequence number (LE): 0 (0x0000)
    Timestamp from icmp data: Jul 16, 2015 13:22:31.57
    [Timestamp from icmp data (relative): 0.350050000
  ▷ Data (48 bytes)
0020  0a 07 00 00 26 23 75 0a  00 00 55 a7 62 bf 00 08
0030  c1 60 00 09 0a 0b 0c 0d  0e 0f 10 11 12 13 14 15
Figure 9 : ICMP reply
                                                           Position and Size
```

Figure 2.9: ICMP reply

Let's try to apply the same to Wireshark; we will then ping `www.google.com` to check whether it works.

Figure 2.10 : ICMP capture filter

Let's ping `www.google.com` and check whether it works.

```
charits-MacBook-Pro:~ NotFound$ ping www.google.com
PING www.google.com (74.125.130.104): 56 data bytes
64 bytes from 74.125.130.104: icmp_seq=0 ttl=40 time=350.085 ms
64 bytes from 74.125.130.104: icmp_seq=1 ttl=40 time=559.549 ms
64 bytes from 74.125.130.104: icmp_seq=2 ttl=40 time=282.911 ms
64 bytes from 74.125.130.104: icmp_seq=3 ttl=40 time=420.467 ms
64 bytes from 74.125.130.104: icmp_seq=4 ttl=40 time=311.638 ms
64 bytes from 74.125.130.104: icmp_seq=5 ttl=40 time=539.921 ms
```

Figure 2.11: Browse google.com

As a result, Wireshark will capture only the ICMP reply packets. Using the same technique, you can filter out traffic on the basis of the protocol header value:

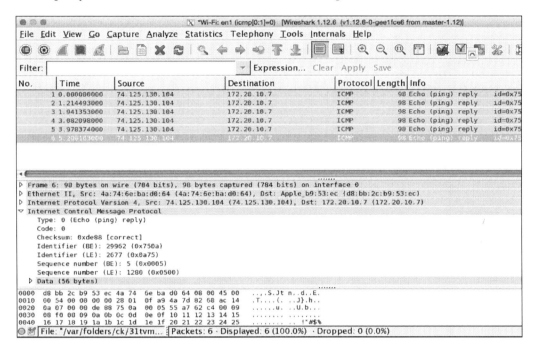

The following table lists some sample bytes-based capture filters for TCP and ICMP; try practicing them too:

Filter	Description
icmp[0] = 0	ICMP request packets
icmp[0:1] = 8	ICMP reply packets
icmp[0:1] = 3	ICMP destination host unreachable packets
tcp[13] = 2	TCP SYN flag packets only
tcp[13] = 18	TCP SYN/ACK flag packets only
tcp[13] = 32	TCP URG flag set packets only

Display filters

Display filters are much more flexible and powerful when compared to capture filters. Display filters do not discard any packets; instead, the packets are hidden to make viewing convenient or convenience. Discarding packets is not a very effective practice because, once the packets are dropped, they cannot be recovered. When you apply the display filter, only those packets that meet the specification of your filter will be displayed. In the the second column of the status bar of the Wireshark window, you will see a number of packets displayed after you apply a filter.

A display filter can be used for a capture file in the **Filter** dialog box located above the **Packet List Pane**. Display filters are more popular than capture filters. The syntax used for display filters can be easily adapted and applied. For new users, a display filter is like a super power that gives you the functionality of hiding inappropriate packets in run-time that do not meet your requirements as per the current scenario.

Display filters can be created on the basis of several different constraints such as the IP address, protocols, port numbers, and header values in specific protocols. There are lot of conditional tools and concatenation operators that can be used to create complex expressions. You can combine different sets of expressions to get more specific sets of packets that we are looking for. Each and every packet shown in the **Packet List Pane** can be filtered using the fields that a packet contains.

Display filters do not delete data; instead, packets are hidden, which can be made visible again once the filter in the **Filter** dialog above the list pane is cleared. For instance, to display only ICMP packets, just enter ICMP in the filter dialog and click on **Apply**; it's really simple, isn't it? If you want to see all packets again, just click on the **Clear** button and everything will be back to normal.

Wireshark has a very awesome feature that can assist you while creating your filter. Just click on the **Expression** button at the end of the **Filter** dialog box, choose the protocol you want to filter, and specify the value if there is one.

Using the **filter expression** dialog is really easy, and if you are a beginner, then this is a boon for you. Let's learn how to use the expression dialog.

Figure 2.12 : The filter expression

1. As show in the preceding screenshot, click on the **Expression** button.

2. Now, you will be presented with the **Expression** window like the one shown in the following screenshot:

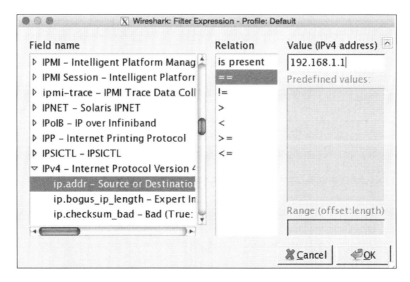

3. For example, if you want to see only packets associated with `ip:192.168.1.1`, then just scroll down in the **Field Name** to find **IPv4**. Then, expand the section and choose the **ip.addr** option.

4. Then, from the **Relation** box next to it, choose the operator you wish to add in your expression.

5. At last, write the IP you are looking for in the **Value (IPv4 address)** box.

6. At last, just click on **OK**. If you've followed all the steps up to here correctly, then you would be able to see the packets originated from the `ip` that you mentioned (change **192.168.1.1** to your IP address).

7. Below the **Value** box, there is a **Predefined value** box that is used when a certain protocol restricts us to use only a specific set of values. You can choose a value form here.

8. Below the **Predefined Value** box, there is a **Range** box that allows us to enter a range of values such as `1-78`, `0-5`, `120-255` if the protocol allows the same.

This is one of the easiest ways to create a display filter; there is one more way following which we can also create such filters. Entering filters manually can drastically increase the speed of your work, but it requires a bit more skill than there are in a novice user.

Before we start digging into creating filters manually, I want you to know about a few more things, such as comparison and logical operators. These can be used to create simple and the most complex filters for Wireshark.

The following table lists the comparison operators used to create display filters:

Operator	Description
==/eq	Equal to
!=/ne	Not equal to
</lt	Less than
<=/le	Less than equal to
>/gt	Greater than
>=/ge	Greater than equal to

Next, let's have a look at the logical operators that are used to combine different conditions together. The following table lists all of them:

Operator	Description
AND/&&	The AND logical operator is used when we want both parts of the expression to state `true`. For example, the `ip.src==192.168.1.1` and `tcp` filters would only display packets originated from `ip 192.168.1.1` and associated with the `tcp` protocol. Only the packets that match both the expressions will be shown.
OR/||	The OR logical operator is used when we just focus on one condition to be true at a time; if both are true, even then it's ok. For example, the `port 53` or `port 80` filters would display all packets associated with port 53 (DNS) along with all packets associated with port 80 (`http`).
NOT/!	The NOT logical operator is used when we want to exclude some packets from the list pane. For example, the `!dns` filter would hide all the packets associated with the DNS protocol.

Retaining filters for later use

Sometimes, you will have a requirement where having access to previously created filters would make your work easy and fast enough. Wireshark gives you the facility where you can retain your display filters through their saved names and use them at a later point of time whenever required. This option will save you the great amount of time and effort required to type some of the complex display filters. To create one for yourself, follow the given steps:

1. Go to **Analyze | Display filters**; this will give you a window like the one shown in the following screenshot:

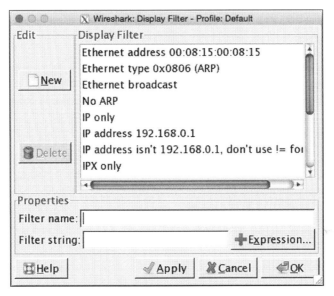

Figure 2.13: Adding Display Filters

2. Now, click on **New**, enter the values in the **Filter name** and **Filter string** fields. For instance, we want to create a display filter for no ARP packets. Then, the values will look something like the following screenshot:

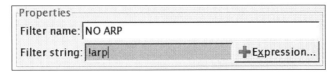

Figure 2.14 : Creating a new filter

3. After entering the same, click on **Apply**. Now, in the list of default filters present you would be able to see **NO ARP**, which can be used later.

4. Make sure that the **Filter String** box is shown with a green background, which denotes that your expression is correct; if it is in red color, then you need to recheck it, and if it is in yellow, this denotes that the results can be unexpected. Now, you can click on **Apply** and then click on **Ok**.

5. If you need assistance to create any filter you want, simply click on the **Expression** button next to the **Filter string** box, where all the protocols and majorly used filter expressions can be found.

6. The **Delete** button will assist you in deleting an existing filter from the list.

7. The **Cancel** button will discard any unsaved changes and close the window.

8. The **Ok** button commits **Save** and will close the window.

9. Now, let's try applying the filter we just created. Navigate to **Analyze | Display Filter |** (Scroll and select) **Display Filter | Apply**.

Try following the same and create your own display filter that you might want to reuse.

Searching for packets using the Find dialog

If you want to find a packet for a particular criterion, you can use the Find dialog. It has a couple of useful search techniques that can be applied easily and effectively on an already captured file or on a live running capture. You can access the Find utility by navigating to **Edit | Find packets** or using the shortcut *Ctrl + F*.

Figure 2.15: The Find Packet dialog

Let's see some more configurable options in it:

- The **display filter**: After capturing the traffic, while analyzing whether you just want to see some specific packets based on a certain IP /Port/ Protocol, those packets that meet a certain criteria will be displayed in the list pane, for example:

    ◦ The `ip.addr == 192.168.1.1` (based on an IP address)

    ◦ The `port 8080` (based on a port number)

    ◦ `http` (based on a protocol)

- The **Hex value**: If you have the hex value for a certain packet that you are looking for, then this option can be selected. Just write the physical address separated by colons, for example:

    ◦ `0A:C4:22:90:45:00`

    ◦ `AA:BB:CC`

- **String**: The next and last option is a text-string-based search where you can enter the name of the DNS server, name of the machine, and any resolved name that you know about (enter any string or word), for example:

    ◦ Cisco

    ◦ An administrator

    ◦ A web server

    ◦ Google

- **Search In**: This feature gives us the ability to search in a specific pane. For instance, if you are looking for a packet in the **bytes** pane, which matches the value **Google** (the ASCII value in the packet bytes pane will be matched), then we can go ahead and first choose the **String** option and then check the **Search In** box and choose **Packet Bytes**.

- **String Options**: To use this, first select the **String** option and then select **Case-Sensitive** and then if you want, choose the character width as well (but I would suggest not changing this unless until you have a specific reason to do so).

    ◦ **Direction**: This last option changes the direction of a search; you can change it to upward or downwards.

Once you have customized the options, enter the text and click on **Find**. This will give you the first exact capture that matches your criterion. To move back and forth between the matched packets, you can use *Ctrl* + *N* (next) and *Ctrl* + *B* (previous).

Colorize traffic

For better and convenient viewing experience, Wireshark gives us a feature where we can colorize a certain type of traffic that we want to highlight. Colorization of traffic is done in order to distinguish between different sets of traffic. Coloring a specific set of traffic with a different rule other than the default one will be like finding a needle in a haystack.

The default profile for most protocols is already created because of which we are able to see traffic in the packet list pane in different colors. You can access it by navigating to **View** | **Edit coloring rules** or clicking on the **Edit coloring rules** button from the main toolbar to open a window as shown in the following screenshot:

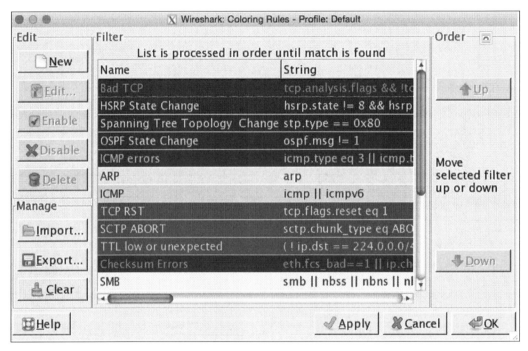

Figure 2.16: Coloring rules

All rules that are currently saved as part of your global configuration file to colorize traffic with certain foreground and background colors are listed in this dialog. Every packet listed in the packet list pane follows a certain rule, which gives them a unique and distinguished look and feel.

Let's use this feature and color the `http error` packets with a color of our choice. Say, for instance, I've a web server running on my machine that is used by the clients connected for file accessing purpose. Now, one of the clients in my network is trying directory listing and gets `HTTP 404` error messages. These error messages will pop up in my packet list pane but will be colored using the same `http` coloring rule that makes these errors less visible to me. To make this more visible, I want to colorize the `HTTP 404` error messages with a `black` background and with a `cyan` foreground. Follow the steps shown here that will achieve the same:

1. I have configured a Linux box running on `172.16.136.129`, and my Mac OS is running on `172.16.136.1` that serves as a web server for Linux, as Shown in the following screenshot:

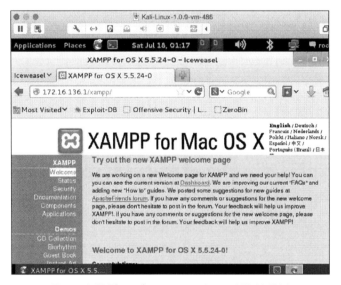

Figure 2.17: The web server running on 172.16.136.1

Normal traffic from a Linux-accessing web server looks something like the screenshot here:

No.	Time	Source	Destination	Protocol	Length	Info
1	0.000000000	172.16.136.129	172.16.136.1	TCP	60	55658→80 [SYN] Seq=0 Win=2920
2	-950618696.077286000	172.16.136.1	172.16.136.129	TCP	64	80→55658 [SYN, ACK] Seq=0 Ack
3	-2021440336.836621000	172.16.136.129	172.16.136.1	TCP	52	55658→80 [ACK] Seq=1 Ack=1
4	-1898165200.561362000	172.16.136.1	172.16.136.129	TCP	52	[TCP Window Update] 80→55658
5	41863044.612094000	172.16.136.129	172.16.136.1	HTTP	355	GET /xampp/ HTTP/1.1
6	0.001038000	172.16.136.1	172.16.136.129	TCP	52	80→55658 [ACK] Seq=1 Ack=304
7	0.084997000	172.16.136.1	172.16.136.129	HTTP	940	HTTP/1.1 200 OK (text/html)
8	0.085422000	172.16.136.129	172.16.136.1	TCP	52	55658→80 [ACK] Seq=304 Ack=88
9	381882809.099438000	172.16.136.129	172.16.136.1	HTTP	400	GET /xampp/head.php HTTP/1.1
10	0.106560000	172.16.136.1	172.16.136.129	TCP	52	80→55658 [ACK] Seq=889 Ack=65
11	-1437096632.918449000	172.16.136.129	172.16.136.1	TCP	60	55659→80 [SYN] Seq=0 Win=2920
12	-950618696.095408000	172.16.136.1	172.16.136.129	TCP	64	80→55659 [SYN, ACK] Seq=0 Ack
13	-136085583.409139000	172.16.136.129	172.16.136.1	TCP	52	55659→80 [ACK] Seq=1 Ack=1 Wi
14	-1321431907.061550000	172.16.136.1	172.16.136.129	TCP	52	[TCP Window Update] 80→55659

Figure 2.18: ormal traffic on a web server running on 172.16.136.1

2. Now that everything is up and running, we will try to do some directory listing manually from Linux, which will give eventually `HTTP 404` error messages.

The traffic generated through this request is captured, which can be seen in the following screenshot:

No.	Time	Source	Destination	Protocol	Length	Info
92	675.958501000	172.16.136.129	172.16.136.1	TCP	52	55667→80 [ACK] Seq=1 Ack=1
93	-1270177470.593326000	172.16.136.1	172.16.136.129	TCP	52	[TCP Window Update] 80→556
94	675.958885000	172.16.136.129	172.16.136.1	HTTP	362	GET /xampp/abc.jpg HTTP/1.
95	238258651.845389000	172.16.136.1	172.16.136.129	TCP	52	80→55667 [ACK] Seq=1 Ack=3
96	-456584943.391379000	172.16.136.1	172.16.136.129	TCP	657	[TCP segment of a reassemb
97	675.981774000	172.16.136.1	172.16.136.129	TCP	483	[TCP segment of a reassemb
98	675.981788000	172.16.136.1	172.16.136.129	TCP	282	[TCP segment of a reassemb
99	-511200557.945201000	172.16.136.1	172.16.136.129	TCP	273	[TCP segment of a reassemb
100	-1437100881.841330000	172.16.136.1	172.16.136.129	HTTP/XML	60	HTTP/1.1 404 Not Found
101	-1177513788.717358000	172.16.136.129	172.16.136.1	TCP	52	55667→80 [ACK] Seq=311 Ack
102	-1177513788.717358000	172.16.136.129	172.16.136.1	TCP	52	55667→80 [ACK] Seq=311 Ack
103	675.982078000	172.16.136.129	172.16.136.1	TCP	52	55667→80 [ACK] Seq=311 Ack
104	-1177513788.717358000	172.16.136.129	172.16.136.1	TCP	52	55667→80 [ACK] Seq=311 Ack

Figure 2.19: HTTP 404 Traffic

We can see, in the preceding captured traffic, that the client requested the **abc.jpg** resource, which was not available; thus, the client received a **404 Not found** error.

3. We figured out easily because there is just one client requesting a single resource. Consider a production environment where thousands of clients are present and they might do the same. In such cases, coloring a specific set of packets with a different rule is a game changer.

4. Navigate to **Edit Coloring Rules | New**. Type **HTTP 404** in the **Name** box. Type `http.response.code==404` in the **String** box. Choose the **Foreground Color** option as Cyan, and choose the **Background Color** option as Black. Then, click on **OK** and navigate to **Apply | OK**.

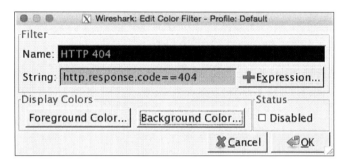

5. Once you click on **Apply**, you will see that only the HTTP 404 error packets will be colored according to your new coloring rule.

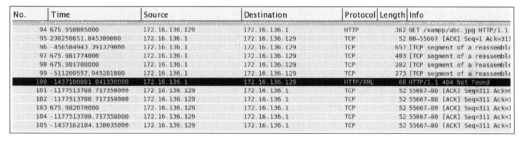

Figure 2.20: After applying the new coloring rule

Try the same using a virtual environment to give yourself more insight into the topic.

Coloring rules listed in the **Edit Coloring Rules** dialog will be checked in a top-to-bottom manner. With every packet, there is coloring rule information attached that can be listed from the **Packet Details Pane** under the **Frame** section. Consider the following screenshot illustrating the same:

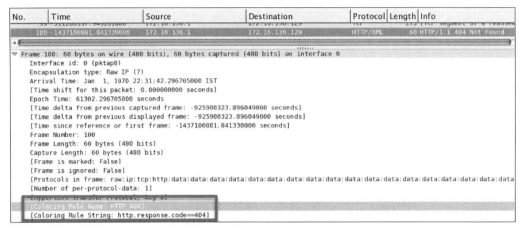

Figure 2.21: Coloring info in a frame header

Create new Wireshark profiles

Profiles in Wireshark are like customized environments, which can save a significant amount of time while auditing a network. A profile is a set of different components, such as capture filters, display filters, time preferences, column preferences, protocol preferences, color profiles, and so on, that fit together and give you a case-specific scenario, which you might require instantly.

Importing and exporting profiles is very easy in Wireshark, which is pretty useful while auditing a network where you don't have your preinstalled tools. Just copy and paste the Profile configuration files in a certain directory to use them. To create a profile, follow these steps:

1. Right-click on the **Profile** column in **Status Bar**.

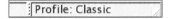

2. Click on **New...** in the pop-up dialog.

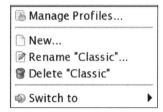

3. Now, choose any profile you wish to use as a template and type the name of the new profile.

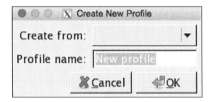

4. And then, click on **OK**.

Now, in the status bar, you will see the the same profile has been activated. The changes that you are going to make in this profile stay here, for example, you can create capture/display filters, change protocol preferences, and change color preferences. This means that any changes in a profile do not alter the contents of other profiles that are saved.

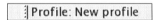

This way, we can create different profiles for case-sensitive scenarios that can save time and make the task easy.

Summary

Using the Find utility can be pretty useful sometimes, and can be accessed from the Edit menu in Wireshark. The Find utility gives us various vectors to search the packet content.

Filtering traffic lets you see only those packets that you are interested in; there are two types of filters: display filters and capture filters.

Display filters hide the packets, and once the expression you made is cleared, all packets can be seen again. However, capture filters discard the packets that do not meet the expression that you created. Discarded packets are not passed to the capturing engine.

Capture filters use the BPF syntax, which is an industry standard and is used by several other protocol analyzers.

Coloring preferences can be really useful while filtering a certain set of traffic based on a specific expression. Distinguishing packets will be become easy, as the matched packets will be shown with a different coloring scheme.

Profiles are like case-sensitive scenarios that can save your time and workload. Changes made to the profiles with respect to its different components, such as display/capture filter and color/protocol/time preferences, stay within the same.

Exporting profiles and various settings from Wireshark is very simple, which make the software more portable.

In the next chapter, you will learn how to work with Wireshark's advanced features such as graphs and statistical options.

Practice questions

Q.1 Explain the difference between display filters and capture filters, and which is more efficient in terms of system resource utilization.

Q.2 Explain the difference between **Find Utility** and **Filters**. Use the Find utility to search using hex values.

Q.3 Create a capture filter to capture only ARP broadcast packets.

Q.4 Create a capture filter to capture all packets except the packet destined to and originated from your physical address.

Q.5 Create a capture filter to capture only TCP SYN packets and TCP ACK packets.

Q.6 Create a capture filter to capture HTTP traffic sent only from you machine.

Q.7 Create a display filter to show packets originating only from your IP.

Q.8 Create a display filter to see packets that are only related to the protocol Secure Socket layer.

Q.9 Create a display filter to see only the ICMP destination host's unreachable packets.

Q.10 Create a display filter to see only TCP packets with a FIN and ACK flags set.

Q.11 Create a display filter to show TCP packets with header length greater than 40.

Q.12 Change the coloring scheme for all the DNS query Type A packets to the color of your choice.

Q.13 Change the coloring scheme of all HTTP error messages to the color of your choice.

Q.14 Create a profile with the name DNS using a default profile, and create a capture filter in this profile that will capture DNS traffic. Then, change the coloring scheme of all DNS response packets to the color of your choice.

Mastering the Advanced Features of Wireshark

In this chapter, we will look under the hood of the Statistics menu in Wireshark and work with different command-line utilities that come pre-packaged with Wireshark. Here, we will cover the following topics:

- Collecting network stats using Wireshark's Statistics menu
- LabUp—Summary, Protocol Hierarchy, Conversations, and Endpoints
- Mapping overall traffic in graphical form
- LabUp—Graphs
- View network traffic in plain-text form
- LabUp—TCP Streams
- Learn how to view logged anomalies in your trace file
- LabUp—Expert Infos
- Using command-line tools for protocol analysis
- LabUp—CommandLine
- Practice questions

With Wireshark, you can access a variety of statistics about the packets and protocols involved in the communication between two hosts. We can collect basic as well as advanced and specific information about protocols that are involved in the communication process. We will discuss most of the useful tools available in this menu, which can give us a better insight into dealing with day-to-day complex situations.

The Statistics menu

Statistics in Wireshark are not presented to you just through recorded figures; there are graphical features too, which can present the figures in terms of graphs. Using this, the analysis process becomes easier and much efficient. Multiple types of graphs are available, which we can use to collect valuable information.

Command-line tools are like a samurai's sword, which will enhance the capability of a moderate user to become and act like an advanced user. In this chapter, we will see a couple of inbuilt tools that are command based.

Using the Statistics menu

A wide range of tools related to network stats is available in the menu, which facilitate users in gaining information ranging from general info to specific protocol related info in detail.

The general details with respect to the packets captured, filters applied, marked packets, and various other stats can be checked in the Statistics menu. Though this option is just for informational purpose, at times this can be pretty much useful.

To access the summary stats, click on **Statistics | Summary**; now, you will be able to see a window, as shown in the upcoming screenshot.

The Summary dialog is partitioned into a couple of sections, which are as follows:

- **File**: General information, such as the name of the file, location of the file, format used, and encapsulation, is listed under this
- **Time**: This section will tell you the time when the first and the last packets were captured and the time elapsed (total capture duration)
- **Capture**: This lists the name of the OS along with the version used and the interface used to dump packets from the live network traffic
- **Comments**: This shows any comments that the user mentioned for reference
- **Interface(s)**: This lists the details of every interface, using which the traffic is captured

- **Display**: This section gives statistics regarding any display filter that has been used and the percentage of ignored packets after a filter was applied

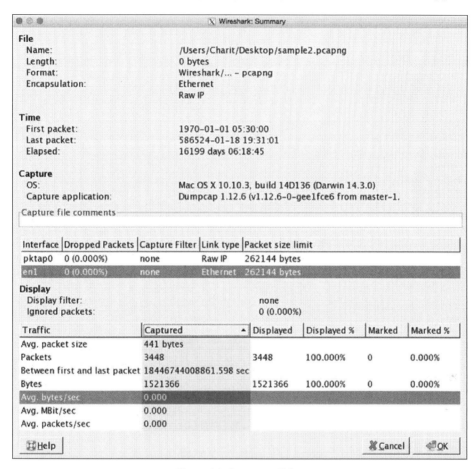

Figure 3.1: Summary dialog

Just below the **Display** section, you must see a few columns listing various details, which include a summary in a tabular format that is grouped on the basis of different categories, such as average packet size, total number of packets captured, time elapsed between the first and last packet captured, and so on.

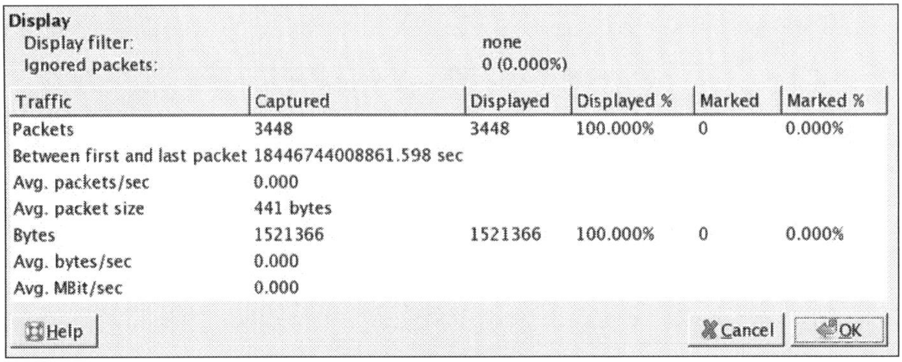

Display
  Display filter: none
  Ignored packets: 0 (0.000%)

Traffic	Captured	Displayed	Displayed %	Marked	Marked %
Packets	3448	3448	100.000%	0	0.000%
Between first and last packet 18446744008861.598 sec					
Avg. packets/sec	0.000				
Avg. packet size	441 bytes				
Bytes	1521366	1521366	100.000%	0	0.000%
Avg. bytes/sec	0.000				
Avg. MBit/sec	0.000				

Help   Cancel   OK

Figure 3.2: Without display filter(screenshot 1)

Let's say, for instance, we have a capture file over which we have applied the display filter **http**. After this, we can access the **Summary** option. Take a look at the following screenshot and try to compare them in order to understand the difference a display filter would make in the representation of the packets related summary.

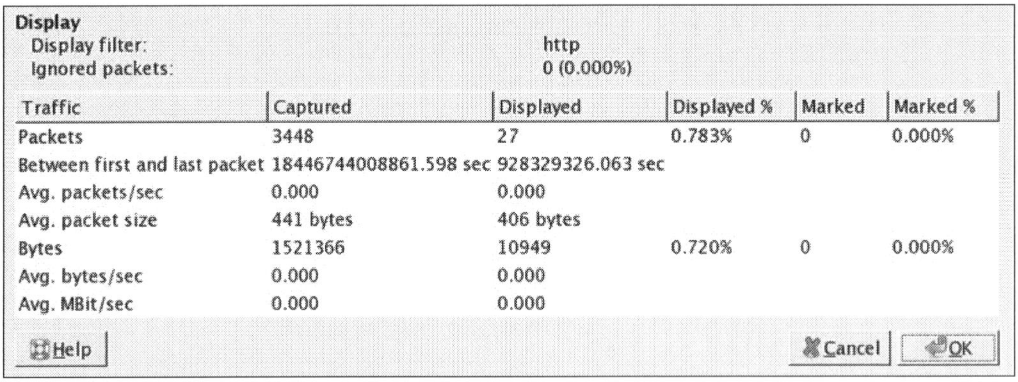

Display
  Display filter: http
  Ignored packets: 0 (0.000%)

Traffic	Captured	Displayed	Displayed %	Marked	Marked %
Packets	3448	27	0.783%	0	0.000%
Between first and last packet 18446744008861.598 sec	928329326.063 sec				
Avg. packets/sec	0.000	0.000			
Avg. packet size	441 bytes	406 bytes			
Bytes	1521366	10949	0.720%	0	0.000%
Avg. bytes/sec	0.000	0.000			
Avg. MBit/sec	0.000	0.000			

Help   Cancel   OK

Figure 3.3: With display filter(screenshot 2)

Now, after applying the filter, the variance among the values listed in the stats can be observed. That is, after applying the display filter **http**, the **Displayed**% column has a different set of values as compared to the previous one without display filter.

Protocol Hierarchy

The Protocol Hierarchy window provides us with an overview regarding distribution of protocols used in the communication process and how to spot unusual activities in your network that do not follow the benchmark as expected. By distribution of protocols, I mean in what percentage a certain protocol has been used in the communication between two hosts, and statistics, for example, how many bytes and packets are being sent and received for every protocol, are collected easily. Any form of unusual activity can be easily figured out by matching our current traffic with the baseline created.

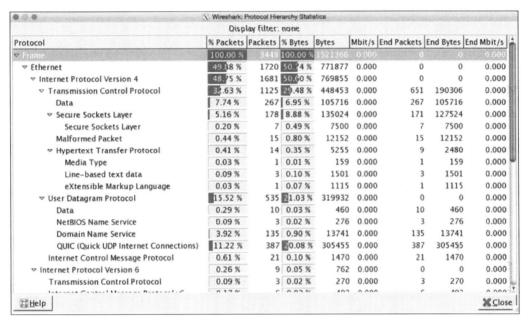

Figure 3.4: Protocol Hierarchy window

If you want to check the protocol distribution for a specific host, then before you open the Protocol Hierarchy window, apply a display filter, for example, **ip.addr==172.20.10.1**. The same filter will be visible at the top of the Hierarchy window just below the title bar. This makes it easy for us to figure out what kind of traffic is actually generated from a certain host, and any malicious traffic from a certain host can be easily figured out.

Refer to the following screenshot:

Protocol	% Packets	Packets	% Bytes	Bytes	Mbit/s	End Packets	End Bytes	End Mbit/s
▽ Frame	100.00 %	328	100.00 %	28766	0.000	0	0	0.000
▽ Ethernet	50.00 %	164	53.99 %	15531	0.000	0	0	0.000
▽ Internet Protocol Version 4	50.00 %	164	53.99 %	15531	0.000	0	0	0.000
▽ User Datagram Protocol	44.21 %	145	49.37 %	14201	0.000	0	0	0.000
Data	3.05 %	10	1.60 %	460	0.000	10	460	0.000
Domain Name Service	41.16 %	135	47.77 %	13741	0.000	135	13741	0.000
Internet Control Message Protocol	5.79 %	19	4.62 %	1330	0.000	19	1330	0.000
▽ Raw packet data	50.00 %	164	46.01 %	13235	0.000	0	0	0.000
▽ Internet Protocol Version 4	50.00 %	164	46.01 %	13235	0.000	0	0	0.000
▽ User Datagram Protocol	44.21 %	145	42.31 %	12171	0.000	0	0	0.000
Data	3.05 %	10	1.11 %	320	0.000	10	320	0.000
Domain Name Service	41.16 %	135	41.20 %	11851	0.000	135	11851	0.000
Internet Control Message Protocol	5.79 %	19	3.70 %	1064	0.000	19	1064	0.000

Wireshark: Protocol Hierarchy Statistics — Display filter: ip.addr==172.20.10.1 — Help — Close

Figure 3.5: Protocol Hierarchy window after applying display filter

Using the **Protocol Hierarchy** window, you can create filters too. Just right-click on the protocol you wish to use and then go ahead and specify the expression, as shown in the following screenshot:

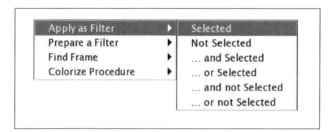

There will be situations when a certain host in your network has been breached and you might be observing some unusual traffic associated with a particular host. In such situations, the **Protocol Hierarchy** window will prove worthy.

Conversations

When two devices are connected to each other on the network, they are supposed to communicate; this is considered normal behavior. However, suppose you have thousands of devices connected to your network and you want to figure out the most active device that is generating too much traffic, then in that instance, the **Conversations** window will be quite useful.

To access this nice tool, click on **Statistics | Conversations**. After this, you will be presented with a window like the one shown in the following screenshot, which lists various details in terms of several columns listing the packets that were transferred, the bytes that were transferred, the flow of traffic, devices' MAC addresses, and various other details. At the top, you will observe various protocols displayed individually in separate tabs, and along with each active protocol tab, you will notice a number that denotes the number of unique conversations.

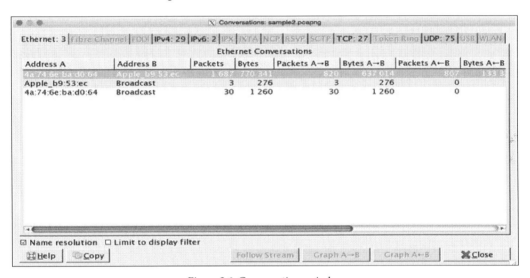

Figure 3.6: Conversations window

For example, if you are looking for the devices that generated a lot of packets and from where major data transfer has happened, then open the **Conversations** dialog, go to the **IPv4** tab, and sort the packets column in a descending order. Here, the device listed in the first row is your answer. Take a look at the following screenshot that illustrates the same.

Address A	Address B	Packets ▲	Bytes	Packets A→B	Bytes A→B	Packets A←B	Bytes A←B
172.143.162.208	172.20.10.7	900	229 312	366	172 714	534	56 59
172.20.10.7	216.58.220.46	430	256 350	204	27 884	226	228 46
172.20.10.1	172.20.10.7	366	31 160	172	17 970	194	13 19
172.20.10.7	173.194.126.120	364	296 096	144	28 864	220	267 23
54.231.136.106	172.20.10.7	276	220 766	158	212 544	118	8 22
172.20.10.7	216.58.196.99	186	128 678	82	14 340	104	114 33
172.20.10.7	216.58.196.110	130	83 634	58	13 692	72	69 94

Figure 3.7: Busiest devices

In the first row, we can see how many packets/bytes have been sent and received by each endpoint and the total elapsed duration. If you wish to create a filter for the same, right-click on the first row and then create the respective expression you are thinking about. I chose the first option, **A<->B**, which only shows packets that are associated with Address **A** and Address **B**:

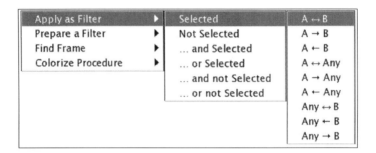

The respective filter will be inserted in the **Display Filter** dialog, as shown in the following screenshot:

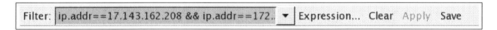

The **Conversations** dialog will let us collect and analyze details in a more granular form, which can be used in various scenarios while troubleshooting and auditing networking infrastructures.

Endpoints

Two devices that share data with each other are often referred to as endpoints with reference to Wireshark. As we have noticed and observed, if a host intends to talk to another host on the network, they would require some form of address to send and receive packets — yes, I am talking about the physical address that every device holds.

Every host is able to communicate with the help of an **Network Interface Card** (**NIC**) that holds a physical address (often termed as a MAC address), and the same address is used for communication over a local network. Devices that communicate in this kind of infrastructure are termed as endpoints. Wireshark gives us the facility of analyzing and collecting information regarding these two devices.

Let's say, for example, that we are observing heavy network traffic flowing across a network, which is kind of unusual according to our daily traffic pattern. Now, we want to figure out due to which device(s) the traffic pattern differs. For us, the **Endpoints** dialog comes to the rescue, which can be accessed from the **Endpoints** menu under **Statistics**, which looks something like the following screenshot. Before you go ahead and open the **Endpoints** dialog, simply click on any TCP packet from the **Packet List** pane. What you will see is a list of tabs visible at the top, each stating a different a protocol. Some of them will be shown as active, and some of them will be shown as inactive because if in your traffic you have a packet relating to a certain protocol, the tab listing that particular protocol will be shown as active; otherwise, it will be shown as inactive.

By default, you will be presented with the **Ethernet** tab (lists the Layer-2 MAC address) in most cases. Along with the protocol, you must observe a number that states the number of endpoints captured for that specific protocol. As in our case, we are seeing **3** and the same number of rows are visible in the **Main** pane.

In the **Main** pane, many more specific details can be seen for every endpoint, such as the total number of packets transferred, total number of bytes transferred, and total bytes and packets received and transmitted for an individual endpoint.

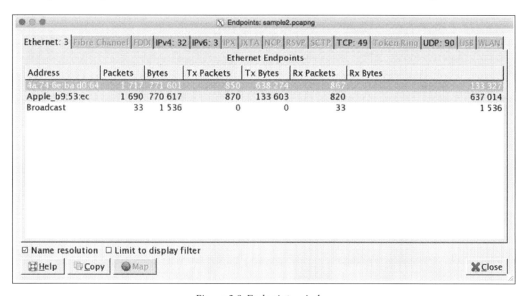

Figure 3.8: Endpoints window

Now, if you want to analyze other protocols, then simply click on any tab of your choice. I clicked on the **IPv4** tab and sorted the main pane using the **Packets** column, which looks like the one shown in the following screenshot:

By just looking at the **Endpoints** dialog, I can now easily figure out that maximum data was transferred from IP **172.20.10.7**. This could be a one single IP talking to some server or probably a server talking to multiple machines on our network at a moderate rate.

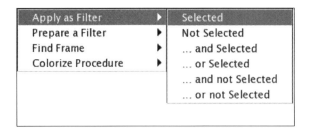

Address	Packets ▲	Bytes	Tx Packets	Tx Bytes	Rx Packets	Rx Bytes	Latitude	Longitude
172.20.10.7	3 404	1 518 822	1 752	255 718	1 652	1 263 104	–	–
17.143.162.208	900	229 312	366	172 714	534	56 598	–	–
216.58.220.46	430	256 350	226	228 466	204	27 884	–	–
172.20.10.1	366	31 160	172	17 970	194	13 190	–	–
173.194.126.120	364	296 096	220	267 232	144	28 864	–	–
54.231.136.106	276	220 766	158	212 544	118	8 222	–	–
216.58.196.99	186	128 678	104	114 338	82	14 340	–	–
216.58.196.110	130	83 634	72	69 942	58	13 692	–	–
17.178.104.39	114	45 990	52	29 624	62	16 366	–	–
216.58.196.97	104	34 162	44	19 058	60	15 104	–	–
17.151.236.24	90	28 432	40	20 386	50	8 046	–	–
216.58.196.109	80	35 144	36	17 770	44	17 374	–	–
216.58.196.98	72	28 854	32	16 536	40	12 318	–	–
17.167.194.236	60	14 250	28	10 820	32	3 430	–	–

Figure 3.9: Endpoints dialog — IPv4v tab

If you would like to dig more into it, we have an interesting option that can be taken advantage of; simply create a display filter for the same. To do so, right-click on the first row with most packets transferred and choose **Selected** under **Apply as Filter**, as shown in the following screenshot:

You will be able to see a display filter for the same **Endpoint** in the **Display Filter** dialog above the **List** pane, like the one shown here:

Apply as Filter ▶	Selected
Prepare a Filter ▶	Not Selected
Find Frame ▶	… and Selected
Colorize Procedure ▶	… or Selected
	… and not Selected
	… or not Selected

This facilitates us to quickly analyze traffic for a certain endpoint and hence increases the speed of analysis for users. Once you click on **Clear**, you will be presented with the same **Endpoint** dialog. At the bottom of the window, you will see two check boxes and a few buttons. The purpose of each is listed in the following:

- **Name Resolution**: This resolves the name of each of the Ethernet addresses listed in the **Ethernet** tab. But in some scenarios, it might affect the performance of the application adversely too, for example, when trying to resolve the unique IP addresses from a huge `pcap` file.

- **Limit to display filter**: This limits the results of the Endpoint window on the basis of a display filter that you already applied before accessing the Endpoints window.

- **Copy**: This copies the content of the current Endpoints window tab in a CSV format (comma-separated values).

- **Map**: This maps the selected endpoint's location in your browser on the basis of its actual geographical location.

Working with IO, Flow, and TCP stream graphs

Among various other reporting tools, Wireshark offers graphing capabilities too, which can present captured packets in an interesting format that makes the analysis process much more effective and easy to adapt. The graphing feature is much more effective in comparison to scrolling thousands of packets to figure out the cause of any network-related problem. If you have an overwhelming number of packets to be analyzed, then graphs can be seriously productive. There are multiple types of graphs available that we will discuss, starting with the IO graph.

IO graphs

This is one of the basic graphs that are created using the packets available in the capture file. To create the IO graph, select any TCP packet in your capture file and then click on **IO Graph** under **Statistics**. Refer to the following screenshot:

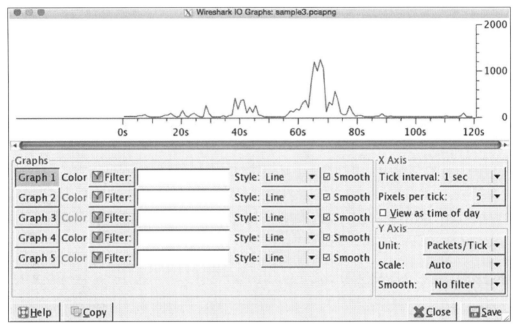

Figure 3.10: IO graphs

This way, you can see the highs and lows in your traffic, which can be used to rectify problems or can even be used for monitoring purpose. In the preceding graph, the data on the x axis represents the time in seconds and the data on y axis represents the number of packets per tick. The scale for the x and y axis can be altered if needed, where x axis will have a range between 10 and 0.001 seconds and y axis values will range between packets/bytes/bits.

From the preceding graph, we can easily depict that between sixtieth to eightieth second of the capture process, the network was most active, which generated approximately 1000 packets each second of the capture process. Now, you will be realizing how easy it was to gather that specific information from thousands of packets in merely 4-5 seconds; this is what graphing makes you capable of.

Just below the plotted area, you can see the **Graph** section, which lists various tools, such as Graphs 1-5, several filters, and the line format, and various other details. Let's take an example and try to understand the functioning of each of them.

The preceding graph displays the generalized form of our network traffic. Now, my requirement is that I just want to see the frequency of the UDP traffic separately in the same graph plotted with a red line. For such specifications, follow these steps:

- Write UDP as a filter in the second filter box from the top
- Click on the **Graph 1** button to deactivate it
- Click on the **Graph 2** button to activate it
- Now, you will see the same window as shown in the following screenshot:

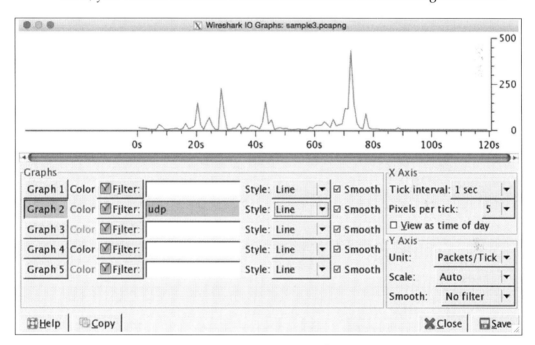

Figure 3.11 : IO graph-UDP traffic only

Analyzing specifically UDP traffic becomes easier in just a few steps. It is clearly visible from the preceding graph that most of the UDP traffic was generated between the seventieth to eightieth second of the capture process, and more than 250 packets were received during the capture process. If you want to compare both TCP and UDP traffic in the same graph, take a look at the following screenshot:

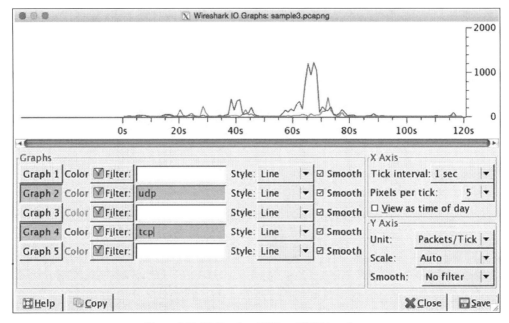

Figure 3.12: IO Graphs—TCP and UDP together

Comparing two things gives us a new angle to view regular things, and generally speaking, the learning process becomes better when we start comparing.

Flow graphs

This is one of the nicest features in Wireshark, where we are assisted with troubleshooting capabilities in scenarios like facing a lot of dropped connections, lost frames, retransmission traffic, and more. Flow graphs let us create a column-based graph, which summarizes the flow of traffic between two endpoints, and it even lets us export the results in a simple text-based format. This is the easiest way of verifying the connection between client and server.

For instance, I have a web server running at **172.16.136.1** and a client running at **172.16.136.129**. The client will request the web server for a certain resource. Let's see what the flow graph looks like for such kind of requests. There will be hundreds of packets generated, but we will look only at HTTP packets, just to make the results more confined and understandable. Click on **Flow Graph** under **Statistics**, and then from the pop-up dialog, choose **Displayed Packet**. Click on **OK**. Refer to the following screenshot that illustrates the same:

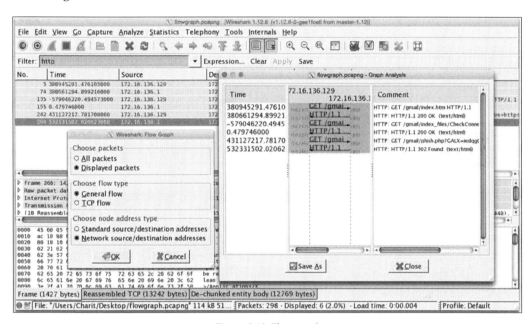

Figure 3.13: Flowgraph

Now, from the **Graph Analysis** window, we can see at what time a certain request was made and what response did we receive, which TCP port was used, along with some plain English comments, and the flow of traffic is also marked. This makes it simple for us to understand how TCP packets flow around.

TCP stream graphs

There are a couple of graphs that come in this section. Each of them depicts the network traffic in a graphical form differently. Let's start by taking a look at each one of them.

Round-trip time graphs

Round-trip time (**RTT**) is the duration in which the ACK for a packet that is sent is received, that is, for every packet sent from a host, there is an ACK received (TCP communication), which determines the successful delivery of the packet. The total time that is consumed from the transfer of the packet to the ACK for the same is called round trip time. Follow these steps to create one for yourself:

- Select any TCP packet in your **packet list** pane.
- Navigate to **Statistics | TCP Stream Graph | Round Trip Time Graph**.
- The x axis represents the TCP sequence number and the y axis represents the RTT in seconds.
- Each plotted point on the graph represents the RTT of a packet. If you are not seeing anything in your graph, then you might have selected an opposite directional packet.
- RTT graphs are often used by network admins to identify any congestion or latency that can make your network perform slowly.
- To investigate further, just click on any plotted RTT dot in your graph, and Wireshark will point you to that specific packet in the list pane.

The following RTT graph represents normal web traffic, and at some points in the graph, latency can be observed:

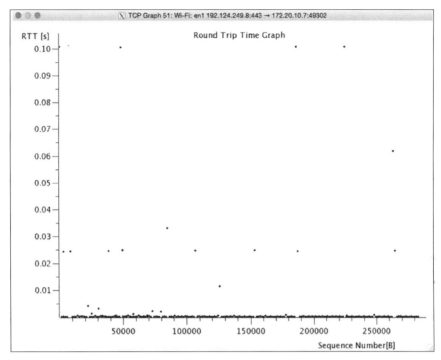

Figure 3.14: Round Trip time Graph

Bottleneck and latency can often be identified with a vertical line of plotted RTT dots, which depicts whether the packet from the sending device is first queued up and then sent all at once or whether the packets are suffering with duplicate ACKs or packet loss, where retransmission was required, thus increasing the RTT time.

Throughput graphs

This graph is very similar to the IO graph that depicts the traffic flow. However, it is different in one important aspect that Throughput graphs depict the unidirectional traffic whereas IO graphs depict the traffic in both directions. For every TCP packet that you select in the list pane, the Throughput graph can be different. If you are seeing a blank graph, then just select another TCP packet and try to create the graph again. Follow these steps to create one for yourself:

1. Open the trace file that contains your packets.
2. Apply a display filter if required.
3. Select any TCP packet from the list pane.
4. Navigate to **Statistics | TCP Stream graphs | Throughput graph**.
5. Voila! It's done.

In the title bar, the IP address of the communicating hosts is present, along with the direction of traffic. The x axis represents the time in seconds, and the y axis represents throughput in bytes/seconds. Refer to the following graph (*Figure 3.15*) that illustrates the same:

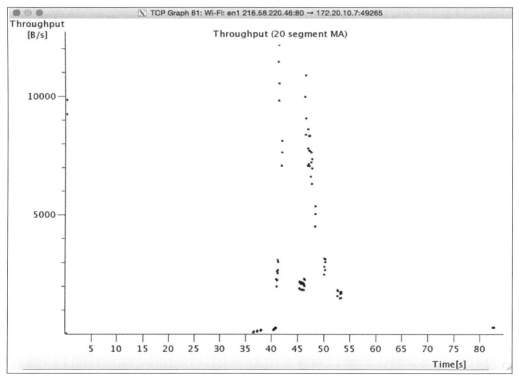

Figure 3.15: Throughput Graph

The Time-sequence graph (tcptrace)

This graph depicts the stream of TCP data over time. The traffic that will be presented is unidirectional (moving in one direction). Time-sequence graph gives us an idea about the segments that are currently traveling, the acknowledgements for segments that we've received, and the buffer area that the client is capable to hold. To create this graph, follow these steps:

1. Open the capture/trace file you want to work with.

2. Click on any TCP packet from the list pane.

3. Navigate to **Statistics | TCP Stream Graphs | Time sequence graph (tcptrace)**.

4.   You must now see something like the following:

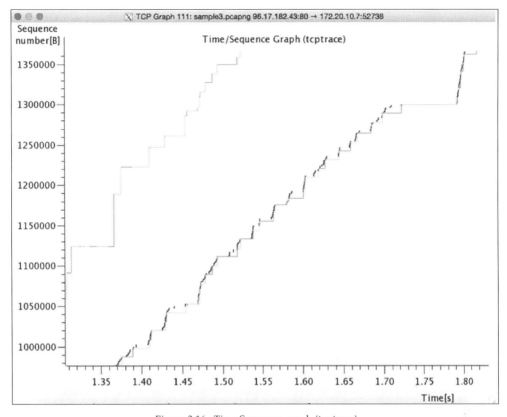

Figure 3.16 : Time Sequence graph (tcptrace)

The x axis of the graph represents the time in seconds and the y axis represents the TCP sequence number. TCP sequence numbers are incremented by the bytes of data sent with every packet, that is, if the sequence number is 1 and the packet we are sending holds 10 bytes of data, then the sequence number will be incremented by 10. Hence, the sequence number for the next packet to be sent will be 11. The throughput of the data is more when we have steeper lines plotted, normally, the graph plotting starts from the lower-left corner to upper-right corner.

There are actually three lines plotted on every graph. The line with multiple I written is the TCP data segment, and the longer the I stream, the more the data in the packet. The line below the TCP segment is the ACK stream for data sent, and the line at the top represents the calculated client-receiving window.

The distance between the client-receiving window line and the TCP segment line is the window size. The closer the line, the less data can be buffered, and vice versa. Consider the following zoomed-in screenshot for more understanding:

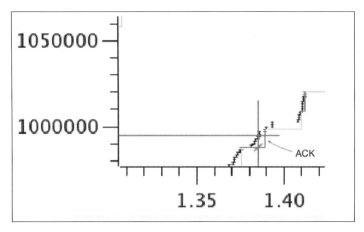

Figure 3.17: Throughput graph

Let's suppose that at 1.38 seconds Host A is sending byte 995,000, and at the same time, host A received an ACK for byte 990,000, which states that 5,000 bytes are still unacknowledged (in-flight). A point to be noted here is that the dark grey lines denote the ACKs received.

Follow TCP streams

Wireshark provides the feature of reassembling a stream of plain text protocol packets into an easy-to-understand format.

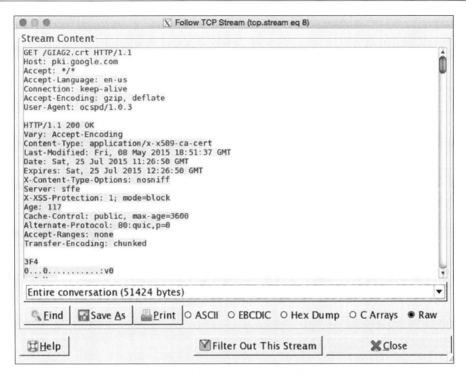

Figure 3.18: Follow TCP Stream window

For instance, assembling an HTTP session will show you the GET requests sent from the client and the responses received from the server accordingly. There is specific color coding that is followed by the requests and responses shown in the Follow TCP stream dialog. Any text in red color denotes a request that a client has sent, and any text in blue color denotes the response received from the server. If the protocol is HTTP, then you can view almost everything in plain text; if the protocol is HTTPS, then most of the things will be encrypted, hence giving ambiguous text on the screen (there is a way to decrypt HTTPS traffic too, which we will discuss in the upcoming chapters). The Follow TCP stream option can be of great help while troubleshooting any HTTP session, which is the same with most of the application layer protocols.

At the bottom of the dialog, you have a drop-down menu from where you can choose to view either side of communication or you can choose the entire communication, consisting of requests and responses that are shared between the client and the server at the same time. Instead of just viewing the data in RAW format, you can choose between ASCII, EBCDIC, Hex dump, and C arrays format.

If you wish to save the content shown in the dialog, then click on **Save as**, which will save the content in a simple text format. Similarly, to print, you can click on **Print**. And if you want to view everything except the Follow TCP stream packets that you are viewing currently, then click on **Filter out this stream**. To close the dialog, click on **Close**.

To view the TCP stream, follow these steps:

1. Open the capture/trace file.
2. Apply the display filter if required.
3. Select any packet from the list pane.
4. Right-click on the selected packet and click on **Follow TCP stream**.

Following the preceding steps gives a simple view of viewing data. Now, figuring out who initiated the connection will be quite easy.

Expert Infos

The information in the **Expert Infos** dialog is populated by the dissectors that enable the translation of every protocol that is well known to Wireshark. The **Expert Infos** dialog keeps you aware of the specific states that users should know about. Presently, expert infos is available only for TCP-based communication. Maybe for other protocols, the **Expert Info** dialog will be available by the time you read this.

You can access the **Expert Info** dialog by clicking on **Expert Info** under **Analyze**, or you can click on the bottom-left corner on the colored dot just before the status bar. Refer to the following screenshot, which illustrates the same:

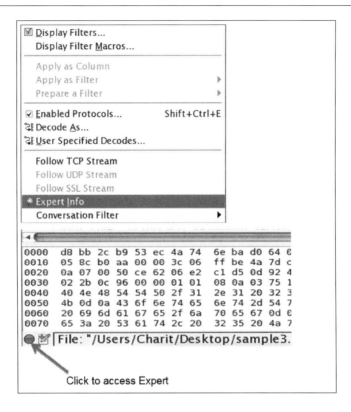

The red dot at the bottom-left corner can be colored with different colors, such as cyan, yellow, green, blue, and grey, where each of them has a specific meaning, which is listed as follows:

- **Red**: This indicates errors
- **Yellow**: This refers to warnings
- **Cyan**: This refers to a note
- **Blue**: This refers to chats
- **Green**: This refers to comments
- **Grey**: This means none

Now, let's have a look at the Expert Infos dialog and discuss various other elements residing within. Refer to the following screenshot for illustration purposes:

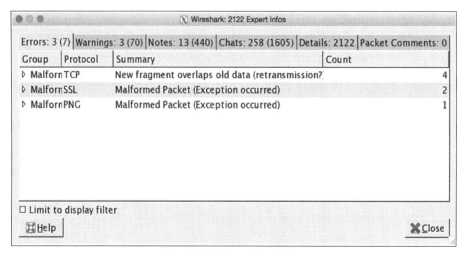

Figure 3.19: Expert Infos dialog

As you can observe, there are multiple tabs listed just below the title bar that consist of packets listed depending on their severity level and category of information. There are mainly four sections in the Expert Infos dialog that point to the likely cause of the problem, so double-checking it will be helpful. Each tab contains the name of the section and two numbers: one inside the parenthesis and one outside. The number inside the parenthesis denotes the total number of packets that have been flagged for the containing category, and the number outside denotes the total number of unique categories for the packets flagged.

We will go through each section one by one, and we will also summarize the criteria by which packets are flagged and listed under different categories, such as chat, note, warnings, details, and so on:

- **Chat**: These are general messages concerning the current communication. A packet that falls under this section is listed as follows:
    - ○ **Window Update**: This makes the sender aware that the TCP receive window size has been updated.

- **Note**: These are unusual messages that may or may not be part of the current normal communication. Packets that fall under this section are listed as follows:

  ° **The Zero Window Probe**: Suppose that the server receiving the packets from the client is not able to process the packets received at the same speed that the client is sending them, thus causing packet loss. In such cases, a server will send a Zero Window packet to the client to halt the process of sending packets for sometime while keeping the connection alive.

  ° **The Keep Alive ACK**: The receiver of the Keep Alive packets sends this ACK as a response.

  ° **The Zero Window Probe ACK**: This relates to the Zero Window Probe example. The Zero Window Probe ACK will be sent by the client in response to the server's request.

  ° **Window is full**: This notifies the sending host that the TCP-receiving window is currently full.

  ° **TCP retransmission**: The TCP packet is retransmitted again because of a duplicate ACK, packet loss, or if the timer for retransmission expires.

  ° **The duplicate ACK**: If you think about the TCP three-way handshake communication, for every packet received at the other end, the sender should get an ACK packet. If the receiver gets the packet with the sequence number that has already been received, then duplicate ACKs will be generated. This will happen in case of packet loss as well.

- **Warning messages**: These are unusual messages that are probably not a part of your general communication. Packets that fall under this section are listed as follows:

  ° **Zero Window**: These messages have been observed when the receiving side tries to notify the sender to stop sending for a while as the TCP-receiving window is full.

  ° **Keep Alive**: These messages will be observed when any Keep Alive messages have been captured in the communication.

  ° **ACKed Lost Packet**: These messages will be observed when an ACK for some lost packet is received.

  ° **Previous Segment Lost**: These messages will be observed when an unexpected packet is received out of sequence.

  ° **Out of Order**: These messages will be observed when are packets received in some random sequence, thus signifying no sequence.

- ○ **Fast Retransmission**: These messages will be popped up when, in a short time of 20 milliseconds, duplicate ACKs have been transmitted again.

- **Error**: These are general error messages in the packets or are thrown by the dissector of a specific protocol translating it. There is no specific category in error messages.

- **Details**: Collectively, all Expert Info dialogs can be viewed in the details tab. However, it is advisable to look into each tab individually on the basis of their severity level. Pointing out the problems can be sometimes easy because the entries made in the **details** tab are lined up in the sequence as they were captured. Viewing anomalies through the details tab can be a bit time consuming and disadvantageous.

- **Packet Comments**: This refers to any annotations given regarding the trace file that can be used to share any interpretations further. Adding comments to the trace file can be really useful while documenting for future references. To add a comment to any packet of your choice, just right-click on the selected packet and click on **Packet Comment**. You will be presented with a dialog where you can add a comment of your choice, and the same comment will be visible in the Packet Comments section of the Expert Infos dialog. Adding a comment will also affect how a certain packet is shown in the Details pane. Generally, an extra field will be added to the details pane highlighted with a green background color.

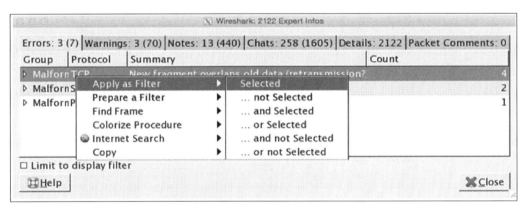

Figure 3.20: Create filter using Expert Infos dialog

Unique categories presented in every section can be expanded to get more information about a specific packet. When you expand and click on the packet listed in the **Expert Infos** dialog, Wireshark will point you to the corresponding packet in the list pane that can be investigated further. Creating a display filter for every category is also possible; just right-click on the selected category and choose the type of filter you want to create. Refer to the following screenshot for illustration purposes:

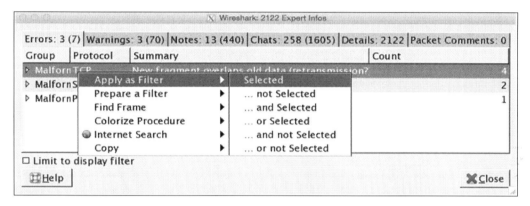

The main motive of the **Expert Infos** dialog is to find the anomalies present in a trace file. Finding the network problems in the trace file for a novice user becomes a lot easier and faster. Viewing the **Expert Infos** dialog can give a better idea about the unusual behavior of network packets. As we already discussed, the **Expert Infos** dialog is available for protocols based on TCP/IP; for the rest, there is not much info available.

The best way to figure out juicy info is to look into the tabs separately instead of looking into the **details** tab because, as we discussed, it can be time consuming and can lead to various misunderstandings. Users like you are not supposed to rely completely on **Expert Infos**; sometimes, the file you trace will contain anomalies that won't be listed in the **Expert Infos** dialog. May be, manual analysis will be required as well.

The protocol field that is shown in the details pane of the selected packet will be colored as per the severity level of the **Expert Infos** dialog; take a look at the following screenshot for further reference:

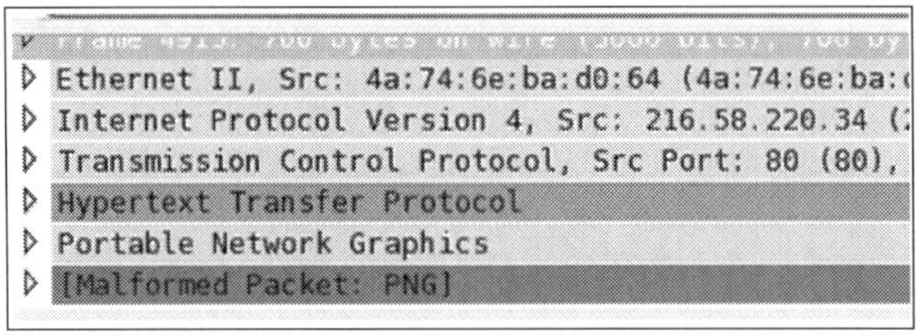

Figure 3.21: Colorization rules in protocol field

We can easily identify from the preceding screenshot that for this particular packet, there is an entry in the Error and Chat sections (red color denotes Error and blue denotes Chats). It is also possible that a single packet is listed in two sections of the Expert Infos dialog.

Command Line-fu

With the default installation of Wireshark, there are couple of command-line tools that get installed. These command-line tools are some sort of protocol analyzers, which can be taken advantage of when you don't have a GUI interface to work with or you don't have an option to install the GUI. There are good number of tools available in Wireshark to do this, which are Capinfos, Dumpcap, Editcap, Mergecap, Rawshark, Reordercap, Text2pcap, and Tshark.

The most common and widely used command-line tool for protocol analysis purposes is Tshark, which is capable of capturing data through listening to a live wire, and it can even analyze your already saved trace files. The captured packets are translated into an understandable form and printed to the standard output, or you can save them to the file of your choice. Dissectors that are used by Wireshark the same Tshark utilizes.

Tshark uses the pcap library to capture and translate the packets from the live wire or from the already saved files. Just like Wireshark's filtering option, we can enable filters in Tshark. There are multiple customizable options present in Tshark that can be leveraged to use it in a more advanced fashion.

Wireshark has a CLI version, which is almost similar to Tshark in terms of the syntax and various options that both of them support equally. Let's understand this topic better with an example. Say, for instance, we have an Apache web server and FTP running on a Windows XP box located at `172.16.136.128` and a Macintosh client running at `172.16.136.1`. Using our custom infrastructure, we will generate some network packets and try to use Tshark for capturing and analysis purposes.

When working on a Windows PC, you might have to create the environment variable before you can start using Tshark. The following screenshot belongs to Tshark, displaying `tshark -h (help options)` within the CLI:

```
Anonymous:Desktop NotFound$ tshark -h
TShark 1.12.6 (v1.12.6-0-gee1fce6 from master-1.12)
Dump and analyze network traffic.
See http://www.wireshark.org for more information.

Copyright 1998-2015 Gerald Combs <gerald@wireshark.org> and contributors.
This is free software; see the source for copying conditions. There is NO
warranty; not even for MERCHANTABILITY or FITNESS FOR A PARTICULAR PURPOSE.

Usage: tshark [options] ...

Capture interface:
  -i <interface>           name or idx of interface (def: first non-loopback)
  -f <capture filter>      packet filter in libpcap filter syntax
  -s <snaplen>             packet snapshot length (def: 65535)
  -p                       don't capture in promiscuous mode
```

Figure 3.22: Tshark help

We will start with the basics and eventually move toward the creation of filters, and then we will collect statistics using the CLI-based tool Tshark:

- The first thing we should know is how many interfaces do we have available to capture packets. Use the following command to check `tshark -D`:

```
Anonymous:Desktop NotFound$ tshark -D
1. en0 (Ethernet)
2. fw0 (FireWire)
3. bridge0 (Thunderbolt Bridge)
4. utun0
5. pktap0
6. en1 (Wi-Fi)
7. en2 (Thunderbolt 1)
8. lo0 (Loopback)
```

Figure 3.23: Interfaces available

If you do not specify any interface for capturing, `tshark` will choose the first interface that is available on its own. Interfaces can be chosen by their names and also by the sequence number they appear in. Refer to the preceding screenshot, which shows all the interfaces that are available.

- I have a custom interface `pktap0` that will listen to the connection between my client and the server. So, the command to initiate the capture process will be `tshark -i pktap0` or `tshark -i 5`:

```
Anonymous:Desktop NotFound$ tshark -i pktap0
Capturing on 'pktap0'
```

- Now, let's generate some HTTP traffic by visiting the web page hosted on our server from the client (I am using the `curl` command-line tool for browsing purpose):

```
Anonymous:Desktop NotFound$ curl http://172.16.136.128
```

- As soon as the preceding command has been issued, a couple of packets are captured by `tshark` on the `pktap0` interface. And a summary of translated packets for better understandability can be seen. Refer to the following screenshot that illustrates the same:

```
Anonymous:Desktop NotFound$ tshark -i pktap0
Capturing on 'pktap0'
  1   0.000000 172.16.136.1 -> 172.16.136.128 TCP 64 51816→80 [SYN] Seq=0 Win=65535 Len=0 MSS=1460 WS
  2 -745883619.604183 172.16.136.128 -> 172.16.136.1 TCP 64 80→51816 [SYN, ACK] Seq=0 Ack=1 Win=64240
  3 -733373297.062554 172.16.136.1 -> 172.16.136.128 TCP 52 51816→80 [ACK] Seq=1 Ack=1 Win=131744 Len
  4 -1830766245.431098 172.16.136.1 -> 172.16.136.128 HTTP 130 GET / HTTP/1.1
  5 -1830766245.129806 172.16.136.1 -> 172.16.136.128 HTTP 130 [TCP Retransmission] GET / HTTP/1.1
  6 -1664501840.066843 172.16.136.128 -> 172.16.136.1 TCP 52 80→51816 [ACK] Seq=1 Ack=79 Win=64162 Le
  7 -392509417.396438 172.16.136.128 -> 172.16.136.1 TCP 52 [TCP Dup ACK 6#1] 80→51816 [ACK] Seq=1 Ac
  8 -2027256734.439159 172.16.136.128 -> 172.16.136.1 HTTP 345 HTTP/1.1 302 Found
  9 -179068134.420122 172.16.136.1 -> 172.16.136.128 TCP 52 51816→80 [ACK] Seq=79 Ack=294 Win=131456
 10 -2067155579.763355 172.16.136.1 -> 172.16.136.128 TCP 52 51816→80 [FIN, ACK] Seq=79 Ack=294 Win=1
 11 -1830766248.828112 172.16.136.128 -> 172.16.136.1 TCP 52 80→51816 [ACK] Seq=294 Ack=80 Win=64162
 12 -392509283.614170 172.16.136.1 -> 172.16.136.128 TCP 52 [TCP Dup ACK 10#1] 51816→80 [ACK] Seq=80
 13 -1830766248.686849 172.16.136.128 -> 172.16.136.1 TCP 52 80→51816 [FIN, ACK] Seq=294 Ack=80 Win=6
 14 -392569681.317465 172.16.136.1 -> 172.16.136.128 TCP 52 51816→80 [ACK] Seq=80 Ack=295 Win=131456
```

Figure 3.24: Packets captured at pktap0

If you want to stop the capture process at any point, press *Ctrl + C*.

- To save the translated packets to a file, we need to specify the -w switch, along with the command that will save the raw data packets to the specified file:

```
Anonymous:Desktop NotFound$ tshark -i pktap0 -w http.txt
Capturing on 'pktap0'
11
```

A total of 11 packets have been captured, and a text file is being created on the desktop with the name `http.txt`, which will contain raw data as shown in the following screenshot:

```
Anonymous:Desktop NotFound$ cat http.txt


?M<+????????.Mac OS X 10.10.3, build 14D136 (Darwin 14.3.0)4Dumpcap


D136 (Darwin 14.3.0)``???@@E@f?@@k???????lP??f??????
???x``dA???_@@E@?@?},?????P?l?&j?f????a??
@@q??????lP??f??♦¡?
???xT??4??9??E??@@H???????lP??f??♦¡?h
???xGET / HTTP/1.1
User-Agent: curl/7.37.1
Host: 172.16.136.128
Accept: */*
```

Figure 3.25: Raw data stored in file

- If you want to save the normal translated form (like the one shown in the list pane in Wireshark), as shown in the standard output, then just redirect the output of the tshark command to a file of your choice, as shown in the following screenshot:

```
Anonymous:Desktop NotFound$ tshark -i pktap0 >> http2.txt
Capturing on 'pktap0'
11
```

As you can see, 11 packets are captured and redirected to the text file http2. Let's see what is stored in the http2.txt file:

```
Anonymous:Desktop NotFound$ cat http2.txt
  1   0.000000 172.16.136.1 -> 172.16.136.128 TCP 64 51821+80 [SYN] Seq=0 Win=65535 Len=0 MSS=1460 WS=32
  2 -1830767469.040043 172.16.136.128 -> 172.16.136.1 TCP 64 80+51821 [SYN, ACK] Seq=0 Ack=1 Win=64240 L
  3 -1830767469.040009 172.16.136.1 -> 172.16.136.128 TCP 52 51821+80 [ACK] Seq=1 Ack=1 Win=131744 Len=0
  4 -2016764535.847514 172.16.136.1 -> 172.16.136.128 HTTP 130 GET / HTTP/1.1
  5 -2027256734.427691 172.16.136.128 -> 172.16.136.1 HTTP 345 HTTP/1.1 302 Found
  6 -1830767469.037172 172.16.136.1 -> 172.16.136.128 TCP 52 51821+80 [ACK] Seq=79 Ack=294 Win=131456 Le
  7 -1830767469.037084 172.16.136.1 -> 172.16.136.128 TCP 52 51821+80 [FIN, ACK] Seq=79 Ack=294 Win=1314
  8 -1935145592.773838 172.16.136.128 -> 172.16.136.1 TCP 52 80+51821 [ACK] Seq=294 Ack=80 Win=64162 Len
  9 -1830767469.036949 172.16.136.1 -> 172.16.136.128 TCP 52 [TCP Dup ACK 7#1] 51821+80 [ACK] Seq=80 Ack
 10 -1935145592.773838 172.16.136.128 -> 172.16.136.1 TCP 52 80+51821 [FIN, ACK] Seq=294 Ack=80 Win=6416
 11 -1830767469.036570 172.16.136.1 -> 172.16.136.128 TCP 52 51821+80 [ACK] Seq=80 Ack=295 Win=131456 Le
```

Hopefully, by now you must have clearly understood the difference between both ways of saving the raw data packets and translated packets. Both of the techniques can be used in multiple scenarios.

- The next big thing you will learn is the different filters (Capture, Read, and Display) available in Tshark. We know about Capture and Display filters already, but here we have one more category, that is, the **Read filter**. The Read filter is closely similar to the Capture filter, as both of them can filter packets from the live network. However, the Read filter is also capable of filtering packets out of a saved file. Using the Read filter could be processor intensive, and things like packet loss can happen, so think twice before using it. To display the filter, the -f switch is used; -R is used for the Read filter; and -Y is used for the display filter. Now, I am going to capture only FTP packets using the following syntax:

```
Anonymous:Desktop NotFound$ tshark -i pktap0 -f "port 20"
Capturing on 'pktap0'
    1    0.000000 172.16.136.1 -> 172.16.136.128 TCP 64 51852→20 [SYN] Seq=0 Wi
    2    0.000151 172.16.136.128 -> 172.16.136.1 TCP 64 20→51852 [SYN, ACK] Sec
    3 -1438261061.117554 172.16.136.1 -> 172.16.136.128 TCP 52 51852→20 [ACK]
    4 -565845755.905104 172.16.136.128 -> 172.16.136.1 FTP-DATA 94 FTP Data: 4
    5    0.330476 172.16.136.1 -> 172.16.136.128 TCP 52 51852→20 [ACK] Seq=1 Ac
    6 -1438260168.702253 172.16.136.128 -> 172.16.136.1 FTP-DATA 97 FTP Data:
    7 -776735948.749363 172.16.136.1 -> 172.16.136.128 TCP 52 51852→20 [ACK] S
```

While applying a filter, there is a restriction that the filter expression must be specified as a single argument if it has spaces in between. Then, we need to write the expression within double quotes. Refer to the preceding screenshot that illustrates the same.

- Now, let's try to create one display filter using the http.pcap file. I want to filter all packets originating from the web server located at 172.16.136.128 using the http protocol.

- First I captured the communication between the client and server. And save the traffic in file HTTP.pcap.

  Once I have enough packets to work with, I will apply display filters, as shown in the following screenshot:

```
Anonymous:Desktop NotFound$ tshark -r http.pcap -Y "ip.src==172.16.136.128 and http"
  31 -2027256734.408549 172.16.136.128 -> 172.16.136.1 HTTP 345 HTTP/1.1 302 Found
  42 -2027256734.408549 172.16.136.128 -> 172.16.136.1 HTTP 345 HTTP/1.1 302 Found
  71 -1899318681.597223 172.16.136.128 -> 239.255.255.250 SSDP 161 M-SEARCH * HTTP/1.1
  76 -1899318681.597223 172.16.136.128 -> 239.255.255.250 SSDP 161 M-SEARCH * HTTP/1.1
  81 -1899318681.597223 172.16.136.128 -> 239.255.255.250 SSDP 161 M-SEARCH * HTTP/1.1
  90 -1899318681.597223 172.16.136.128 -> 239.255.255.250 SSDP 161 M-SEARCH * HTTP/1.1
 467 -2027256734.408549 172.16.136.128 -> 172.16.136.1 HTTP 345 HTTP/1.1 302 Found
 619 -2027256734.408549 172.16.136.128 -> 172.16.136.1 HTTP 345 HTTP/1.1 302 Found
 653 -2027256734.408549 172.16.136.128 -> 172.16.136.1 HTTP 345 HTTP/1.1 302 Found
1925 -1830772787.988137 172.16.136.128 -> 172.16.136.1 HTTP 345 HTTP/1.1 302 Found
```

Figure 3.26: Tshark display filter

- Suppose you want to quickly collect statistics about the http protocol from the `http.pcap` file. For such a requirement, we can use this command:

```
tshark -r <file-name> -q -z <expression>
```

```
Anonymous:Desktop NotFound$ tshark -r http.pcap -q -z http,tree

HTTP/Packet Counter:
Topic / Item           Count      Average      Min val      Max val      Rate (ms)      Percent

Total HTTP Packets     17                                                              100%
 HTTP Request Packets  11                                                              64.71%
  GET                  7                                                               63.64%
  SEARCH               4                                                               36.36%
 HTTP Response Packets 6                                                               35.29%
  3xx: Redirection     6                                                               100.00%
   302 Found           6                                                               100.00%
  ???: broken          0                                                               0.00%
  5xx: Server Error    0                                                               0.00%
  4xx: Client Error    0                                                               0.00%
  2xx: Success         0                                                               0.00%
  1xx: Informational   0                                                               0.00%
 Other HTTP Packets    0                                                               0.00%
```

The `-q` switch keeps it silent over the standard output (this is generally used while working with statistics in Wireshark) and the `-z` switch for activating various statistics options available. Both of these switches are often used together.

- Let's take one more simple example before wrapping this up; from the http.pcap file, I want to figure out how many hosts there are in total during the whole capture time. For such a requirement, refer to the following screenshot:

```
Anonymous:Desktop NotFound$ tshark -r http.pcap -q -z hosts
# TShark hosts output
#
# Host data gathered from http.pcap

172.16.158.1     Anonymous.local
172.16.136.1     Anonymous.local
```

Here, you learned about the basic theoretical and practical concepts of the CLI utility Tshark, along with how to capture and filter data as per our requirements. With the help of Tshark, it becomes really easy to understand how protocols work; we saw various techniques to collect and analyze the packets. Statistical features in Tshark are rich, which helps a moderate user become advanced with an better understanding of how to analyze network packets.

Summary

The Statistics menu in Wireshark contains options that can give us insight from a unique perspective. In this chapter, we've discussed features such as Summary, Conversations, Endpoints, and Graphs.

Summary is an informational feature, which offers a granular form of data, filters, and the trace file that you are working with. The Conversations window details data regarding the communication that happens between two or more hosts. The Endpoints dialog gives an overview of the devices connected to the network and communicating. The Protocol Hierarchy window gives an idea about the protocols being used in the communication, that is, it gives us a picture of the distribution of protocols used by the hosts for communication.

Graphs are a pictorial way of representing the statistics regarding packets. We can easily figure out if something is wrong with our network; we can match network performances and troubleshoot general day-to-day problems that occur.

IO graphs tell us the basic status of a network, and let us create filters. Matching network performances and differentiating a specific protocol becomes easy due to these. The Flow graph depicts the flow of data in a column-based manner and creates a simple interface to understand the flow of packets in a network. TCP stream graphs are a couple of types, but their objective is to depict the throughput of our network, that is, to know how much data is traveling over a particular period of time.

Using the Follow TCP Stream option, you can reassemble the packets listed in a raw data form, which can be easily read. There are different options that are available to change the form to ASCII, Hex, and many others.

The Expert Infos dialog tells you the information that can be usual and unusual. All of them are related to your packets; information is generated with the help of protocol dissectors, which translate the packets to a normal form, and if they find something unusual, then it will be listed in a section and under a category inside the dialog.

Command-line tools also get installed when you install Wireshark. The most common tool used is Tshark, which works in a similar way to Wireshark and tcpdump. It uses the pcap library that is used by other major protocol analyzers. With tshark, you can listen to live networks or work along with an already saved capture file. The Filtering and Statistical features are really efficient when dealing with any network analysis process. In the next chapter, we will dive into analyzing the commonly used application layer protocols.

Exercise

Q.1. What is the purpose of the Statistics menu and what tools does it contain?

Q.2. Using the Conversations dialog, can you figure out the busiest host on the network? If yes, how?

Q.3. Think of a scenario where using the Endpoints window can be useful.

Q.4. Is it possible to create a display filter using the Endpoints window?

Q.5. Switch the name resolution feature off while viewing the conversations window. What difference does it make if it is switched on?

Q.6. Can using the Summary option from an already saved capture file help you figure out the total number of ignored packets after you apply a display filter?

Q.7. Describe the benefits of using different graphing techniques while analyzing data.

Q.8. Using an IO graph, create a filter to plot the DNS traffic in a green line.

Q.9. Create an IO graph and show UDP traffic in red along with general TCP traffic. Then, change the y axis unit to per bytes.

Q.10. Create a display filter for FTP packets, and apply the same in a Flow graph. Then, customize it to check the SEQ number and ACKs instead of details.

Q.11. Using a previously captured file, create a Round Time Trip graph and figure out the packet whose RTT is the highest. Then, check the sequence number of that packet and verify its sequence number by comparing it with the graph.

Q.12. Create a Throughput graph between a server and your client. Try to figure out at what time the throughput was at its peak and also try to check the average throughput in bytes/seconds.

Q.13. If you have a requirement to view TCP packets in a raw data form, then which option will you opt for to customize the same window in order to view just the responses from the server side?

Q.16. Point out at least 5 benefits of using the Follow TCP Stream dialog.

Q.17. Explain the significance of the Expert Info dialog and figure out how many categories are there in a Warnings section.

Q.18. Using a command-line protocol analyzer, start sniffing your currently working network interface and save all traffic to a file named `traffic.pcap` (capture traffic at least for a minute).

Q.19. Capture only DNS traffic using tshark and save all the capture packets to a file named `DNS.pcap`.

Q.20. Create a display filter to filter HTTP and SSL traffic from the traffic.pcap file we created earlier and save the filtered traffic to a new file called `HTTP.txt`.

Q.21. Using the statistical features available in tshark, figure out the total number of hosts in the `traffic.pcap` file and save all the IP addresses that belong to one single host of your choice (Google, Yahoo, Apple, and so on) to a file named `hosts.txt`.

Q.22. Using the statistical feature available in tshark, check the Ethernet address of the hosts participating in the communication process from the `traffic.pcap` file and figure out the most communicating host from the list.

Q.23. View the protocol distribution using tshark statistical functions for the `traffic.pcap` file.

4
Inspecting Application Layer Protocols

This chapter will lead you through the common application layer protocols and will make it easy for you to find any anomalies. You will understand and analyze the normal behavior of application layer protocols by looking at the most common protocols and understand their usual and unusual behaviors.

- DNS—normal and unusual
- Lab Up—DNS
- FTP—normal and unusual
- Lab Up
- HTTP—normal and unusual
- Lab Up—HTTP
- SMTP—normal and unusual
- Lab Up—SMTP
- SIP—normal and unusual
- Lab Up—SIP
- VoIP—normal and unusual
- Lab Up—VoIP
- Decrypting encrypted traffic
- Practice questions

We will cover some of the most common application layer protocols that govern today's networks, whether small or big. Without spending too much time, let me take you on this wonderful journey of protocols.

Domain name system

Imagine a world of Internet where you have to type a random numerical value (IP address), instead of a name, to visit a website. Also, assume that each numerical figure is different. Considering this, how many IP addresses can you memorize? 5? 10? Perhaps, 50 at max? So, now, you are confined to visiting just 50 websites. This doesn't really sound feasible.

Suppose instead of just memorizing the IP addresses, you note down each of them, followed by the name that you want to give to the website to figure out which website is for what purpose. Now, you can create an Excel file for yourself, consisting of the IP addresses written next to the name of the website you gave. This way, probably, you can collect more than a thousand website addresses for later use.

For the sake of your unlimited web experience, DNS comes to your rescue, and it does exactly what you did in the preceding example. DNS creates a database of websites with their IP addresses, along with the name of the domain, A single row of record is often termed as resource records in a zone file. Each entry in the zone file is termed as a resource record. DNS uses TCP and UDP, both for different purposes, over the port 53 by default.

As a client, when you try to visit a website from your LAN environment, your request is being sent through an internal DNS server that looks up the resource records it contains. The request is termed as a DNS query. If your DNS server has already saved the IP address for the domain you are looking for, your client machine will get a reply from the internal DNS server that contains the IP address of the website you are trying to visit. Thus, you can form IP packets and start communicating. This reply is termed as a DNS response.

Dissecting a DNS packet

A DNS packet consists of a couple of unique fields that are briefly discussed here:

- **Transaction ID**: This is a number that keeps the dots connected between a particular domain query and it's corresponding response.
- **Query/response**: Every DNS packet is marked as a query or a response, depending on the details it contains.
- **Flag bits**: Each query and response contains different flag bits set, which are as follows.
    - ° **Response**: The message is a query or a response.

○ **Opcode**: This determines the type of query contained. Opcode ranges between 0–15. Refer to the following table:

Opcode	Description
0	Standard query
1	Inverse query
2	Server status request
3	Unassigned
4	Notify
5	Update
6-15	Unassigned

○ **Truncated**: This determines whether the packet is truncated if its size is large (greater than 512 bytes).

○ **Recursion desired**: The query sent by your client is supposed to go on a recursive search procedure from one DNS server to another if the resource record you are looking for is not present.

○ **Recursion available**: If this bit is set, then it means the recursion that your client requested is available, and if what you are looking for is not present on one server, then your query would be transferred to another DNS for lookup procedure.

○ **Reserved (z)**: .As defined by RFC 1035; Reserved for future use, must be set to zero for all queries and responses.

○ **Response code**: The values in this field signifies the response.

• **Response code**: This field is used to signify whether errors and the type of error. Here are the possible code values that you can receive:

Code	Description
0	No error
1	Format error
2	Server failure
3	Name error
4	Not implemented
5	Refused

• **Questions**: Indicates the number of queries present in the packet.

• **Answers**: Indicates the number of answers in response to the query sent.

- **Authority RRs**: Indicates the number of authority resource records sent as response.

- **Additional RRs**: Indicates the number of additional resource records sent as response.

- **Query section**: The query sent to the DNS Server, it should be the same in the response received as well.

- **Answer section**: The answer that came as a response to our query. The response can be multiple too. The answer basically consists of the resource records that came in response to our query.

- **Type**: This field indicates the type of query sent. Refer to the following table for common query types.

Type	Description
A	Host address
NS	Name server
MX	Mail exchange
SOA	Start of zone authority
PTR	Pointer record
AAAA	IPv6 address
AXFR	Full zone transfer
IXFR	Incremental zone transfer

- **Additional info**: This field includes additional info containing resource records. It is not required to answer the query.

Dissecting DNS query/response

A client sends a query to the DNS server that possesses the name resolution information. Using this information, the client can start IP-based communication. Sometimes, the information the client is looking for is not available with the DNS server it requested. In this case, the DNS server itself transfers the query to any neighbor DNS it knows about, if recursion is desirable. The whole query and response thing is completed within two packets only. Refer to the following *Figure 4.1* where I am trying to visit `https://www.google.co.in`. A request from my client located at `192.168.1.103` is sent to the default gateway at `192.168.1.1`. This gateway will forward my query to the DNS server it knows about:

```
▷ Frame 9: 74 bytes on wire (592 bits), 74 bytes captured (592 bits) on interface 0
▷ Ethernet II, Src: Apple_b9:53:ec (d8:bb:2c:b9:53:ec), Dst: Zte_07:73:6c (d0:5b:a8:07:73:6c)
▷ Internet Protocol Version 4, Src: 192.168.1.103 (192.168.1.103), Dst: 192.168.1.1 (192.168.1.1)
▷ User Datagram Protocol, Src Port: 65382 (65382), Dst Port: 53 (53)
▽ Domain Name System (query)
      [Response In: 10]
      Transaction ID: 0x2b4a
   ▷ Flags: 0x0100 Standard query
      Questions: 1
      Answer RRs: 0
      Authority RRs: 0
      Additional RRs: 0
   ▽ Queries
      ▽ www.google.com: type A, class IN
            Name: www.google.com
            [Name Length: 14]
            [Label Count: 3]
            Type: A (Host Address) (1)
            Class: IN (0x0001)
```

Figure 4.1: DNS query

If you notice, here, DNS is using UDP as an underlying protocol. If you want to know more about the DNS query being generated, just expand the flags section. This section will list various details such as whether recursion is available, whether recursion is desired, whether the query is truncated, what the response code is, what the Opcode for the query is, and so on. Please refer to the following screenshot.

```
▽ Flags: 0x0100 Standard query
      0... .... .... .... = Response: Message is a query
      .000 0... .... .... = Opcode: Standard query (0)
      .... ..0. .... .... = Truncated: Message is not truncated
      .... ...1 .... .... = Recursion desired: Do query recursively
      .... .... .0.. .... = Z: reserved (0)
      .... .... ...0 .... = Non-authenticated data: Unacceptable
```

The expanded `Flags` section depicts that the type of DNS packet is a query, the packet data is not truncated, and recursion is desirable if available.

In response to this query, you will be seeing one more packet with the same transaction ID that denotes the association of a particular query. It is the response packet. Response for our query will usually consist of IPv4 address for the domain we are trying to look for. We'll be returned with a single IP, or maybe multiple IPs available to it. If the domain we are looking for is not available, then its probable CNAME's will be returned in as favor.

Refer to *Figure 4.2* to understand this:

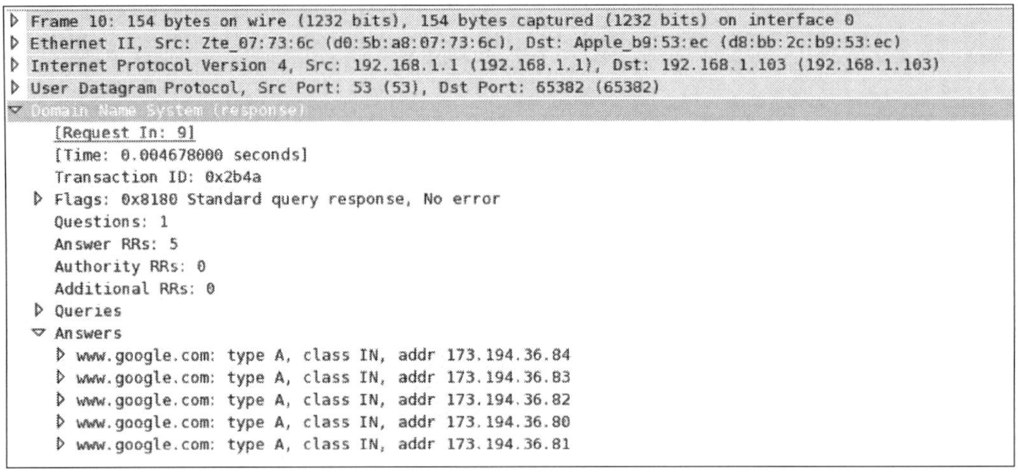

```
▷ Frame 10: 154 bytes on wire (1232 bits), 154 bytes captured (1232 bits) on interface 0
▷ Ethernet II, Src: Zte_07:73:6c (d0:5b:a8:07:73:6c), Dst: Apple_b9:53:ec (d8:bb:2c:b9:53:ec)
▷ Internet Protocol Version 4, Src: 192.168.1.1 (192.168.1.1), Dst: 192.168.1.103 (192.168.1.103)
▷ User Datagram Protocol, Src Port: 53 (53), Dst Port: 65382 (65382)
▽ Domain Name System (response)
    [Request In: 9]
    [Time: 0.004678000 seconds]
    Transaction ID: 0x2b4a
  ▷ Flags: 0x8180 Standard query response, No error
    Questions: 1
    Answer RRs: 5
    Authority RRs: 0
    Additional RRs: 0
  ▷ Queries
  ▽ Answers
    ▷ www.google.com: type A, class IN, addr 173.194.36.84
    ▷ www.google.com: type A, class IN, addr 173.194.36.83
    ▷ www.google.com: type A, class IN, addr 173.194.36.82
    ▷ www.google.com: type A, class IN, addr 173.194.36.80
    ▷ www.google.com: type A, class IN, addr 173.194.36.81
```

Figure 4.2: DNS response

As I said, we could get multiple replies. If you notice the **Answer RRs** section, we have received 5 replies for the `www.google.com` domain. For verification that the response received belongs to the previous query only, just match the `Transaction ID`. Expand any section in the answers category to view more details. Refer to the following image:

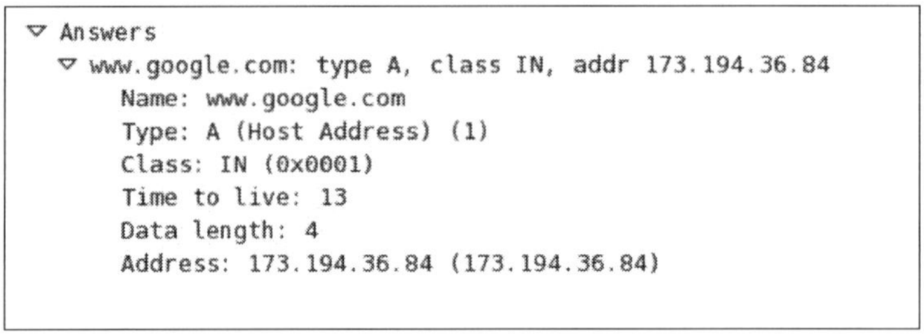

```
▽ Answers
  ▽ www.google.com: type A, class IN, addr 173.194.36.84
      Name: www.google.com
      Type: A (Host Address) (1)
      Class: IN (0x0001)
      Time to live: 13
      Data length: 4
      Address: 173.194.36.84 (173.194.36.84)
```

Unusual DNS traffic

Name resolution problems can have a significant impact on the performance of a network. One of the most common DNS problems you can face is when looking for something that does not exist in the DNS server's database. Sometimes, you are trying to visit a website that exists, but your DNS server is not able to resolve the domain you gave. It could also be a timed-out situation where your client waited more than the expected time for a DNS response.

In the following *Figure 4.3*, I am trying to check the type A record for the `http://google.com` domain, which is actually an incorrect syntax. Hopefully, it won't be resolved:

```
Anonymous:~ NotFound$ host -t a http://google.com
Host http://google.com not found: 3(NXDOMAIN)
```

Figure 4.3: Type A record for `http://google.com`

As expected, we got a `Not Found` error. I only tried once, but the client tried it twice to resolve the domain given. What got captured is depicted in *Figure 4.4* here:

No.	Time	Source	Destination	Protocol	Length	Info
1	0.000000000	192.168.1.103	192.168.1.1	DNS	77	Standard query 0xcdc1 A http://google.com
2	0.009283000	192.168.1.1	192.168.1.103	DNS	77	Standard query response 0xcdc1 No such name
3	0.053794000	192.168.1.103	192.168.1.1	DNS	77	Standard query 0xbb93 A http://google.com
4	0.056583000	192.168.1.1	192.168.1.103	DNS	77	Standard query response 0xbb93 No such name

Figure 4.4: DNS Response-No Such Name

There can be multiple situations where you can get stuck. The best option is to first have a benchmark set for your own network, and then try comparing your problem with the benchmark you created. For example, check the name you are trying to resolve, launch a protocol analyzer, and dig into the name resolution queries and responses. Understand how long it is taking to complete the query, the response process, and so on. Every device on the network maintains a local DNS cache (host file), which is initially used to resolve any domain you request. If the local DNS cache does not have the entry for that domain, then the request will be forwarded to the local network's DNS server, which will perform the lookup. If found, their response will be sent. Otherwise, the request from the local DNS server will be forwarded to an external DNS server, which the local DNS server is configured to look for.

File transfer protocol

Since the Internet came into existence, we have been working with FTP. It was in the limelight even when the Internet was still a closed network used by the government and other corporate organizations.

FTP uses the TCP protocol to initiate and transfer files over a designated channel. There will be two channels created; one is the command channel, and the other one is specifically a data channel. The command channel will be used to send and receive the commands and their responses. The data channel is used to send data between the client and the server.

Commonly, port 21 is used by the FTP server to listen for the connection, and any random port on the client to send and receive data. As per the standard, port 21 will be used for the command channel and port 20 for the data channel. However, you will observe random port numbers used to transfer TCP data segments.

Dissecting FTP communications

There are two types of mode a client uses to communicate with the server: active and passive. Both of them have a different approach to send and receive data. In earlier versions, active mode was in use by default, but these days, you can see passive mode in use by default. I will discuss each of them using my own virtual network where I have a FTP server (VSFTPD) configured on the 172.16.136.129 IP and a client at 172.16.136.1. The following sections described the flow and show how the client and server will behave in the active and passive modes.

Passive mode

- The client sends a SYN request to the server running at port 21.

- The client receives SYN/ACK from the server over a temporary port used.

- The client sends ACK to the server to confirm that the channel will be used for sending commands. Refer to the following screenshot:

```
1 0.000000000        172.16.136.1     172.16.136.129    TCP      64 56982→21 [SYN] Seq=0 Win=65535
2 0.000187000        172.16.136.129   172.16.136.1      TCP      60 21→56982 [SYN, ACK] Seq=0 Ack=1
3 1846322634.413041000  172.16.136.1  172.16.136.129    TCP      52 56982→21 [ACK] Seq=1 Ack=1 Win=
```

- Now, the client will be shown a welcome banner and will be asked for the assigned credentials:

```
 4 0.018723000          172.16.136.129  172.16.136.1     FTP      88 Response: 220 Welcome to Charit's FTP se
 5 555032032.287455000  172.16.136.1    172.16.136.129   TCP      52 56982→21 [ACK] Seq=1 Ack=37 Win=131728 L
 6 -952210303.718297000 172.16.136.1    172.16.136.129   FTP      62 Request: USER abc
 7 -143593220.746255000 172.16.136.129  172.16.136.1     TCP      52 21→56982 [ACK] Seq=37 Ack=11 Win=29696 L
 8 4.629189000          172.16.136.129  172.16.136.1     FTP      86 Response: 331 Please specify the passwor
 9 4.629206000          172.16.136.1    172.16.136.129   TCP      52 56982→21 [ACK] Seq=11 Ack=71 Win=131696
10 5.732635000          172.16.136.1    172.16.136.129   FTP      62 Request: PASS abc
11 -1086390884.249094000 172.16.136.129 172.16.136.1     FTP      75 Response: 230 Login successful.
12 2070317539.792672000 172.16.136.1    172.16.136.129   TCP      52 56982→21 [ACK] Seq=21 Ack=94 Win=131672
```

Figure 4.5: Server showing welcome banner and asking for credentials

- Normally, passive mode must be on by default. Performing a directory listing will tell you that the **Extended passive (ESPV)** mode is in use. In this mode, the client requests the server to listen on the data port and wait for the connection. In return, the server informs the client about the TCP port number used for the connection. Please refer to the below screenshot.

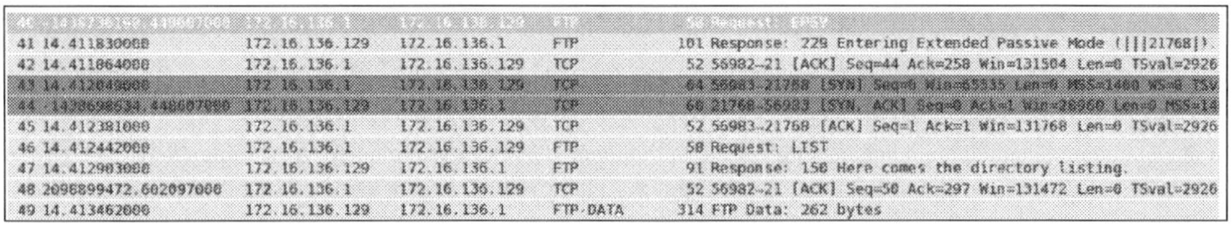

Figure 4.6: client sends ACK to the server

In frame 42, the server informs about the IP address and the port number that the client has to use while creating any data connection to the server.

- In frame 42, the server informs us about the IP address and the port number that the client has to use while creating any data connection to the server. Followed by a sequence of SYN, SYN/ACK, and ACK, packets which us required to create a data channel between both the devices. After this, the LIST command is executed as seen in frame 46. Then data is transferred using the temporary ports used by both the client and the server.

- As soon as the data transfer is complete, the sending host closes the connection by transmitting a FIN packet which is addressed by the receiving side using an ACK packet. The receiving side also sends a FIN packet that is acknowledged too. If both the devices want to share more data, then a new data channel will be created using random port numbers.

Active mode

- The client sends a SYN request to the server running at port 21.
- The client receives SYN/ACK from the server over a temporary port used by the client.
- The client sends ACK to the server to confirm that the channel will be used to send commands. Refer to the following screenshot:

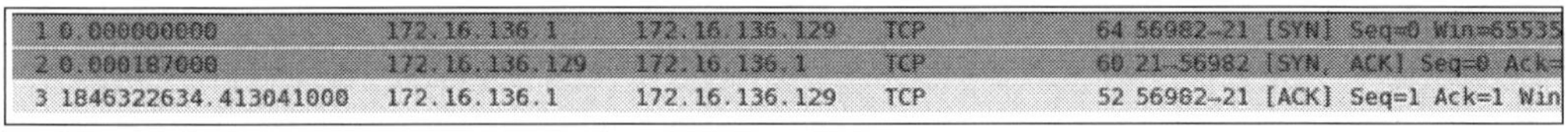

- Now, the client will be shown a welcome banner and will be asked for the assigned credentials:

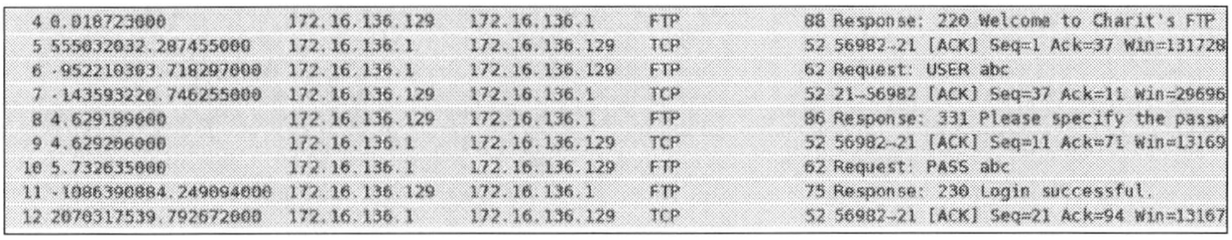

Figure 4.7: Client is shown a welcome banner and asked for credentials

- Now, we have to turn passive mode off, because, as usual, it will be on by default. Once done, we can create a data channel for transferring purposes, refer to the following screenshot:

40 894485615.991284000	172.16.136.1	172.16.136.129	FTP	81 Request: EPRT |1|172.16.136.1|57197|
41 894485615.991670000	172.16.136.129	172.16.136.1	FTP	103 Response: 200 EPRT command successful.
42 290386415.628665000	172.16.136.1	172.16.136.129	TCP	52 57196→21 [ACK] Seq=67 Ack=260 Win=13150
43 -544276953.032968000	172.16.136.1	172.16.136.129	FTP	58 Request: LIST
44 894485615.992341000	172.16.136.129	172.16.136.1	TCP	60 20→57197 [SYN] Seq=0 Win=29200 Len=0 M
45 894485615.992407000	172.16.136.1	172.16.136.129	TCP	64 57197→20 [SYN, ACK] Seq=0 Ack=1 Win=65
46 894485615.992662000	172.16.136.129	172.16.136.1	TCP	52 20→57197 [ACK] Seq=1 Ack=1 Win=29696 Le
47 894485615.992690000	172.16.136.1	172.16.136.129	TCP	52 [TCP Window Update] 57197→20 [ACK] Seq=
48 -540049189.689031000	172.16.136.129	172.16.136.1	FTP	91 Response: 150 Here comes the directory
49 894485615.993039000	172.16.136.1	172.16.136.129	TCP	52 57196→21 [ACK] Seq=73 Ack=299 Win=13140
50 894485615.993489000	172.16.136.129	172.16.136.1	FTP-DATA	314 FTP Data: 262 bytes
51 349348548.220939000	172.16.136.1	172.16.136.129	TCP	52 57197→20 [ACK] Seq=1 Ack=263 Win=13150
52 323940847.628665000	172.16.136.129	172.16.136.1	TCP	52 20→57197 [FIN, ACK] Seq=263 Ack=1 Win=
53 366125747.443723000	172.16.136.1	172.16.136.129	TCP	52 57197→20 [ACK] Seq=1 Ack=264 Win=13150
54 894485615.994235000	172.16.136.129	172.16.136.1	FTP	76 Response: 226 Directory send OK.

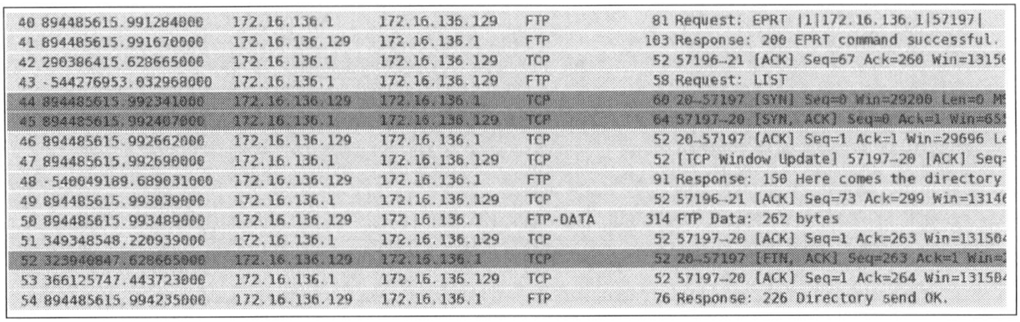

Figure 4.8 Creating data channel for transferring purpose

Frame `40` shows that the client is requesting to switch the passive mode off using the `EPRT |1|172.16.136.1|57197|` command. **Extended Port (EPRT)** helps in specifying an extended address that can be used for data connection. The command accepts three arguments: network protocol, network address, and the port number.

- Now, whenever the client tries to initiate a connection, it has to be destined for the particular address specified by the EPRT command. Before, every data connection server informed the client about the temporary port to be used.

You learned about the active and passive modes of communication that the FTP servers support. You also learned how they behave. Whenever troubleshooting any FTP connection, checking the mode will be useful and saves time.

Dissecting FTP packets

In general, every request sent from the client is a specific command set to which the server responds with a numerical value followed by a text message. See the following screenshot:

```
62 Request: PASS abc
75 Response: 230 Login successful.
```

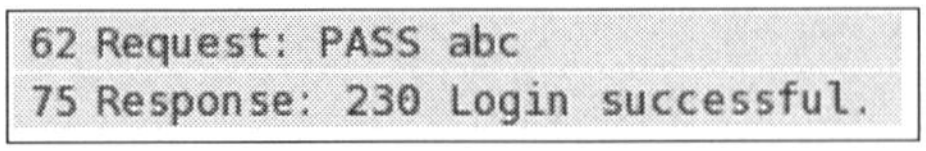

As you can see, the server requested for the password, which the client provides. It can be seen over the wire in plain text in the list pane itself. Once the server receives and verifies that the password is correct, the respective message will be shown. In our case, the password is correct, so the client receives 230 as a response code followed by a Login Successful message.

The command issued from the client side can have arguments or no arguments, and the data flowing across between the devices can be simply seen in the TCP header of the packet. Refer to the following *Figure 4.9*:

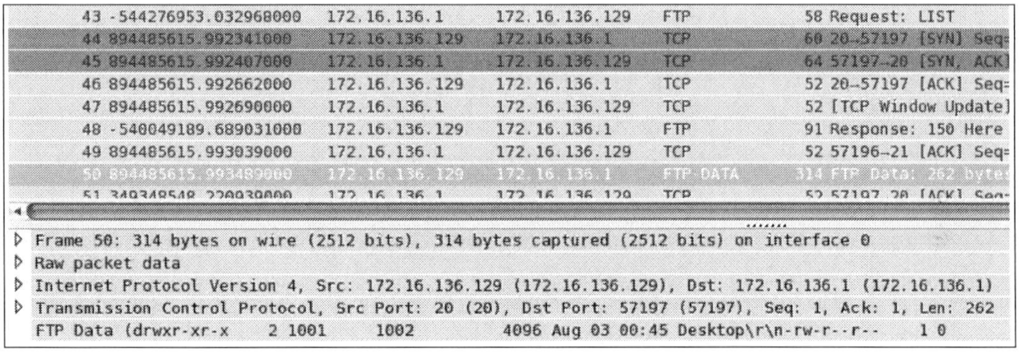

43	-544276953.032968000	172.16.136.1	172.16.136.129	FTP	58	Request: LIST
44	894485615.992341000	172.16.136.129	172.16.136.1	TCP	60	20→57197 [SYN] Seq=
45	894485615.992407000	172.16.136.1	172.16.136.129	TCP	64	57197→20 [SYN, ACK]
46	894485615.992662000	172.16.136.129	172.16.136.1	TCP	52	20→57197 [ACK] Seq=
47	894485615.992690000	172.16.136.1	172.16.136.129	TCP	52	[TCP Window Update]
48	-540049189.689031000	172.16.136.129	172.16.136.1	FTP	91	Response: 150 Here
49	894485615.993039000	172.16.136.1	172.16.136.129	TCP	52	57196→21 [ACK] Seq=
50	894485615.993489000	172.16.136.129	172.16.136.1	FTP-DATA	314	FTP Data: 262 byte
51	349349548.229039000	172.16.136.1	172.16.136.129	TCP	52	57197→20 [ACK] Seq=

▷ Frame 50: 314 bytes on wire (2512 bits), 314 bytes captured (2512 bits) on interface 0
▷ Raw packet data
▷ Internet Protocol Version 4, Src: 172.16.136.129 (172.16.136.129), Dst: 172.16.136.1 (172.16.136.1)
▷ Transmission Control Protocol, Src Port: 20 (20), Dst Port: 57197 (57197), Seq: 1, Ack: 1, Len: 262
  FTP Data (drwxr-xr-x   2 1001   1002   4096 Aug 03 00:45 Desktop\r\n-rw-r--r--   1 0

Figure 4.9: FTP-DATA returned

Frame 43 shows that the client issued the LIST command that was processed by the server, and 262 bytes of data was returned back to us. Select frame 50 to further investigate the contents of the TCP header. One of the biggest disadvantages of using FTP is that all data travels in plain text, even the usernames and passwords.

Reassembling the FTP data stream is easy because except the data, there is nothing that travels around. There is no code or command that gets appended to the packets travelling, thus making it easy for Wireshark and the user to understand things easily. To reassemble the TCP stream of FTP packets, just right-click on the selected packet, choose the **Follow TCP Stream** option, and view it in raw form. Refer to the following *Figure 4.10*:

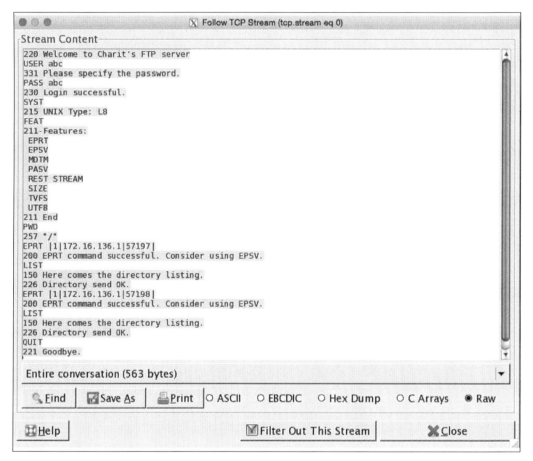

Figure 4.10: FTP stream

The entire communication between the client and the server that happened over the data and command channels is translated into human-readable format. Text in red color is what the client sent, and text in blue color is what the client received. These days, we have a couple of advanced protocols that can create an encrypted channel. One of them is **Secure File Transfer Protocol (SFTP)**.

Unusual FTP

There can be multiple scenarios, which generate FTP traffic of an unusual type. I will use a couple of scenarios to explain this and will show you how a certain traffic type looks. An example would be brute force attacks where a malicious user tries different passwords again and again, until the exact password is matched. This is the most common traffic type that you will see while working with FTP. Applying a `ftp.request.command=="PASS"` filter will show all the password attempts that have been made to your server. If you see an unusual number of attempts in a short span of time, then it can be a brute-force attempt against your server. Refer to the following screenshot:

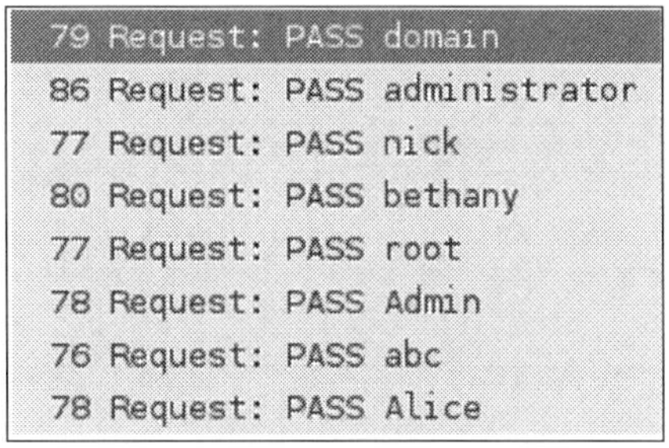

```
79 Request: PASS domain
86 Request: PASS administrator
77 Request: PASS nick
80 Request: PASS bethany
77 Request: PASS root
78 Request: PASS Admin
76 Request: PASS abc
78 Request: PASS Alice
```

Figure 4.11: FTP brute force

I applied the same display filter mentioned earlier, and you can see the results. Someone was trying to brute force my FTP server. To secure your server from such brute force or dictionary attacks, you can limit the server to maximum login attempts, after which the server should lock down the respective account for a particular amount of time.

You could also colorize the brute force traffic if you want. This will eventually give you a better overview of your capture file or live traffic. Try it out using the code that the server sends back to the clients in response.

Another example is a malicious device that is infected by some malware. Due to the malware, the device is trying to contact a command and control-center server to download some payload, perhaps for privilege escalation purpose or to launch further attacks. There is even a possibility where an attacker sitting on the other side is trying to download or upload something. Let me take an example to explain. I have a Kali Linux box running at `192.168.1.105` and a Windows box at `192.168.1.104`. Through Kali, I created a small malware that was downloaded and installed by the victim (Windows). Once executed, we will get the shell from the device. Then, we can launch FTP from within the shell to connect our Kali box for privilege escalation purposes.

Refer to the following screenshot that captures the FTP traffic between the attacker and the victim:

5 0.77097600	192.168.1.105	192.168.1.104	FTP	90 Response: 220 Welcome to charit's FTP server
6 0.97935700	192.168.1.105	192.168.1.104	FTP	90 [TCP Retransmission] Response: 220 Welcome to charit's FTP server
8 3.01186800	192.168.1.104	192.168.1.105	FTP	64 Request: USER abc
10 3.02034200	192.168.1.105	192.168.1.104	FTP	88 Response: 331 Please specify the password.
12 4.89021500	192.168.1.104	192.168.1.105	FTP	64 Request: PASS abc
13 4.99799600	192.168.1.105	192.168.1.104	FTP	77 Response: 230 Login successful.
15 20.7320120	192.168.1.104	192.168.1.105	FTP	60 Request: XPWD
16 20.8443810	192.168.1.105	192.168.1.104	FTP	63 Response: 257 "/"
21 26.3072450	192.168.1.104	192.168.1.105	FTP	79 Request: PORT 192,168,1,104,4,77
22 26.3814360	192.168.1.105	192.168.1.104	FTP	105 Response: 200 PORT command successful. Consider using PASV.
23 26.3908600	192.168.1.104	192.168.1.105	FTP	60 Request: NLST
27 26.4087450	192.168.1.105	192.168.1.104	FTP	93 Response: 150 Here comes the directory listing.
31 26.4120250	192.168.1.105	192.168.1.104	FTP	78 Response: 226 Directory send OK.
41 85.1657690	192.168.1.104	192.168.1.105	FTP	79 Request: PORT 192,168,1,104,4,78
42 85.2421850	192.168.1.105	192.168.1.104	FTP	105 Response: 200 PORT command successful. Consider using PASV.
43 85.2533840	192.168.1.104	192.168.1.105	FTP	72 Request: RETR payload.txt
47 85.2589130	192.168.1.105	192.168.1.104	FTP	121 Response: 150 Opening ASCII mode data connection for payload.txt (3 bytes).
51 85.2629570	192.168.1.105	192.168.1.104	FTP	78 Response: 226 Transfer complete.

Figure 4.12: victim FTP capture

As you can clearly see, the attacker connected to the FTP server and downloaded the payload.txt file, which might be used to gain root privileges over the box.

If something of this nature is able to bypass your firewalls and other security appliances in place, then consider improvising the configuration you created and try to avoid these things in future. Sometimes, activity of this kind can be legitimate as well, but it should not stop you from investigating further. A small file of a few kbs is enough to compromise your whole network.

Hyper Text Transfer Protocol

Data on the web is transferred using the HTTP application layer protocol. Normal communication in HTTP is a request/response model where the communication between a client and a server is coordinated by a set of rules. The client requests for a certain resource to the server and then receives a status code that specifies the current status of the requested resource. If available then, the resource is also sent along with the status code. HTTP is one of the most popular and most widely used protocols to transfer data requested by browsers from the respective servers. The world of Internet is mostly governed by HTTP that runs on the transport layer.

How it works – request/response

Every time you visit a website, this smart protocol takes care of your web-browsing experience. Web server utilizes the HTTP protocol to serve web pages they contain to the requesting clients. At the beginning of every HTTP session, the TCP three-way handshake takes place. It creates a dedicated channel between the communicating hosts followed by HTTP and data packets, which are sent in and received while the session is active. For instance, you are visiting a web server located at `http://172.16.136.129` and the client at `172.16.136.1`. Using our client-server infrasrtucture, we will try to capture the requests sent and responses received.

I will try to visit the home page located at the server mentioned earlier and will capture the traffic generated for the whole session, that is, requests sent and responses received. Follow the actions mentioned here to replicate the scenario.

Request

- Open your browser, and type the **Uniform Resource Locator** (**URL**) of any website that you want to visit. In my case, the website is located at `http://172.16.136.129` (Don't get confused because of the IP address I am using to visit a webserver. While studying DNS remove, we discussed that it is just a way to locate a webserver that is assigned with an IP address.). Press *Enter* to go to the home page. Here is the screenshot of the home page I am visiting:

- Due to the our preceding actions, a couple of packets are generated that are captured by Wireshark. Let's have a look at the list pane shown in the following screenshot:

1 0.000000000	172.16.136.1	172.16.136.129	TCP	64 59781→80 [SYN] Seq=0 Win=65535
2 -1438998251.586830000	172.16.136.129	172.16.136.1	TCP	60 80→59781 [SYN, ACK] Seq=0 Ack=1
3 0.000146000	172.16.136.1	172.16.136.129	TCP	52 59781→80 [ACK] Seq=1 Ack=1 Win=
4 0.000035000	172.16.136.1	172.16.136.129	HTTP	467 GET / HTTP/1.1
5 -1439017790.883535000	172.16.136.129	172.16.136.1	TCP	52 80→59781 [ACK] Seq=1 Ack=416
6 548191280.817750000	172.16.136.129	172.16.136.1	HTTP	262 HTTP/1.1 304 Not Modified
7 0.070913000	172.16.136.1	172.16.136.129	TCP	52 59781→80 [ACK] Seq=416 Ack=211
8 5.073679000	172.16.136.129	172.16.136.1	TCP	52 80→59781 [FIN, ACK] Seq=211 Ack
9 5.073739000	172.16.136.1	172.16.136.129	TCP	52 59781→80 [ACK] Seq=416 Ack=212
10 29.999840000	172.16.136.1	172.16.136.129	TCP	52 59781→80 [FIN, ACK] Seq=416 Ack
11 30.000161000	172.16.136.129	172.16.136.1	TCP	52 80→59781 [ACK] Seq=212 Ack=417

Figure 4.13: Packets captured by Wireshark

All these packets get generated as soon as you press *Enter*. As you can see, the first three packets are TCP three-way handshake packets where our client is requesting the server to create a dedicated channel. In our case, the connection was successful. However, if the server daemon wasn't running or because of any reason the server is not accepting our requests, then we could have seen RST ACK packets, like the one shown here:

1 0.000000000	172.16.136.1	172.16.136.129	TCP	64 59783→80 [SYN] Seq=0
2 0.000315000	172.16.136.129	172.16.136.1	TCP	40 80→59783 [RST, ACK]

Figure 4.14:RST and ACK packets, as server not accepting the requests

This error states that the server is out of service or perhaps the server is not supposed to respond to our requests.

- After the TCP packets, you can see the first HTTP request sent by our client. Every request comprises a couple of elements that are sent to the server:

```
GET / HTTP/1.1\r\n
Host: 172.16.136.129\r\n
If-None-Match: "12625d-bc-51c6ab45063d1"\r\n
Accept: text/html,application/xhtml+xml,application/xml;q=0.9,*/*;q=0.8\r\n
If-Modified-Since: Mon, 03 Aug 2015 16:31:40 GMT\r\n
User-Agent: Mozilla/5.0 (Macintosh; Intel Mac OS X 10_10_3) AppleWebKit/600.6.3
Accept-Language: en-us\r\n
Accept-Encoding: gzip, deflate\r\n
Connection: keep-alive\r\n
```

Figure 4.15: HTTP request

- This is how a request looks. In the first line, there are three things passed on to the server as the arguments, which are HTTP method and requested resource location "/" (root directory)

- The second line specifies the `Host` argument that is required by the `HTTP/1.1` protocol requests. The value of this field is the webserver's address that you typed in the address bar of the browser.

- The fourth line is the `ACCEPT` parameter that mentions what kind of content is acceptable by the requesting client in response.

- The `If-modified-since` parameter is sent from the client to the server, which includes the date and time of your previous request made to the server. If the server contents have been changed since your previous request, then you will receive the new updated page. Otherwise, your system will present you with the locally cached page that will eventually save some resources.

- The next field is `User-Agent`, which specifies the browser-related information that you are using to visit the webpage. This information will be used by the server to present you with browser-compatible content.

- Parameters such as `Accept-Language` and `Accept-Encoding` are passed on to the server to inform us of what type of content is acceptable to the client. So, while the server prepares the response material, these things should be taken into consideration.

- The `Connection-Alive` parameter specifies that the client wishes to keep the connection working after this particular request has been processed.

All the HTTP packets are sent most commonly to the webserver at port `80` (other common webserver ports are `8080, 3132, 8088` and so on. which are being dissected by Wireshark as per HTTP protocol preferences).

Response

- As you can see, after the fourth packet, the server acknowledges the client's request to get to the server's web root directory. The server starts transmitting the resource that client requested for. The sixth packet in the list pane is what the client received, a status code followed by a short message, including the content of the resource requested. Refer to the following *Figure 4.16* illustrating the HTTP response:

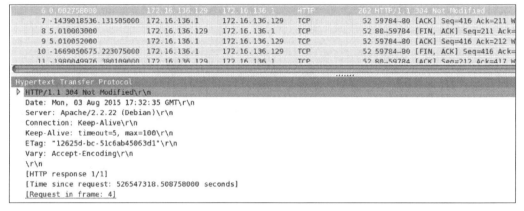

Figure 4.16: HTTP response

- As a part of TCP communication, the client will acknowledge every packet sent by the server. It can be seen in the seventh packet that the client is trying to send an ACK for the resource it received.

- Let's dissect the response elements for packet number six. The first line consists of three arguments sent in response. They denote the HTTP protocol version in use, the status code (304 in our case, which specifies that the requested resource did not change since the time mentioned in the Date parameter), and finally, a brief description about the status code (Not Modified in our case).

- In the third line, the Server parameter mentions the name and version of the web server running. We can see that Apache/2.2.22 is the server that is located at 172.16.136.129.

- The fourth and fifth lines state that the server wishes to keep the connection alive. The duration for which the server wishes to do so is also mentioned in the next line of the parameters sent in response to us. Rest of the content is mentioned in the next few lines are some configuration parameters.

This is a very basic example to check out the request and responses exchanged between the client and the server. However, this basic thing is what actually happens every time you visit a website. As stated earlier, we receive a status code followed by a brief description in response. With every tab you open in your browser, there will be a new socket created between a client and a server connected through an IP address and the port number on which the web server runs.

Unusual HTTP traffic

All the details mentioned earlier are part of a normal traffic pattern. What we are about to witness is some unusual traffic pattern that you might face while dealing with HTTP. I will try to mention some do's and don'ts, which might prove helpful to you while troubleshooting and analyzing HTTP. Most of the HTTP problems revolve around errors such as 404, some kind of redirection, DNS resolution problems, and server-related issues. Let me explain each scenario in detail.

For instance, you are visiting a web server, and you are looking for something that is currently not available or the requested resource's location has been changed. In such cases, you will receive a 404 status code, which denotes that the requested resource is not found on the server. Refer to the following screenshot where I tried to request for a file named abc.txt on a web server that does not exist:

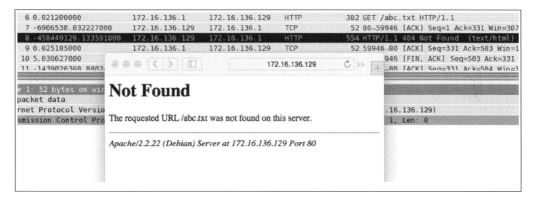

Figure 4.17 : HTTP 404

On the list pane, you can see that the requested resource is not available. So, we get 404 Not Found Error. Such errors could be malicious too if someone is trying to perform directory listing on your webserver. Changing the coloring rules of such 404 packets to something different other than the normal HTTP packets rules will get our attention quickly. As you can see, packet number eight is a HTTP packet, applied with a different coloring scheme.

Redirection of the user's request is often done when a certain requested resource location has been changed to another address or the resource isn't available. Now, to make you understand redirection, I have made some changes in our infrastructure that can be easily seen in the diagram shown here:

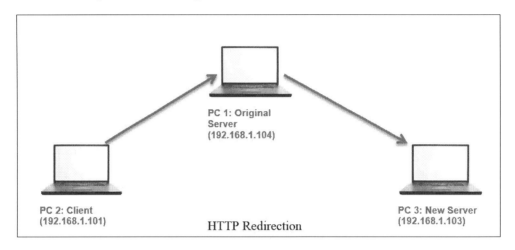

Now, the request from the client sent to the original server at `192.168.1.104` will be redirected to a new server located at `192.168.1.103` without any further efforts by the client. To configure redirection, you have to modify your server's configuration file. The following captured packets depict the redirection happened. Refer to the next list pane in *Figure 4.18*:

```
16 -894755292.094458000   192.168.1.101   192.168.1.104   TCP    64 60068-80 [SYN] Seq=0 Win=65535
17 -1439017251.826457000  192.168.1.104   192.168.1.101   TCP    60 80-60068 [SYN, ACK] Seq=0 Ack=
18 5.015205000            192.168.1.101   192.168.1.104   TCP    52 60068-80 [ACK] Seq=1 Ack=1 Win
19 225473059.936095000    192.168.1.101   192.168.1.104   HTTP  466 GET / HTTP/1.1
20 66295390.403899000     192.168.1.104   192.168.1.101   TCP    52 80-60068 [ACK] Seq=1 Ack=415 W
21 5.016916000            192.168.1.104   192.168.1.101   HTTP  580 HTTP/1.1 302 Found (text/html)
22 -1439036540.123162000  192.168.1.101   192.168.1.104   TCP    52 60068-80 [ACK] Seq=415 Ack=529
29 -77577563.228889000    192.168.1.104   192.168.1.101   TCP    52 80-60068 [FIN, ACK] Seq=529 Ac
30 -1354952914.826457000  192.168.1.101   192.168.1.104   TCP    52 60068-80 [ACK] Seq=415 Ack=530
31 -894755292.083749000   192.168.1.101   192.168.1.103   TCP    64 60069-80 [SYN] Seq=0 Win=65535
32 10.040659000           192.168.1.103   192.168.1.101   TCP    60 80-60069 [SYN, ACK] Seq=0 Ack=
33 190061013.628710000    192.168.1.101   192.168.1.103   TCP    52 60069-80 [ACK] Seq=1 Ack=1 Win
34 10.041701000           192.168.1.101   192.168.1.103   HTTP  466 GET / HTTP/1.1
35 -1700935729.321851000  192.168.1.103   192.168.1.101   TCP    52 80-60069 [ACK] Seq=1 Ack=415 W
36 10.045989000           192.168.1.103   192.168.1.101   HTTP  262 HTTP/1.1 304 Not Modified
37 -506133590.227039000   192.168.1.101   192.168.1.103   TCP    52 60069-80 [ACK] Seq=415 Ack=211
51 -1793850626.523174000  192.168.1.103   192.168.1.101   TCP    52 80-60069 [FIN, ACK] Seq=211 Ac
52 15.056875000           192.168.1.101   192.168.1.103   TCP    52 60069-80 [ACK] Seq=415 Ack=212

Frame 21: 580 bytes on wire (4640 bits), 580 bytes captured (4640 bits) on interface 0
Raw packet data
Internet Protocol Version 4, Src: 192.168.1.104 (192.168.1.104), Dst: 192.168.1.101 (192.168.1.101)
Transmission Control Protocol, Src Port: 80 (80), Dst Port: 60068 (60068), Seq: 1, Ack: 415, Len: 528
Hypertext Transfer Protocol
  ▷ HTTP/1.1 302 Found\r\n
```

Figure 4.18: HTTP redirection

As you can see, a TCP handshake was initiated with the old server at 104 followed by an HTTP GET request. The server at 104 responded with a 302 Found response in packet 21, which is an indication of redirection. Our request was sent to the new server located at 103 with whom we again initiated the TCP three-way handshake (packet 31). After packet 31, the destination field was changed to the new server's address.

On investigating packet 21 further, we can see the content that redirected our request to the new server. Expand the Line-based text data section under the HTTP section of the details pane for packet 21. Refer to the following screenshot:

```
Line-based text data: text/html
    <!DOCTYPE HTML PUBLIC "-//IETF//DTD HTML 2.0//EN">\n
    <html><head>\n
    <title>302 Found</title>\n
    </head><body>\n
    <h1>Found</h1>\n
    <p>The document has moved <a href="http://192.168.1.103">here</a>.</p>\n
    <hr>\n
    <address>Apache/2.2.22 (Debian) Server at 192.168.1.104 Port 80</address>\n
    </body></html>\n
```

We have already discussed DNS resolution problems in the DNS protocol section. For example, if the requested web server is not able to resolve your request using your internal DNS server as well as other external servers, then you won't be able to visit the website. Even if the DNS servers are working fine and you are not able to visit the site, then congestion can be the problem, where a server is not able to process multiple requests at the same time. This will result in errors such as 408 time-out requests, 429 Too Many requests, or even 404 not found. The world of HTTP is enormous, and day-to-day situations can differ from person to person. The most important fact that you should keep in mind is that if all your basic-level concepts are clear, then only it would be an easy to do the job you have been assigned. Nothing can beat common sense with out-of-the-box thinking.

Simple Mail Transfer Protocol

SMTP is used widely to send and receive emails over small, as well as large, infrastructures (can be public or private). The protocol uses the Sender-SMTP process to send e-mails and the Receiver-SMTP process to receive emails. This makes SMTP a client-server-based protocol that runs over port 25. However, many mail server admins follow the secure practice of changing the default port number for SMTP to any other random port that prevents the server from sending any spams out there in the wild and even keep the server out-of-reach from malicious users.

Most commonly, an SMTP channel for mail transfer is created using a TCP three-way handshake that happens between two hosts, which is followed by a series of SMTP packets. For illustration purpose, I configured one SMTP server on `192.168.1.105` and a client on `192.168.1.104`. The client will request the server to send an e-mail to an address known to the client. The server will respond to this request with numerical code, followed by a brief response parameter. For understanding the real functioning of the protocol, I will be using the following architecture.

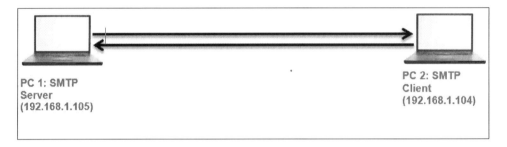

Usual versus unusual SMTP traffic

Using the netcat client from Kali Linux, I will try connecting to the SMTP mail service running on a Windows machine. Once a dedicated channel is created between the server and the client, the server indicates that it is ready to accept any commands sent in. Also, the server will respond with numerical codes with a short summary. I followed these steps to connect and send an e-mail:

1. Open a connection using netcat `nc -nv 192.168.1.105 25`.

2. Initialize an SMTP session using the `HELO testmail` command.

3. Specify the `from` address using the `MAIL FROM:<abc@charit.com>` command.

4. Specify the recipient's address using the `RCPTS TO:<efg@charit.com>` command.

5. To enter data into the mail body, type `DATA` and press *Enter*. Now, type the message you wish to send. Once you are finished writing your email, type a `.` to mark the ending and press *Enter*.

6. Now, your message will be sent. If you wish to send more emails, follow the same procedure; or else, you can close your connection with the mail server. Type `QUIT` to do so.

The series of commands I followed generated a couple of packets that contain details about the session in a very granular form. I also created a capture filter, which captured only the packets associated with the client and server that would help me in closely analyzing the packets related to the session; and preventing other packets entering the list pane. All of these commands mentioned will only work when the server is configured to permit clear text message communication without any authentication, refer to the following screenshot depiction for similar behavior.

1	0.000000000	192.168.1.104	192.168.1.105	TCP	60 57073-25 [SYN] Seq=0 Win=29200 Len=0 MSS
2	1439081651.426767000	192.168.1.105	192.168.1.104	TCP	60 25-57073 [SYN, ACK] Seq=0 Ack=1 Win=1638
3	-41448.227586000	192.168.1.104	192.168.1.105	TCP	52 57073-25 [ACK] Seq=1 Ack=1 Win=29696 Len
4	4205130.997054000	192.168.1.105	192.168.1.104	SMTP	90 S: 220 Charit's.com ESMTP server ready.
5	1439081652.143751000	192.168.1.104	192.168.1.105	TCP	52 57073-25 [ACK] Seq=1 Ack=39 Win=29696 Le
6	-287363963.384218000	192.168.1.104	192.168.1.105	SMTP	61 C: helo abc
7	1744899513.488830000	192.168.1.105	192.168.1.104	SMTP	82 S: 250 Charit's.com Hello, abc.
8	1439081657.529807000	192.168.1.104	192.168.1.105	TCP	52 57073-25 [ACK] Seq=10 Ack=69 Win=29696 L
9	1744901809.636862000	192.168.1.104	192.168.1.105	SMTP	79 C: mail from:<abc@charit.com>
10	1744899513.488830000	192.168.1.105	192.168.1.104	SMTP	81 S: 250 Sender OK - send RCPTs.
11	1439081671.468558000	192.168.1.104	192.168.1.105	TCP	52 57073-25 [ACK] Seq=37 Ack=98 Win=29696 L
12	1439081686.949708000	192.168.1.104	192.168.1.105	SMTP	78 C: rcpts to:<efg@charit.com>
13	4206566.333758000	192.168.1.105	192.168.1.104	SMTP	91 S: 250 Recipient OK - send RCPT or DATA.
14	1439081687.064346000	192.168.1.104	192.168.1.105	TCP	52 57073-25 [ACK] Seq=63 Ack=137 Win=29696
15	1439081688.805525000	192.168.1.104	192.168.1.105	SMTP	57 C: data
16	4207044.779326000	192.168.1.105	192.168.1.104	SMTP	91 S: 354 OK, send data, end with CRLF.CRLF
17	2122359292.356797000	192.168.1.104	192.168.1.105	TCP	52 57073-25 [ACK] Seq=68 Ack=176 Win=29696
18	1439081690.221834000	192.168.1.104	192.168.1.105	SMTP	55 C: DATA fragment, 3 bytes
19	1439081690.447064000	192.168.1.104	192.168.1.105	SMTP	55 [TCP Retransmission] C: DATA fragment,
20	1439081690.454208000	192.168.1.105	192.168.1.104	TCP	52 25-57073 [ACK] Seq=176 Ack=71 Win=16314
21	1439081690.455528000	192.168.1.105	192.168.1.104	TCP	64 [TCP Dup ACK 20#1] 25-57073 [ACK] Seq=17
22	168258645.511998000	192.168.1.104	192.168.1.105	SMTP	54 C: DATA fragment, 2 bytes
23	419451065.438925000	192.168.1.105	192.168.1.104	SMTP	75 S: 250 Data received OK.
24	1439081690.858935000	192.168.1.104	192.168.1.105	TCP	52 57073-25 [ACK] Seq=73 Ack=199 Win=29696
25	168257924.091710000	192.168.1.104	192.168.1.105	SMTP	57 C: DATA fragment, 5 bytes
26	1439081694.129351000	192.168.1.105	192.168.1.104	SMTP	95 S: 221 Charit's.com Service closing chan
27	850006670.085950000	192.168.1.105	192.168.1.104	TCP	52 25-57073 [FIN, ACK] Seq=242 Ack=78 Win=1
28	850006670.085950000	192.168.1.104	192.168.1.105	TCP	52 57073-25 [ACK] Seq=78 Ack=242 Win=29696

Figure 4.19: SMTP session

Packets from 1-3 are TCP-handshake packets. The handshake is happening between the client and the server. In the fourth packet, the client receives a message stating 220 as the response code. This means the server is ready and available to respond to the client's request. In the sixth packet, the client initializes the standard SMTP session using the HELO command (You must be wondering why most of the packets listed in the list pane start with C or S. Requests sent from the client are marked with the character C, and server responses are marked with character S.). Then, enter the sender's and recipient's e-mail addresses, which were confirmed to be correct by the server, with response code 250 in packets 10 and 13. After that, enter the e-mail body using the DATA command, which was successfully received by the server in packet 23. In the end, the user gracefully closes the connection by issuing the QUIT command, which the server confirmed in packet 26, thus sending the FIN, ACK.

Now, I will introduce you to the dark side of SMTP that you might have witnessed, or you will someday. By dark side, I meant the packets that are not supposed to pop up inside the list pane usually. However, if they do, then you have to look into your protocol configuration. For this, I would like to introduce you to some quite common scenarios that you should be aware of.

The first and foremost case I can think of is when the server and the client are not able to create a dedicated channel for communication; in short, the TCP handshake did not go well. This can happen because of many reasons, such as the mail server daemon is not running, the mail server is not running on the default port, the mail server daemon has reached the maximum simultaneous client connections allowed or connections from a particular subnet are not allowed there can be multiple scenarios related to this. The following list pane depicts two kinds of traffic abnormalities:

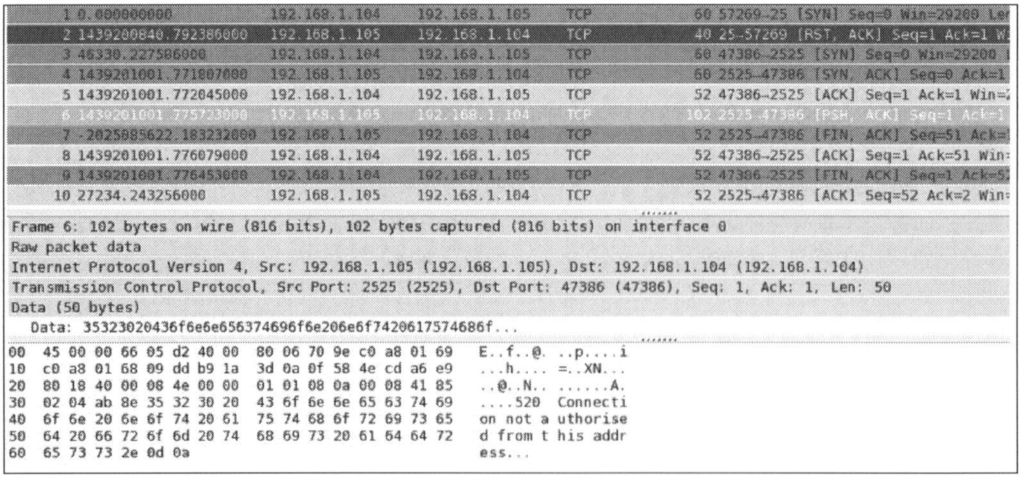

Figure 4.20: SMTP unusual traffic

The first two packets were generated due to an error, which stopped the TCP handshake from occurring. This error can be generated due to many factors, some of which are mentioned here:

- Mail server daemon is not running
- Mail server daemon default port is changed
- Mail server daemon has reached the maximum simultaneous connections limit (DDoS attack).
- Mail server's configuration has been tampered with

Let's suppose now, that the client came to know about the correct port number to which the connection should be initiated, but still, the session was not created successfully. Observe the traffic starting from packet 3 to the packet 10, the last packet. A TCP three-way handshake happened, but then, suddenly, the client was kicked off from the session. What could be the possible reason for such a response from the server? Perhaps the client is not allowed to get connected because of some restrictions in place, such as IP or MAC filtering.

1	0.000000000	192.168.1.104	192.168.1.105	TCP	60 57230-25 [SYN] Seq=0 Win=29200 Len=0 MSS=1460
2	-1439191021.671720000	192.168.1.105	192.168.1.104	TCP	60 25-57230 [SYN, ACK] Seq=0 Ack=1 Win=16384 Len
3	-299332529.969384000	192.168.1.104	192.168.1.105	TCP	52 57230-25 [ACK] Seq=1 Ack=1 Win=29696 Len=0 TS
4	-1435002675.066153000	192.168.1.105	192.168.1.104	SMTP	90 S: 220 Charit's.com ESMTP server ready.
5	0.144765000	192.168.1.104	192.168.1.105	TCP	52 57230-25 [ACK] Seq=1 Ack=39 Win=29696 Len=0 T
6	2.062258000	192.168.1.104	192.168.1.105	SMTP	61 C: helo abc
7	2.199304000	192.168.1.105	192.168.1.104	SMTP	82 S: 250 Charit's.com Hello, abc.
8	2.199772000	192.168.1.104	192.168.1.105	TCP	52 57230-25 [ACK] Seq=10 Ack=69 Win=29696 Len=0
9	212289295.064342000	192.168.1.104	192.168.1.105	SMTP	76 C: mail from: <efg@abc.com>
10	12.450170000	192.168.1.105	192.168.1.104	SMTP	81 S: 250 Sender OK - send RCPTs.
11	12.450646000	192.168.1.104	192.168.1.105	TCP	52 57230-25 [ACK] Seq=34 Ack=98 Win=29696 Len=0
12	22.846623000	192.168.1.104	192.168.1.105	SMTP	75 C: rcpts to: <abc@abc.com>
13	566789423.708283000	192.168.1.105	192.168.1.104	SMTP	90 S: 553 we do not relay non-local mail, sorry
14	23.255494000	192.168.1.104	192.168.1.105	TCP	52 57230-25 [ACK] Seq=57 Ack=142 Win=29696 Len=0
15	53.669236000	192.168.1.105	192.168.1.104	TCP	52 25-57230 [FIN, ACK] Seq=142 Ack=57 Win=16328
16	-700612319.058152000	192.168.1.104	192.168.1.105	TCP	52 57230-25 [FIN, ACK] Seq=57 Ack=143 Win=29696
17	53.671389000	192.168.1.105	192.168.1.104	TCP	52 25-57230 [ACK] Seq=143 Ack=58 Win=16328 Len=0

Figure 4.21: Client not allowed to get connected due to some restrictions

Another type of abnormal traffic that can be seen widely these days is harvesting of e-mails used by spammer and spamming botnets roaming in the wild. A spammer tries to harvest emails from the publicly accessible mail servers to verify which email address is valid and which isn't. For example, look at the following screenshot (*Figure 4.15*) where a malicious user tries to verify the existence of an e-mail ID using the **E-mail From** field, verification of e-mail addresses can alos be done using VRFY command. Depending on the response, the user will come to know whether the email is valid or not. Observe packet number 13 for the server's response. These kinds of attacks are done using a custom-made dictionary file, which matches the current domain requirements. Once an email is verified, the spammer can perform various forms of social-engineering attacks. A response code greater than 350 in SMTP protocol is probably some kind of error that can reduce your network performance, thus increasing the latency.

Session Initiation Protocol and Voice Over Internet Protocol

SIP is a part of the VOIP protocol family that is just a signaling protocol used to create, manage, and terminate voice over IP sessions in a networking environment. Examples of SIP can be a two-way phone call or a conference call, including multimedia sessions where multiple hosts can be present. This protocol is generally discussed in regards to the initiation of the session between the remove parties ; hosts/nodes that intend to communicate. After the initiation is completed, the data is transferred over the dedicated channel where the **Real time Transport Protocol** (**RTP**) helps. Basically, the family of RTP governs the transport and the flow control of all of the multimedia items (RTCP controls the flow).

The two most used tools while working with this protocol are the Statistics menu, under which we will cover Protocol Hierarchy, Packet Lengths, and flow graphs, which will give you an idea of data travelling back and forth between two hosts. Under the **Telephony** menu, you will see the RTP and VOIP Calls options that can facilitate us in assembling the VOIP call streams. We can then play them back to hear the conversation, this is what makes me really excited about Wireshark.

SIP runs over the UDP protocol and commonly uses port 5060. All of this together in an IP-based environment makes it possible for us to dial instantly to our friends over a VoIP-enabled device. SIP makes it easy for the VOIP telephony server to establish user locations. It facilitates us with different call-managing features such as initiating calls, disconnecting calls, adding someone to a conference call, transferring calls, and various others. SIP is not going to help you maintain the quality of calls, yet SIP is one of the most important standards used by various services. Before we jump directly into looking and listening to the traffic, let's get ourselves acquainted with how the traffic moves in a voice over IP call.

There will be three parties we will consider: two of them are clients and one is the IP telephony server that helps in transferring the required and necessary packets back and forth between the two communicating hosts. The following figure depicts a small infrastructure telephony architecture and lists the various steps taken:

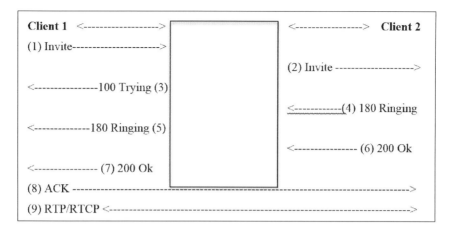

- **Client 1** sends an **Invite** request to initiate the session using SIP.

- The telephony server in between, transfers the request to **Client 2**.

- The telephony server acknowledges **Client 1** with the **100 TRYING** packet.

- **Client 1** receives a **180 RINGING** packet as soon as **Client 2** starts ringing. When **Client** 2 on the other side received the call, it sends the **200 OK** packet, which is forwarded to **Client 1**.

- Now, the client sends the **ACK** packet to acknowledge the receipt of the **200 OK** packet.

- Now, both parties are connected with a dedicated channel over which the RTP/RTCP packet starts flowing back and forth.

- Once both of them are done, there will be a **BYE** packet sent from by the hosts communicating, which is acknowledged by the other end.

- If you observe, most of the packets are passing through the telephony server. Because the telephony server only knows about the exact location of the connected hosts.

- Once the connection is successfully created, all the packets are sent and received directly by the clients without the server's intervention.

I have configured a small VoIP telephony infrastructure using Asterisk PBX that you can download freely from the vendor's website. VOIP server is located at 192.168.1.107, client 1 at 192.168.1.104, and client 2 at 192.168.1.107. Then, I downloaded X-Lite client using which, I tried calling client 2 from client 1. Now, using the real SIP traffic captured, it becomes easy for us to analyze and learn. Interestingly, there is an option using which, we can play back the communication captured (this can be really dangerous and more amazing).

Here is example traffic captured as seen in the list pane of Wireshark:

5 0.001200000	192.168.1.104	192.168.1.107	SIP/SDP	981 Request: INVITE sip:101@192.168.1.107	
5 0.001673000	192.168.1.107	192.168.1.104	SIP	515 Status: 100 Trying	
172 0.085903000	192.168.1.107	192.168.1.106	SIP/SDP	917 Request: INVITE sip:101@192.168.1.106:5621
177 0.087461000	192.168.1.107	192.168.1.104	SIP	531 Status: 180 Ringing	
178 0.652323000	192.168.1.106	192.168.1.107	SIP	348 Status: 100 Trying	
179 0.959210000	192.168.1.106	192.168.1.107	SIP	501 Status: 180 Ringing	
182 0.961010000	192.168.1.107	192.168.1.104	SIP	531 Status: 180 Ringing	
186 3.827648000	192.168.1.106	192.168.1.107	SIP/SDP	782 Status: 200 OK	
188 3.829335000	192.168.1.107	192.168.1.106	SIP	489 Request: ACK sip:101@192.168.1.106:56215;r
205 3.834786000	192.168.1.107	192.168.1.104	SIP/SDP	820 Status: 200 OK	
211 3.839764000	192.168.1.104	192.168.1.107	SIP	482 Request: ACK sip:101@192.168.1.107	
1644 10.852745000	192.168.1.104	192.168.1.107	SIP	641 Request: BYE sip:101@192.168.1.107	
1645 10.853115000	192.168.1.107	192.168.1.104	SIP	489 Status: 200 OK	
1652 10.854002000	192.168.1.107	192.168.1.106	SIP	527 Request: BYE sip:101@192.168.1.106:56215;r
1690 11.042924000	192.168.1.106	192.168.1.107	SIP	467 Status: 200 OK	

Figure 4.22: SIP traffic

One thing you should consider is place the analyzer close to the telephony server so that you can easily capture every bit of packet-level information moving around. While capturing, if you cannot see any SIP packets, then you won't be able to capture VOIP packets as well. You would end up capturing UDP packets only in the list pane, which won't prove very fruitful for your analysis.

Analyzing VOIP traffic

Just for the sake of curiosity, I want to show you the protocol distribution for SIP traffic that can be seen using the **Protocol Hierarchy** dialog from the **Statistics** menu. Refer to the following *Figure 17*:

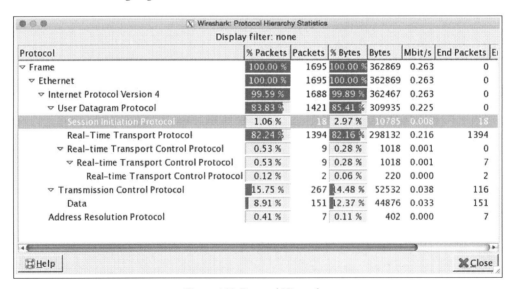

Figure 4.23: Protocol Hierarchy

Major traffic generated during the session is UDP based, and as seen in the preceding screenshot, SIP traffic is a very small part of it. If you observe closely, it is just 1 percent roughly, whereas RTP has a major role here with 82 percent. This gives an overview about the session we captured and tells us which protocol participates in what percentage. As we already know, SIP is used only to create and manage sessions that occur between two users, or it can be a multiuser conference call.

Flow graphs are one more way of getting a summary of the traffic. They help in understanding the movement of request and acknowledgements sent or received. Refer to the following *Figure 4.24*:

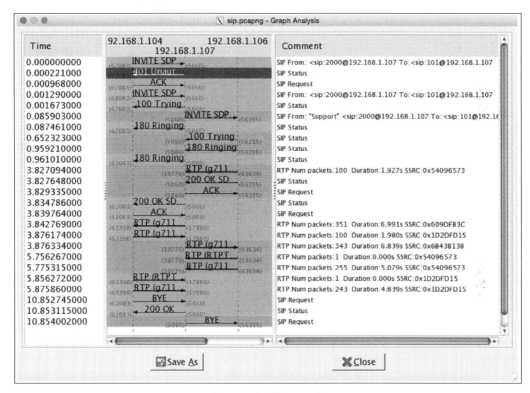

Figure 4.24: Flow graph

There are three IPs listed just below the title bar in the center section. These IPs belong to the server and the two clients that are trying to communicate. The entire request and the responses with their status codes and summary messages can be seen clearly here. Requests sent are colored in orange and the responses with green. This makes every element look more precise and easy to understand.

Reassembling packets for playback

Yes, this is possible. You can assemble the VOIP packets back to listen to either, or both sides of the communication in parallel. Let's suppose I want to listen what message client 1 sitting at `192.168.1.104` sent to the client 2. We can use the **Telephony** menu in Wireshark to reassemble the packets and choose the **VOIP Calls** option from the list. The following screenshot illustrates the resulting dialog.

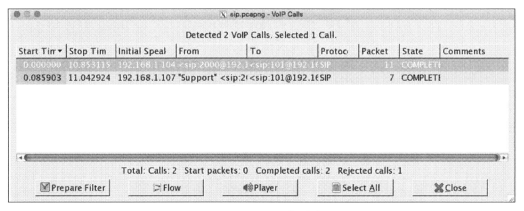

Figure 4.25 : VOIP Calls dialog

Now, choose which side of communication you want to listen to. Then, click on the **Player** button, which will then ask you to provide maximum **Jitter** (Jitter is the variance in packet rate at which the packets are being sent and received. If jitter is high, then there is a chance your network is dealing with congestion. Calls having high jitter values are not feasible to listen to.) in our communication session. The maximum jitter value is `22`. So, by default, there will be **50 ms** value given in the box. You can change this value if your jitter is higher than that; otherwise, just click on **Decode**:

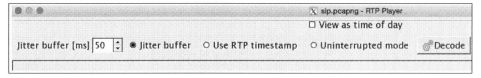

Figure 4.26: Player dialog

I did not change the default value and clicked directly on the **Decode** button, which reassembled all the VoIP packets for the side of communication I chose. Refer to the following screenshot:

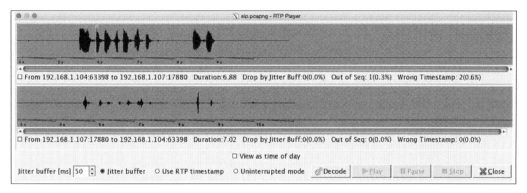

Figure 4.27: RTP Player

If you want to play the message, check the box just below the scrollbar and click on **Play**. Various useful details related to the assembled VOIP stream are listed..

Unusual traffic patterns

Wireshark has numerous tools that help a user in maintaining QS for a certain networking infrastructure and also consists of a tool that helps in identifying various day-to-day traffic anomalies. A common type of traffic when dealing with an SIP server is INVITE requests that are sent from one client to initiate the connection with another client. As you might already know, this process is a three-way handshake where the client who initiated the request is supposed to acknowledge when the session creation is completed. What if the client who requested does not respond with ACK and sends another INVITE request? Normally, the server will try to connect the client to the requested client machine, meanwhile waiting for the ACK response for the previous request. Now, let's suppose the client sent 100 INVITE requests through different clients on the network and did not even bother to send ACK for any one of those sessions created. This can result in a DOS attack (INVITE flood attack) where the SIP server won't be able to process any further requests (the buffer size for INVITE is 100). To resolve this, you can apply a display filter to view the INVITE requests sent from a client or apply a filter where the status code is 200:OK.

Other than DOS attacks, there is a chance that your network may slow down due to packet congestion, or you might not be able to get connected to another client on your network. In other words, your call cannot get through, if there is lag in setting up the call (the average call setup time is high). You will witness multiple cases once you work in a production environment. So, Wireshark and the various powerful tools it contains comes to our rescue.

For instance, if some client is trying to make a call to an invalid extension, they will get an error, and the call won't get through. Such a scenario will generate packets as shown here:

```
12 3.100381000     192.168.1.104    192.168.1.107    SIP/SDP    981 Request: INVITE sip:100@192.168.1.107 |
13 3.100794000     192.168.1.107    192.168.1.104    SIP        515 Status: 100 Trying |
167 3.366362000    192.168.1.107    192.168.1.104    SIP        574 Status: 503 Service Unavailable |
199 3.481824000    192.168.1.104    192.168.1.107    SIP        364 Request: ACK sip:100@192.168.1.107 |
```

I would suggest that you filter SIP packets consisting of error codes greater than 399 and create a display filter using `sip.Status-Code > 399`. See the following screenshot that lists multiple errors generated while client 1 was trying to call:

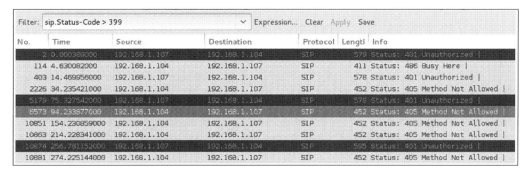

Figure 4.28: SIP error

Decrypting encrypted traffic (SSL/TLS)

Yes, it is possible to decrypt your online TLS traffic into a plain text SSL stream using Wireshark. Google Chrome and Firefox look for a log file, which stores the TLS session keys. Follow these steps to decrypt encrypted traffic:

1. Create an environment variable with the name SSLKEYLOGFILE that will point to a text file. Your browser will look for this file every time it starts up. To create environment variables, right-click on **My Computer** | Go to **Advanced Settings** | **Environment Variables** | **New** | **Specify Name**: SSLKEYLOGFILE and **Value**: C:/Users/username/sslkeylog.txt and click on **Ok**.

2. I have created a blank text file, C:/Users/username/sslkeylog.txt (make your new environment variable point to this file).

3. Now, open your browser and visit a website enabled with TLS/SSL. For demonstration purpose, I have my own SSL webserver located at 192.168.1.105 and a client located at 192.168.1.105.

The certificate I created is self-signed; that's why you are seeing a red diagonal line across `https` in the address bar. After you visit any secure website enabled with SSL, your **sslkeylog.txt** will be populated with some random numbers, as shown in the following screenshot. If not, cross check your settings before moving on:

```
CLIENT_RANDOM 17999a56ea29e69bcb242b441b1b519e
0b3b16e79b9a46bfdcb280fd4eb027e1786e3766c7313f
1117b14
```

4. I captured the whole traffic between my client and server in Wireshark. Now, go to **Edit | Preferences | Protocol tree | SSL | (Pre)-Master-Secret log filename | /path/to/sslkeylog.txt | Ok**. Then, right-click on the SSL packet (Make sure you select **Decrypt packet data**. The option should be present in the bytes pane) and follow the SSL stream. Now, you will see something like *Figure 4.29* here:

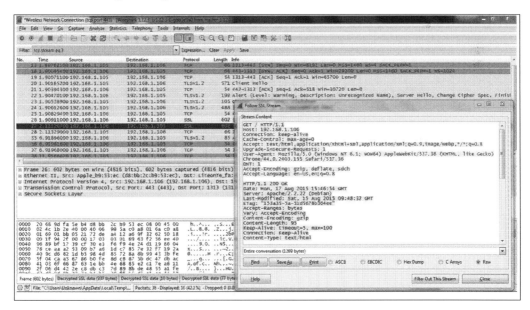

Figure 4.29: Decrypt SSL traffic

This is one of the easiest ways by which you can go ahead and decrypt SSL traffic with just a few clicks. One more way is to feed the RSA private key of the server into the Wireshark SSL preferences, which will give you the same result.

Summary

Domain name system/Service is a protocol used to resolve website names to an IP address. Using this domain name service, your machine can communicate on an IP-based network. Using zone transfer (if enabled), unauthenticated malicious users can ask for zone data form name servers, which is considered highly malicious and dangerous..

File transfer protocol has been used to transfer files from one machine to another since the Internet came into existence and is still being used in today's modern networks. The most unsecure part about FTP is that the data is passed in plain text and can be easily captured using protocol analyzers, unless you are using some encrypted form of the FTP client-server infrastructure.

The web browsers are used to present and transfer the web-based content back and forth uses hypertext transfer protocol. It is commonly also referred to as the request/response model, where a host requests for a certain resource and the server responds with a status code and the resource if available. Status codes greater than 399 should be watched closely, I would suggest is to apply different colorization schemes.

SMTP protocol is used to send e-mails. It is an unencrypted protocol where commonly authentication mechanism is not used. Every SMTP command and its corresponding arguments are passed over the wire in plain text that can be easily sniffed using Wireshark.

VoIP traffic is made up of two things: RTP for data transfer and SIP protocol used to create the session. Signaling protocol creates and manages a session where real-time transport protocol is used to carry the voice itself. Using Wireshark, anyone can capture and reassemble the packets back to listen to a communication session. One should take care of congestion, jitter, lag, and echoing problems while dealing with these protocols in order to maintain the quality of service.

Practice questions:

Q.1 What is the significance of the DNS protocol while you surf the Internet?

Q.2 How would you define zone transfers and recursive DNS queries?

Q.3 What is the difference between recursion desired and recursion available in DNS queries?

Q.4 How many DNS record types exist? Explain the purpose of the AAAA record type and what does non-authoritative answer mean?

Q.5 Differentiate between active and passive modes of FTP. Explain which mode is better.

Q.6 What solution can you come up if you are being asked to make your FTP session encrypted? Explain the difference it would make.

Q.7 Using a virtual infrastructure or a physical one, install the FTP server on any of the machines and then try to communicate with it while capturing live packets in Wireshark.

Q.8 Find out how you can limit the maximum number of login attempts. How can such limitation affect the overall security of your FTP server?

Q.9 Why do we refer to HTTP communication as a request/response approach and what is the purpose of the three-way handshake while initiating the connection?

Q.10 Which version of HTTP are we currently using and what is the difference between the old and new ones?

Q.11 While your browser makes an HTTP request, various other parameters are also sent in your request. Why is it so? What is the purpose of `Accept-Encoding` and `Accept-Language` parameters sent with your request?

Q.12 Visit websites of your choice and browse a couple of pages while capturing all the packets in Wireshark. Then, create a display filter to check whether any redirection was present in your whole session.

Q.13 For what purpose is SMTP on client side used? To send e-mails or receive them? Which protocols are popularly used to receive e-mails?

Q.14 Is it possible to perform a brute force attack on an SMTP server? If yes, then how and how do you identify such traffic pattern?

Q.15 What do you understand by e-mail harvesting and how you can perform an e-mail harvesting attack on an SMTP server? Is there any kind of specific response you will look for?

Q.16 Read about the difference between various email protocols and SMTP?

Q.17 What is the significance of SIP in a VOIP session? What percentage of traffic do you think SIP will have in a whole VOIP session?

Q.18 What is the difference between RTP and RTCP protocols?

Q.19 Download a SIP traffic capture file (`sippcap`) from Wireshark's website and analyze the session using a flow graph. Are you able to the see the process flow we discussed?

Q.20 Filter out all the wrong password attempts using specific code for such responses and apply a different coloring scheme (use the `aaa.pcap capture` file).

5

Analyzing Transport Layer Protocols

This chapter will help you understand TCP and UDP protocols, how they communicate, the problems you can face with these protocols, and how you can use Wireshark to assist them. You will also learn how to analyze TCP and UDP protocols and look for any anomalies that may follow. The following are the topics that we will cover in this chapter:

- Understanding the TCP header and how it communicates
- Understanding the TCP analysis flags
- Lab up — TCP
- How to check for different analysis flags in Wireshark
- Understanding UDP traffic
- Lab up — UDP
- Practice questions

We will discuss TCP and UDP protocols using various practical examples that can give you an insight about how low-layer protocol packets communicate and travel in your network in order to transmit data successfully. We will also look at some common anomalies that you might witness in your day-to-day operations.

The transmission control protocol

A TCP is a connection-oriented protocol used by various other application-layer protocols to ensure data delivery without any loss of packets during transition. On the basis of sequence numbers and acknowledgement numbers, a TCP ensures fail-proof delivery of packets between the hosts that intend to communicate. A TCP is supposed to provide an end-to-end, reliable form of communication, which should be robust at all times. It sits in between the network layer and the application layer and uses the IP datagram to transfer data packets between the sender and receiver. Because of this approach, the TCP and IP are used by various application layer protocols for their reliable delivery.

A TCP is like a two-way communication process where not only the sender is involved in the communication, but even the receiver actively works to make it a successful connection. You can imagine it to be like a landline connection, where you dial a number; if the number you dialed is correct, you will hear a ringtone (if the other side is open to communicate). Only when the receiver responds by picking up the receiver, you can start talking. Likewise, in TCP-based communication, a process called **three-way handshake** takes place between the parties that are involved in the communication to create an independent channel between the two hosts.

Understanding the TCP header and its various flags

The TCP header is normally 20 bytes long, but at times, due to the presence of the options field, the TCP header size can vary up to 60 bytes. Refer to the following illustration of a simplified TCP header:

Source port		Destination port	
Sequence number			
Acknowledgement number			
Data offset	Flags	Window size	
Checksum		Urgent pointer	
Options			

Now, let's get acquainted with the header fields to get a stronger grasp over the basics of a TCP:

- **Source port**: This is the port number associated with the sender side of the communication or you can say the port responsible for listening on the sender side.

- **Destination port**: This is the port number associated with the recipient side of the communication or you can say the port responsible for receiving the transmitted packets.

- **Sequence number**: These are the unique values that are used to ensure reliable delivery of data. TCP tracks each segment using sequence numbers.

- **Acknowledgement number**: These values are sent in response from the receiver side as part of the confirmation process that the packet was successfully received.

- **Data offset:** This indicates where the data packet begins and the length of the TCP header. The size can vary due to the presence of the options field.

- **Flags**: There are various types of flag bits present; each of them has its own significance. They initiate connection, carry data, and tear down connections, and on the basis of their assigned purpose, we've named them as follows:

  - **SYN (synchronize)**: These are the packets that are used to initiate a connection that is commonly known as the handshake process.

  - **ACK (acknowledgement)**: These packets are used to confirm that the data packets have been received, and this also confirms the initiation and tear down of the connections.

  - **RST (reset)**: These packets signify that the connection you were trying to create has been shut down or may be the application we were trying to communicate with is not accepting connections.

  - **FIN (finish)**: These packets indicate that the connection is being torn down after the successful delivery of data packets. Both the sender and receiver send the FIN packets to gracefully terminate the connection. If they want to communicate again, they will start from the beginning, that is, from the three-way handshake process.

  - **PSH (push)**: These packets indicate that the incoming data should be passed on directly to the application instead of getting buffered. To state this simply, the other host should receive data without waiting for it.

  - **URG (urgent)**: Marked packets indicate that the data that the packet is carrying should be processed immediately by the TCP stack and the urgent pointer field should be examined if it is set.

  - **CWR (congestion window reduced)**: These packets are used by the sender to inform the receiver that due to the transmit, the buffer is getting overfilled, and because of congestion, both the parties should slow down the transmission process to avoid any packet loss that might happen.

- **Window size**: This field in the header indicates the amount of data that the sender can send, . The amount is decided during the handshake process where both the hosts that communicate match the buffer size compatible for transmission. Flow control can be achieved through this field.

- **Checksum**: To cross check the integrity of the data that is being received, this field is used, where the contents of the TCP segments are validated.

- **Urgent pointer**: This field tells us about the value that the urgent pointer contains. It specifically indicates the sequence number of the octet that lies before the data.

- **Options**: This field length can vary due to the presence of various options. This field has three parts: the first part specifies the length of the option field, the second part denotes the options being used, and the third actually contains the options in use. One of the important options **maximum segment size (MSS)** is also part of this field.

- **Data**: The last part in the TCP header is the real data that travels around.

The preceding information gives us an overview regarding TCP headers and the significance of various parts of the header. While analyzing TCP sessions, it becomes quite important to know about these details.

How TCP communicates

To understand and analyze the packets in real time, I have configured a server that runs at `172.16.136.129` and a client that runs at `172.16.136.1`, as shown in the following figure. Using Wireshark, I will try to illustrate the three-way handshake process, which happens before the actual data transfer as well as the tear down process (graceful termination). The three-way handshake ensures that the server and client are open to making connections and are ready with resources to create a dedicated channel between each other for a reliable delivery of packets.

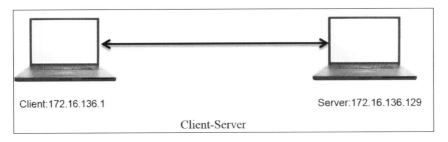

Client:172.16.136.1   Server:172.16.136.129

Client-Server

How it works

The server runs an HTTP server daemon at port 80. On the client, I will visit the default webpage hosted at `http://172.16.136.1` while capturing all the packets taking part in the communication process.

```
ip.addr==172.16.136.129 and ip.addr==172.16.136.1
```

 For the sake of visibility and ease, I've created a display filter to display the traffic between these two hosts specifically.

282 -895706969.756684000	172.16.136.1	172.16.136.129	TCP	64 52138→80 [SYN] Seq=0 Win=65535 Len=0
283 -1439969339.488273000	172.16.136.129	172.16.136.1	TCP	60 80→52138 [SYN, ACK] Seq=0 Ack=1 Win=
284 15.671376000	172.16.136.1	172.16.136.129	TCP	52 52138→80 [ACK] Seq=1 Ack=1 Win=13174
285 15.672063000	172.16.136.1	172.16.136.129	HTTP	375 GET / HTTP/1.1
286 1228372207.391617000	172.16.136.129	172.16.136.1	TCP	52 80→52138 [ACK] Seq=1 Ack=324 Win=307
287 15.672711000	172.16.136.129	172.16.136.1	HTTP	503 HTTP/1.1 200 OK (text/html)
288 15.672725000	172.16.136.1	172.16.136.129	TCP	52 52138→80 [ACK] Seq=324 Ack=452 Win=1
289 -895706969.777480000	172.16.136.1	172.16.136.129	TCP	64 52139→80 [SYN] Seq=0 Win=65535 Len=0
290 15.747286000	172.16.136.129	172.16.136.1	TCP	60 80→52139 [SYN, ACK] Seq=0 Ack=1 Win=
291 714245694.355758000	172.16.136.1	172.16.136.129	TCP	52 52139→80 [ACK] Seq=1 Ack=1 Win=13174
292 378319958.968279000	172.16.136.1	172.16.136.129	HTTP	359 GET /favicon.ico HTTP/1.1
293 1580695018.460033000	172.16.136.129	172.16.136.1	TCP	52 80→52139 [ACK] Seq=1 Ack=308 Win=307
294 -459410977.038322000	172.16.136.129	172.16.136.1	HTTP	556 HTTP/1.1 404 Not Found (text/html)
295 15.754902000	172.16.136.1	172.16.136.129	TCP	52 52139→80 [ACK] Seq=308 Ack=505 Win=1
299 20.679013000	172.16.136.129	172.16.136.1	TCP	52 80→52138 [FIN, ACK] Seq=452 Ack=324
300 609634608.344347000	172.16.136.1	172.16.136.129	TCP	52 52138→80 [ACK] Seq=324 Ack=453 Win=1
301 20.761722000	172.16.136.129	172.16.136.1	TCP	52 80→52139 [FIN, ACK] Seq=505 Ack=308
302 -1931345972.395708000	172.16.136.1	172.16.136.129	TCP	52 52139→80 [ACK] Seq=308 Ack=506 Win=1

Figure 5.1: Connection Process:Three-way handshake, data transfer and tear down process

In the packets 282, 283, and 284, it is clearly visible that the client and server are trying to create a dedicated channel. The client initiated the creation by sending a SYN packet in the 282 packet with the SEQ set to 0. Since the server was open for communication, the server responded with a SYN/ACK packet with ACK set to 1 and SEQ set to 0. This is followed by a confirmation sent from the client side that is seen in the packet number 284 with SEQ=1 and ACK=1. This is what a three-way handshake process looks like. This can be seen before any real data transfer that happens that follows the TCP approach.

After the successful completion of channel creation, the client sends a GET request to access the contents of the web-root directory. The server acknowledged this in the packet number 287 and sent the requested content to the client's machine with the 200 OK status message, which is acknowledged by the client in the next packet. As seen in the list pane again, the client was requesting a new resource, which the server wasn't able to find and thus sent a **404 Not Found** status message, which was acknowledged by the client in the the the packet 295.

After all the data transfer takes place, when the client has nothing left to request, or when the server has nothing left to send, the client sends FIN/ACK packets to properly terminate the connection. The server acknowledges this and sends its own FIN/ACK packets, which are acknowledged by the client as well in the packet number 302. This way of termination is often referred to as the teardown process. Take a look at the following screenshot that illustrates this process:

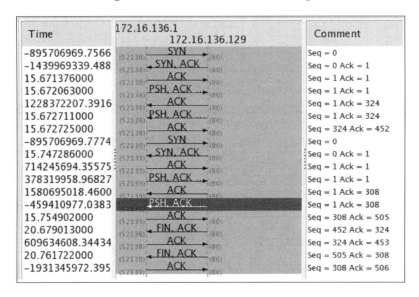

This was a small and sweet conversation that we captured and through which you learned about the process flow. I think I've one more interesting way to illustrate the process flow using graphs that we've already seen in the previous chapters. Refer to the preceding screenshot.

From this flow graph, it becomes more clear and concise to view the requests and responses shared between the two communicating hosts. The most interesting part that I like in the preceding screenshot is the comment section that lists out the SEQ and ACK numbers, which are sent and received by the hosts.

You must be wondering how these are generated and incremented. Let me tell you the trick behind this amazing world of numbers that is used while transferring data. The host that initiates a new connection uses **Initial Sequence Numbers (ISN)** that are generated by the host's operating system. It can be any random number that has no significance with respect to the data. The sequence number we see in the packet one is zero is actually a relative referencing technique used by Wireshark to ease the numbering system for the sake of users. First of all, you should know that the numbers are used to keep track of how much data is being transferred between the two hosts.

Starting from the packet 1, where SEQ=0 (the relative sequence number in real is 704809601), which is received by the server and in return replies with its own SEQ=0 and ACK=1 for the client's SEQ=0. At the end of this three-way handshake, the client replies with SEQ=1 and ACK=1 without any further increments as no data is being transferred during the process.

Then, by the fourth packet, the client sends a GET request with SEQ=1 and ACK=1 where the data payload length equals 323 (refer to the following figure), which the server receives and acknowledges with SEQ=1 and ACK=324. Did you see what just happened? The server replied by adding a total data payload length into ACK to denote that the data was successfully received. Hence, it sends the requested resource to the client with data payload length equals 451, which in return gets acknowledged by the client with ACK=452 and SEQ=324. In the same way, the transmission goes on until the tear down takes place using FIN/ACK packets at the end.

```
▷ Frame 285: 375 bytes on wire (3000 bits), 375 bytes captured (3000 bits) on interface 0
▷ Raw packet data
▷ Internet Protocol Version 4, Src: 172.16.136.1 (172.16.136.1), Dst: 172.16.136.129 (172.16.136.129)
▽ Transmission Control Protocol, Src Port: 52138 (52138), Dst Port: 80 (80), Seq: 1, Ack: 1
     Source Port: 52138 (52138)
     Destination Port: 80 (80)
     [Stream index: 7]
     [TCP Segment Len: 323]
     Sequence number: 1    (relative sequence number)
     [Next sequence number: 324    (relative sequence number)]
```

Graceful termination

We saw, in detail, the process of TCP three-way handshake using the captured packets and the flow graph that gave us insight about the process. Similarly, we should be comfortable about the teardown process, which indicates proper termination of a session between two hosts.

Considering the same scenario that we discussed here, let me show you the packets that were generated to terminate the connection in a proper standardized format. Refer to the following screenshot for this:

```
299 20.679013000     172.16.136.129    172.16.136.1      TCP    52 80→52138 [FIN, ACK] Seq=452 Ack=324
300 609634608.344347000  172.16.136.1   172.16.136.129    TCP    52 52138→80 [ACK] Seq=324 Ack=453 Win=1
301 20.761722000     172.16.136.129    172.16.136.1      TCP    52 80→52139 [FIN, ACK] Seq=505 Ack=308
302 -1931345972.395708000 172.16.136.1   172.16.136.129    TCP    52 52139→80 [ACK] Seq=308 Ack=506 Win=1
```

After the successful delivery of all the required packets, the server initiated the teardown process (as there was nothing left to send or the client was just sitting idle and doing nothing). In the beginning, the server sent its own FIN and ACK packets to the client with SEQ=452 (the client acknowledged the same with ACK) and ACK=324 (this is the client SEQ number when the data transfer was completed). These were acknowledged by the client in the next packet. Following the same approach, the client issued its own FIN and ACK packets (using SEQ and ACK numbers used in the second round of communication, where the client requested something that wasn't available. Refer to the preceding flow graph to know more) to end the connection from its own side (as the connection was bi-directional), which was received and acknowledged by the server. As soon as the client received ACK from the server, the connection between the two hosts was closed completely, and the sockets and other resources involved during the communication were freed up.

RST (reset) packets

Often times, there will be situations when the server daemon is not available, it is not able to process your request due to overload, you are restricted to interact with the server, or the port you are trying to connect to is not open for connections (not associated with any service). There can be a lot of reasons why you will see a RST packet. Let me replicate the scenario and capture the traffic between the client and server I have, which will surely make it easy for you to understand this. An RST packet basically denotes that the connection you were trying to initiate got closed abruptly.

In this scenario, the server daemon is not running and the client is trying to communicate; as a result, it receives RST packets in return for every SYN request sent. I tried visiting the web server just once, but you will notice more than one SYN and RST packets because every browser performs a different number of attempts over a non-responding or a closed socket at a particular interval of time. Hence, in our case, I am using the Apple Safari browser, which made at least three attempts to connect back in a max time of 3-4 minutes. I tried requesting Google Chrome as well, which made approximately 7 attempts to connect back in merely 10 minutes (the browser will continue to make a request at a particular interval of time). Refer to the following screenshot that illustrates the packets captured in the process:

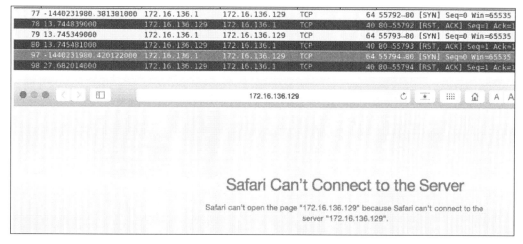

Figure 5.2: RST packets captured

Relative verses Absolute numbers

Wireshark purposefully translates real SEQ/ACK flag numbers to a simpler format, which makes it significantly easier for us to keep track of data sent across the wire. For instance, I've a web server at 172.16.136.129 and a client at 172.16.136.1. Using a web browser, I will try to visit the server that will generate a couple of packets, which will be captured by Wireshark. Refer to the following screenshot illustrating the same packets generated for the session.

I have selected the first packet generated for the session in the list pane and its corresponding details in the packet. The details pane and bytes pane can be seen highlighted as follows:

- **1**: In the list pane, it can be observed that the SEQ number assigned for the SYN packet to begin communication is zero.

- **2**: In the details pane, we can see that the number 0 is a relative sequence number, which is not the real SEQ number and has been changed for our perusal by Wireshark.

- **3**: In the bytes pane, we can see that the corresponding hex value for SEQ=0 is 0x2a028a81, which is equivalent to 704809601 in decimal.

So, the real SEQ number is `704809601`, which was converted to `0` to make our analysis easy.

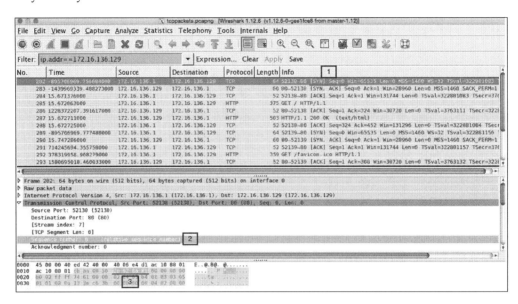

According to our analysis, the ACK value that we must receive should be `704809602` (incremented SEQ value with 1). Let's verify the same using the next packet and its corresponding related information using the details and bytes pane. Refer to the following screenshot for illustration:

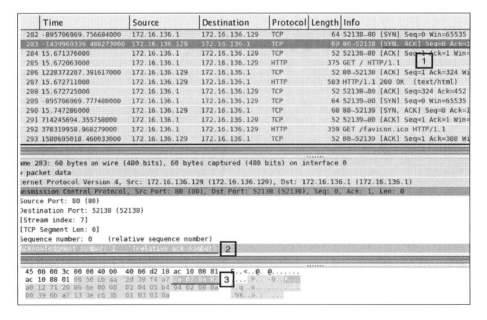

Refer to the following list to understand what each pointers highlights:

- The second packet I selected is the SYN, ACK packet that the client received from the server. It contains the SEQ=0 and ACK=1 (relative numbers) servers.

- The related information for the packet 2 in the communication is shown in the details pane and the bytes pane. If you observe, in the details pane, the ACK server sent for the client's request is 1.

- The hex value for the ACK received is 0x2a028a82, which is equivalent to 704809602 in decimal. This is the same value that we should be expecting.

Now, it would be easy for you to check the absolute numbers translating them from their given hex values. There is one more interesting way by which we can customize the numbering system, where we can view the real absolute numbers directly in the list pane and the details pane. Follow these steps to activate and deactivate it:

1. Navigate to **Edit | Preferences** in the menu bar.

2. Expand the **Protocol** tree and look for TCP.

3. Remove the checkmark from the **Relative sequence numbers** option, as shown in the following figure:

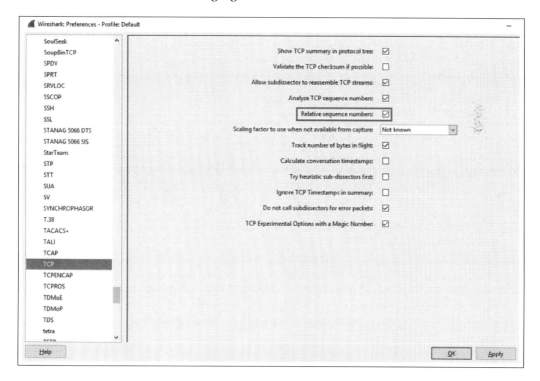

4. Navigate to **Apply | Ok**. That's it. Refer to the following screenshot:

```
282  895706969.756664000  172.16.136.1    172.16.136.129   TCP    64 52138-80 [SYN] Seq=704809601
283 -1439969339.488273000  172.16.136.129  172.16.136.1     TCP    60 80-52138 [SYN, ACK] Seq=7587
284 15.671376000            172.16.136.1    172.16.136.129   TCP    52 52138-80 [ACK] Seq=704809602
285 15.672063000            172.16.136.1    172.16.136.129   HTTP  375 GET / HTTP/1.1
286 1228372207.391617000    172.16.136.129  172.16.136.1     TCP    52 80-52138 [ACK] Seq=758772904
287 15.672711000            172.16.136.129  172.16.136.1     HTTP  503 HTTP/1.1 200 OK  (text/html)
288 15.672725000            172.16.136.1    172.16.136.129   TCP    52 52138-80 [ACK] Seq=704809925
289 -895706969.777480000    172.16.136.1    172.16.136.129   TCP    64 52139-80 [SYN] Seq=1018631651
290 15.747286000            172.16.136.129  172.16.136.1     TCP    60 80-52139 [SYN, ACK] Seq=1324!
291 714245694.355758000     172.16.136.1    172.16.136.129   TCP    52 52139-80 [ACK] Seq=1018631651
292 378319958.968279000     172.16.136.1    172.16.136.129   HTTP  359 GET /favicon.ico HTTP/1.1
293 1580695018.460033000    172.16.136.129  172.16.136.1     TCP    52 80-52139 [ACK] Seq=132490464(
```

```
ame 282: 64 bytes on wire (512 bits), 64 bytes captured (512 bits) on interface 0
w packet data
ternet Protocol Version 4, Src: 172.16.136.1 (172.16.136.1), Dst: 172.16.136.129 (172.16.136.129)
ansmission Control Protocol, Src Port: 52138 (52138), Dst Port: 80 (80), Seq: 704809601, Len: 0
  Source Port: 52138 (52138)
  Destination Port: 80 (80)
  [Stream index: 7]
  [TCP Segment Len: 0]
  Sequence number: 704809601
  Acknowledgment number: 0
```

As we analyzed, the first packet in the TCP handshake process has an SEQ number 704809601 as an decimal equivalent. Now, after deactivating the **Relative sequence numbers** options, we can observe the same in the list and details panes.

There are a few more options that are enabled by default in the TCP **Protocol Preferences** window, which makes the analyses more systematic and advanced. For example, validating the checksum whenever possible and A=analyzing the TCP sequence numbers.

Checksums are generally used during the transmission to ensure the integrity of the data being sent and received. As discussed, there is an extra field in the TCP header. What actually happens is when the sender prepares the packet that needs to be transmitted, the checksum of the packet that contains data is calculated and sent along with the packet. Now, the receiving side will receive the packet and recalculate the checksum using the same algorithm used by the sender. If the checksum value that came along with the packet is identical to the one that the receiver calculated, then the packet is accepted; otherwise, the packet that contains the error (checksum not matched) is discarded and the sender side is not even informed about the error that has taken place. The sender is supposed to know about this by himself. The validation of the checksum is not 100% guaranteed, and even this reduces the performance as TCP packets reassembly won't take place now.

Checksum offloading is a feature that only new network drivers support, where the packets that are ready to be transmitted are passed on to the network hardware that are captured by Wireshark with an empty checksum field that generates the `checksum offloading` error. The reason is that, even before the actual packet transfer happens, Wireshark captures the packet (the packets will contain the valid checksum once the actual transfer happens). This might lead to several confusion. So, the best approach would be to switch off the offloading feature from your interface if available, or to disable the **Validate checksum** feature for TCP protocol preferences. Refer to the following figure that illustrates this:

```
282 -895706969.756684000   172.16.136.1     172.16.136.129   TCP    64 52138-80 [SYN] Seq=704809601
283 -1439969339.488273000  172.16.136.129   172.16.136.1     TCP    60 80-52138 [SYN, ACK] Seq=75877
284 15.671376000           172.16.136.1     172.16.136.129   TCP    52 52138-80 [ACK] Seq=704809602
285 15.672063000           172.16.136.1     172.16.136.129   HTTP  375 GET / HTTP/1.1
286 1228372207.391617000   172.16.136.129   172.16.136.1     TCP    52 80-52138 [ACK] Seq=758772904
287 15.672711000           172.16.136.129   172.16.136.1     HTTP  503 HTTP/1.1 200 OK  (text/html)
288 15.672725000           172.16.136.1     172.16.136.129   TCP    52 52138-80 [ACK] Seq=704809925
289 -895706969.777480000   172.16.136.1     172.16.136.129   TCP    64 52139-80 [SYN] Seq=1018631658
290 15.747286000           172.16.136.129   172.16.136.1     TCP    60 80-52139 [SYN, ACK] Seq=13249
291 714245694.355758000    172.16.136.1     172.16.136.129   TCP    52 52139-80 [ACK] Seq=1018631659
292 373319950.908279000    172.16.136.1     172.16.136.129   HTTP  359 GET /favicon.ico HTTP/1.1
293 1580605018.460033000   172.16.136.129   172.16.136.1     TCP    52 80-52139 [ACK] Seq=1324904640
294 -459410977.038322000   172.16.136.129   172.16.136.1     HTTP  556 HTTP/1.1 404 Not Found  (text
295 15.754902000           172.16.136.1     172.16.136.129   TCP    52 52139-80 [ACK] Seq=1018631966
299 20.679013000           172.16.136.129   172.16.136.1     TCP    52 80-52138 [FIN, ACK] Seq=75877

Header Length: 32 bytes
.... 0000 0001 1000 = Flags: 0x018 (PSH, ACK)
Window size value: 30
[Calculated window size: 30720]
[Window size scaling factor: 1024]
Checksum: 0x9a4b [incorrect, should be 0x9a5b (maybe caused by "TCP checksum offload"?)]
```

The packets with invalid checksums are displayed with a black background and red foreground color. Look at the error highlighted in red color in the details pane; this states that the checksum is incorrect, and this might be because the checksum-offloading feature is activated. The packets with an invalid checksum cannot be reassembled, and it doesn't look nice (a lot of invalid errors on the screen), so the best option is to deactivate this feature if not required.

Another option that you should know about is the **Analyzing TCP sequence numbers** feature, which keeps track of the `SEQ` and `ACK` numbers and keeps you aware of the various types of errors that can take place during transmission, for example, lost frames, duplicate `ACK`, retransmissions, window scaling, and several others. Turning this feature off will also affect the **Expert Info** dialog, where any of the warnings related to transmission errors and other useful information won't be populated.

Unusual TCP traffic

One of the scenarios that commonly falls under this category is the lost connection or unsuccessful connection attempt scenario, which we have already analyzed in the RST packets section. You might observe several other examples, such as high latencies, due to long-distance communications or queuing up of the traffic. To make the analysis easy and to sort out such problems, use the time column by sorting it, and then, you will be able to figure out large time gaps between the packets at the top of the list pane.

Another example can be where a malicious user is trying to perform a port scan on your network and your firewall responds with RST packets to the user to avoid such attacks, or it might also be possible that the port that the malicious user is looking for is closed. A normal scan can generate a lot of traffic and which is quite noisy. This can be easily observed in the list pane of Wireshark. Refer to the following screenshot where I've tried scanning my machine using nmap from another device, and it seems quite visible and hence is easy to track:

Observe `Frame 19`, where the port scan initiated by the malicious user sent a `SYN` packet in order to check whether the port is open or closed. As a result, in our case, port 21 (FTP) was closed; hence our machine sent a `RST` packet, which will be used by the port scanner on the other side to display statistics. If the port was open, the malicious user will be notified with `SYN` and `ACK` (refer to the following screenshot), which signify that our machine is open to a connection over the port 21, and this might become an entry point to the user's malicious attacks.

```
45 · 1440530056.614689000  172.16.136.129   172.16.136.1        TCP      44 39152-21 [SYN] Seq=
46 · 1440530052.614709000  172.16.136.1     172.16.136.129      TCP      44 21-39152 [SYN, ACK]
47 · 1440530056.614709000  172.16.136.129   172.16.136.1        TCP      40 39152-21 [RST] Seq=
Frame 45: 44 bytes on wire (352 bits), 44 bytes captured (352 bits) on interface 0
Raw packet data
Internet Protocol Version 4, Src: 172.16.136.129 (172.16.136.129), Dst: 172.16.136.1 (172.16.136.1)
Transmission Control Protocol, Src Port: 39152 (39152), Dst Port: 21 (21), Seq: 891895594, Len: 0
```

Figure 5.3: Port 21 open, an entry point for malicious attacks

Take a look at `Frame 45`, where the client sent a `SYN` request to the server at `172.16.136.1`, and by this time, the port was open so our server sent `SYN` and `ACK` packets (`Frame 46`), acknowledging the connection initiation attempt with a positive confirmation that the server is open to connection over port 21.

There can be various scenarios other than this half-open scan (the scan shown in the preceding screenshot is called half open because the client who initiated the connection attempt, would never complete the connection by sending `ACK`, which the server will be expecting). If your basics regarding the packet behavior, connection initiation, completion process, TCP headers, flags in packets, and `SEQ-ACK` numbers are clear, then it would be quite easy for you to point out any unusual form of traffic that is flowing around. There is no such automated tool that can point out these abnormalities until you customize your environment about how to react or alarm you to such traffic anomalies. These are some traffic patterns that you can expect to happen on a regular basis.

How to check for different analysis flags in Wireshark

The analysis of the flags present in TCP packets is quite simple while using Wireshark, there is an individual section that is available in the details pane for every TCP packet. Let's take a TCP packet from our previous handshake process that we captured and see how flags are presented in the details pane. Then, we will try to create a display filter corresponding to the same. Refer to the following screenshot that illustrates this:

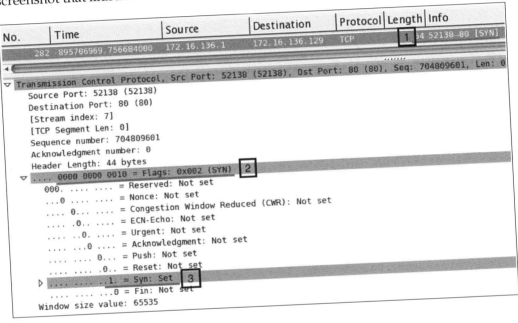

Now, we will see what each pointer signifies:

- Here, the SYN packet sent from the client to the server to initiate the three-way handshake can be seen in the list pane.

- Here, the flags related to the same packet are set and the hex equivalent of 000000000010 is set to 0x002.

- For the corresponding TCP packet, the SYN flag bit is set to 1; the same can be seen in the details pane. The rest of them are still 0.

Now, if you wish to create a display filter to see only the SYN packets that you have in the trace file, then apply the filter shown here. As a result, you will see only SYN packets present in your trace file. The following figure illustrates the same:

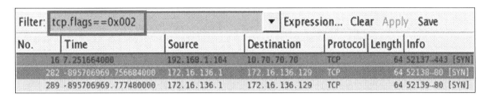

Let's try to create one more filter to view the SYN and ACK packets only in the list pane. Follow these steps to create the filter:

1. Open your trace file.
2. Choose any TCP SYN, or ACK packet.
3. Note the corresponding SYN and ACK hex equivalent values for the flags set.
4. Create your filter using the hex equivalent that you have. Your filter must look something like what is shown in the.

The User Datagram Protocol

As defined in RFC 768, a UDP is a connection-less protocol, which is great for transmitting real-time data between hosts and is often termed as an unreliable form of communication. The reason for this is that UDP doesn't care about the delivery of packets, and any lost packets are not recovered because the sender is never informed about the dropped or discarded packets during transmission. However, many protocols such as DHCP, DNS, TFTP, SIP, and so on rely only on this. The protocols that use a UDP as a transport mechanism have to rely upon other techniques to ensure data delivery and error-checking capabilities. And these protocols are inbuilt with such features, which can provide some level of reliability during the transmission. A point that we should not to forget is that a UDP provides faster transmission of packets as it is not concerned about the initiation of the connection or graceful termination as seen in the TCP. That's why a UDP is also referred to as a transaction-oriented protocol and not a message-oriented protocol like a TCP.

A UDP header

The size of a usual UDP header is 8 bytes; the data that is added with the header can be theoretically 65,535 (practically 65,507) bytes long. A UDP header is quite small when compared to a TCP header; it has just four common fields: **Source Port**, **Destination Port**, **Packet Length**, and **Checksum**. Refer to the UDP header shown here:

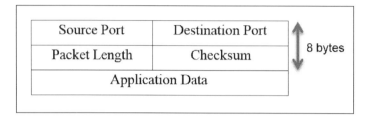

- **Source port**: This is the port number used by the sending side to receive any replies if needed. Most of the time, in a TCP and UDP, the port number chosen to be the part of the socket is ephemeral. On the other side of the communication, the port number comes in the category of well-known port numbers.

- **Destination port**: This field of the header identifies the port number used by the server or receiving side, and all data will be transmitted to this port. This port number is assigned to a particular service by IANA, and definitely, it is permanently assigned to the same service specifically. For example, port 53 is for DNS and cannot be assigned to any other service (not advisable).

- **Packet length**: This field specifies the length of the packet, starting from the header to the end of the data; the minimum length you will observe will be 8 bytes every time, that is, the length of the UDP header.

- **Checksum**: As discussed earlier, checksum is performed over data, that is, the packet of the packet to ensure data integrity that is what is sent from the sender side is the same what receiver got and to verify this there are couple of checksum algorithms which comes to the rescue. Sometimes, while working with a UDP, you will see that the checksum value is 0 in the packet we received. This means that the checksum is not required to be validated.

How it works

To understand the way a UDP works, let's go ahead and analyze some of the protocols that use a UDP as a delivery protocol. First, I would like to discuss DHCP, and then we will see DNS traffic as well. We actually saw UDP traffic before as well while we were going through VOIP and SIP analysis.

For analysis purpose, I have a default gateway configured at `192.168.1.1` and a client at `192.168.1.106`. Using the client, I will try to generate DHCP and DNS traffic, which will be captured in Wireshark, and then, I will try to dissect each protocol's communication process as well as the different components utilized during the whole session. Refer to the following network architecture that I have:

The DHCP

The most common and important protocol that assigns IP addresses to devices and makes them network compatible is **Dynamic Host Configuration Protocol (DHCP)**. Now, from the client, I will try to release the IP address that the client already holds, which will generate a DHCP packet, and the same will be captured by our sniffer. Look at the following figure to understand this:

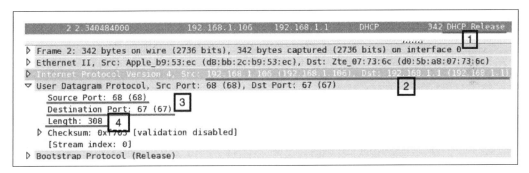

In the list pane, we can see a DHCP release packet that was generated implicitly by the client in order to release the current IP address (I used the `dhclient -v -r` command on the Linux terminal to release the IP address, but be careful while using this command as it may disconnect your machine from the network, hence making it incompatible for network communication). The client from the IP address `192.168.1.106` to the server at `192.168.1.1` initiates the request. The port numbers used by the client and server in case of DHCP are permanent, these won't be changed in your case either unless they are manually configured.

The DHCP server port number is 67 and the DHCP client port number is 68 by default; you can see the same in the preceding figure (highlighted as **3**). There is a fourth field that I have highlighted, the packet length field, which specifies the length of the packet starting from the first byte until the end of data in the packet. However, out of 308 bytes, 8 bytes show the length of the UDP header and the remaining 300 bytes represent the application data that is appended. Interestingly, if a machine is power cycled, it will request the DHCP server to allocate an IP address. This, as a result, will generate a couple of packets related to the DHCP request, release, and offer and various others that will also use the UDP as a transport mechanism.

```
Filter: udp.dstport==67                          ▼  Expression... Clear  Apply  Save

No.      Time               Source           Destination      Protocol Length Info
        19 44.476141000     192.168.1.106    192.168.1.1      DHCP           342 DHCP Release
       103 91.729193000     0.0.0.0          255.255.255.255  DHCP           342 DHCP Discover
       109 93.810969000     0.0.0.0          255.255.255.255  DHCP           342 DHCP Request
                                                        .......
 Frame 19: 342 bytes on wire (2736 bits), 342 bytes captured (2736 bits) on interface 0
 Ethernet II, Src: Apple_b9:53:ec (d8:bb:2c:b9:53:ec), Dst: Zte_07:73:6c (d0:5b:a8:07:73:6c)
 Internet Protocol Version 4, Src: 192.168.1.106 (192.168.1.106), Dst: 192.168.1.1 (192.168.1.1)
 User Datagram Protocol, Src Port: 68 (68), Dst Port: 67 (67)
    Source Port: 68 (68)
    Destination Port: 67 (67)
    Length: 308
  ▷ Checksum: 0x2d5d [validation disabled]
    [Stream index: 1]
 Bootstrap Protocol (Release)
```

I filtered the packets listed to show only DHCP packets using the udp.port==67 filter; as a result, only DHCP packets will be listed in the list pane.

The TFTP

The **Trivial File Transfer Protocol** (**TFTP**) is a lightweight version of the FTP that is used to transfer between hosts. Unlike the FTP protocol, TFTP does not ask users for any credentials. A TFTP uses a UDP as a transport mechanism. Most commonly, a TFTP is used in LAN environments, and when dealing with manageable devices such as switches and routers, network administrators do use TFTP servers to take a back up of configuration files and to update the firmware running in those devices. A TFTP is also used by security professionals to transfer files from their system to yours in order to escalate the privileges (gaining more rights on a compromised system).

I have a TFTP server running at 192.168.1.106 and a client running at 192.168.1.104. There is a text file abc.txt that I've created on the server, and the client will try to download the same. And our sniffer in place will capture the traffic that is generated.

The traffic generated due to the transaction that takes place between two hosts is successfully captured and the packets corresponding to it are shown in the following figure:

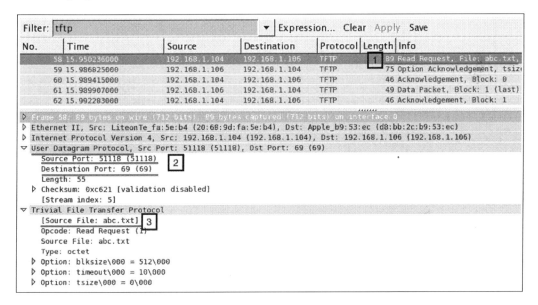

Now, let's see what each pointer signifies:

- This shows that the transfer of the packet is initiated as soon as the client requests the abc.txt file. The request frame can be seen in the list pane.

- As discussed, a TFTP uses a UDP for a transport mechanism. The related details for the request are shown in the details pane, which states that the request was initiated from a ephemeral port number from the client destined to port 69 on the server (69 is a well-known port to the TFTP protocol).

- The request was specific to the abc.txt file that is also shown in the details pane in the TFTP protocol section.

You must be wondering about the acknowledgement packets that are shared between the two hosts. As we discussed, a UDP is an unreliable form of communication, so why are we seeing ACKs in a UDP? The reason is that the TFTP server I am using has some kind of inbuilt reliability feature. Even on the client side, over the standard console, after initiating the request, I received quite interactive messages from the server, such as the file of size 3 bytes has been transferred successfully, and various other details were listed along with the message. The interesting thing to know here is that port 69 was only involved in the first packet, and the rest of the packets were sent and received by the acknowledging feature that the server is embedded with. So, the statement that some protocols use a UDP as a transport protocol and have their own inbuilt feature to ensure delivery is true, as we have just witnessed.

Unusual UDP traffic

Suppose that the resource we are looking for is not available on the server. How will traffic look like then? Refer to the following screenshot to understand this:

As seen in the preceding screenshot, the client requested an invalid resource that the server wasn't able to locate and hence returned with an error code and the summary message `File not found`. The same message was shown over the standard console to the client.

Sometimes, it is also possible that the server daemon may not run and the client may request a certain resource. In such cases, the client would receive the `ICMP destination unreachable` error with the error code 3. Refer to the following figure for the same:

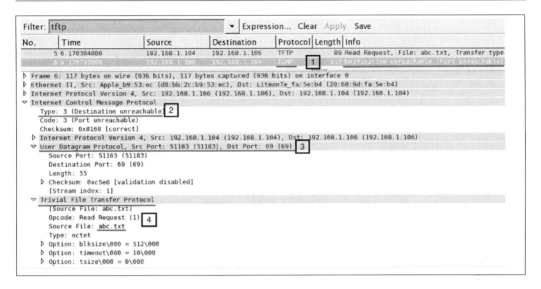

Now, we will see what each pointer signifies:

- The server returned with an ICMP destination unreachable message when the TFTP server daemon was not functional

- The client received an error code of type 3

- The details regarding the request were mentioned in the reply under the UDP protocol section, which stated that the request was sent to port 69, which was currently nonfunctional

- The requested resource was shown under the TFTP protocol section

Unusual DNS requests are also very often seen when a client initiates a request to look for name servers associated with an address. It would look similar to the one shown in the following figure:

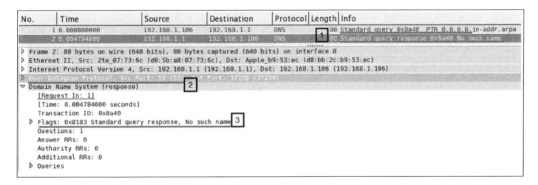

Now, we will see what each pointer signifies:

- **1**: As seen in the list pane, the client at `192.168.1.106` initiated a request to look for the address `8.0.0.0` and received a response in `Frame 2`
- **2**: The request was sent to the default gateway that holds the DNS cache
- **3**: The gateway responded with a `No such name` error

There can be multiple scenarios where you will see unusual traffic related to a UDP. The most important thing to look for is TFTP traffic, which might be generated because of a the TFTP client in your network. It may be malicious traffic that you would like to make a note of.

Summary

TCP is a reliable form of communication that has features like a three-way handshake and a tear down process ensures the connection is reliable and interactive.

A TCP header is 20 bytes long and consists of various fields such as source and destination port, `SEQ` and `ACK` numbers, offset, window size, flag bits, checksum, and options. The presence of various flags and header fields let the sender and receiver be sure about the delivery as well as the integrity of the data being sent.

The `SEQ` and `ACK` numbers are used by TCP-based communications to keep track of how much data is being sent across between the hosts taking part.

A UDP is a connection-less protocol that is a nonreliable means of communication over IP, where the lost and discarded packets are never recovered. A UDP does provide us with faster transmission and easier creation of sessions. A UDP header is 8 bytes long, which has very few fields such as source and destination port, packet length, and checksum. At the end application, the data is appended.

Common protocols such as DHCP, TFTP, DNS, and RTP mostly use a UDP as a transport mechanism, and these services are some of the major services that we deal with in our everyday life. To make the connection reliable, some of these protocols support their own version of acknowledging features that comes inbuilt.

In the next chapter, you will learn the basics of wireless traffic, how to decrypt wireless traffic, and the anomalies that may follow.

Practice questions

Q.1 List at least five differences between TCP and UDP protocols.

Q.2 Capture a three-way handshake and tear down packets using your own FTP server.

Q.3 Explain the purpose of window scaling and checksum offloading and state their corresponding significance in terms of TCP communications.

Q.4 In what way can TCP-based communication can recover from a packet loss or unexpected termination? Imitate any scenarios that can generate such traffic.

Q.5 Create a display filter to show only TCP FIN and ACK packets sent to your machine from your default gateway in the list pane.

Q.6 What is the difference between the absolute and relative numbering system used by Wireshark in order to keep track of packets?

Q.7 What is the purpose of the options field at the end of the TCP header and what kind of arguments does it contain?

Q.8 There is one more way through which you can create filters to view a packet with a specific flags set. Without providing the HEX equivalent, figure out what it is and how you can filter a packets set with a PSH flag set using the same technique.

Q.9 Find out why the length of data can only be 65507 bytes while working with a UDP.

Q.10 What kind of packets you will see in a list pane if the server daemon for a TFTP is not running?

Q.11 Try performing a zone transfer on your locally configured DNS and capture the traffic for analysis. What interesting facts did you notice about the packets? Explain them in brief.

6
Analyzing Traffic in Thin Air

In this chapter, you will learn how to analyze wireless traffic and pinpoint any problems. You will also learn how to analyze wireless traffic using Wireshark. The following are the topics we will cover in this chapter:

- Understanding IEEE 802.11 traffic
- Analyzing normal and unusual behavior
- Lab up — wireless communication
- Decrypting encrypted wireless traffic
- Lab up — decrypting WEP and WPA traffic
- Practice questions

We start from the basics such as how WLAN traffic gets generated and various essential elements responsible for handling the wireless transmission between hosts. Then, moving ahead, we will analyze the usual and unusual forms of packets that can be seen in Wireshark. Side by side, we will identify anomalies and regular traffic patterns. We will also discuss how you can decrypt wireless (WEP) traffic using Wireshark, which can definitely give an advantage while auditing WLAN environment.

What we are going to witness is not much different from the wired networking that we saw earlier; here, we will be quite concerned with the medium through which packets are flying around us. The two layers at the bottom of the OSI model are important as they represent the data link and the physical layer. The data link layer is divided into two parts: **Logical Link Control** (LLC) and **Media Access Control** (MAC).

Understanding IEEE 802.11

At the **Institute of Electrical and Electronics Engineer (IEEE)**, there are several committees working together on several projects, and one of these is 802, which is responsible for developing LAN standards. A free white paper can be downloaded from the IEEE website based on 802 standards. Specifically, 802.11 contains WLAN standards. If you want to analyze what normal traffic looks like, you should be aware of the standards and the present working technologies within 802.11.

There are a couple of 802.11 standards, but the few important ones that we should know about are 802.11b, 802.11a, 802.11g, and 802.11n, which are explained in the following list:

- **802.11**: This only supports a network bandwidth of 1-2 Mbps. This is the reason why many 802.11-compatible devices have become obsolete. Hence, it became necessary to develop other 802.11 standards.

- **802.11b**: This specification uses a signaling frequency of 2.4 Ghz that is similar to the 802.11 standard. A maximum of 11 Mbit transmission rate can be achieved over a 2.4 Ghz band using b specification. As most of the home appliances (microwave, cordless phones, and so on) work over a 2.4 Ghz spectrum, it causes quite dense interference and congestion during WLAN packets transmission. To avoid the interference, the access points can be installed at a reasonable distance. The 802.11b band is divided into 14 overlapping channels, where every channel has 22 Mhz widths. In one instance, there can be a maximum of three non-overlapping channels operating at the same time. This space separation is necessary and required in order to let the channels operate individually. One device can be part of one channel at a time; the same follows when you listen to the packets. Practically, it is possible now to sniff more than one channel at a time, which is facilitated through various tools that are now available; one of them is *Kismet*, which can sniff up to 10 channels at regular short intervals.

- **802.11a**: This is based on **Orthogonal Frequency Division Multiplexing (OFDM)** that was released in 1999 and supports a maximum transmission rate up to 54 Mbps, which also gives us an advantage over 802.11b congested bands. This specification was developed as a second standard to 802.11 standards. It is commonly used in business environments, but because of its high cost, the *b* specification is not best suited for home environments. Though it supports higher speeds around 5 Ghz spectrums than 802.11b, the range of devices falls short if it is configured with *a* specification. The capability of bypassing the obstructions that comes in between is not better than 802.11b. There is no channel overlap that happens in 802.11a. A higher regulated frequency helps in preventing the interferences caused by devices that work on 2.4 Ghz spectrums.

- **802.11g**: Somewhere around the middle of 2002, this specification came into existence, and this tried combining the best features of 802.11a and 802.11b. The signaling frequency used here is 2.4 Ghz, and the bandwidth it supports is upto 54 Mbps. Due to the 2.4 Ghz frequency in use, the range parameter that suffered a decline was improvised. The 802.11g also supports backward compatibility, which means that all 802.11g access points will support network adapters using 802.11b and vice versa. A strong point in this specification is: it won't get easily obstructed.

- **802.11n**: To improve further, the wireless N was introduced. The key area where the improvement was carried on is the range and the transfer rates. The base technology that is implemented to make all this possible is **Multiple-Input Multiple-output** (**MIMO**) communication. There are multiple antennas fitted into the access point that are used to send, receive, and bounce off the signals. This enables a channel frequency of 40 Mhz. The final version of this specification, which was released in 2007, stated a transfer rate up to 600 Mbps. It can be configured with 2.4 or 5 Ghz (if the access point is compatible with both); it can use both frequencies at the same time, thus enabling backward compatibility with network adapters. A maximum of four antennas can be used with the MIMO technology. Once all of this starts working together, users can experience fastest speed and maximum signaling range, and it's not much affected by another device working on the same frequency band. If this network type gets inferred, then it will other specifications such as 802.11b/g.

Various modes in wireless communications

WLANs uses the **Carrier Sense Multiple Access and Collision Avoidance** protocol (**CSMA/CA**) to manage the stations sending data, where every host that wants to send data is supposed to listen to the channel first, that is, if it is free, then the host can go ahead and send the packet; if not, then the host has to wait for its turn. This is because the same medium is being shared by every host, thus avoiding collisions that might happen if two hosts start transmitting at the same time, as a result making the performance of the network go slow and more prone to errors. The 802.11 architecture is composed of several components such as a **station** (**STA**), a wireless **access point** (**AP**), **basic service set** (**BSS**), **extended service set** (**ESS**), **independent basic service set** (**IBSS**), and **distribution system** (**DS**).

There are four common modes of association between the STA and the AP, which are as follows:

- **Infrastructure/managed mode:** A wireless network environment where two devices wish to connect an STA and an AP to share data and network resources is termed as the infrastructure mode. An AP is defined with a **Service Set Identifier** (**SSID**), which is actually just a name given to the access point for identification purpose (for security reasons, sometimes, broadcasting an SSID can be disabled, which will prevent your wireless network from being discovered by unintended users). For example, once you start scanning for available Wi-Fi networks around you to connect to, you'll be shown multiple network names, from which you are supposed to choose a network that you know about. All these names of networks are called SSID. Another useful term to know is **Base Service Set Identifier** (**BSSID**), that is, the access point's MAC address. By default, every access point is supposed to broadcast the SSID and transmit a beacon frame 10 times in a second to let devices know that they are ready to accept connections. Refer to the following diagram that illustrates this example:

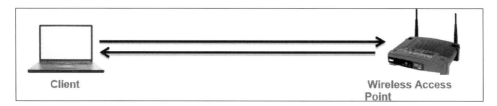

- **Ad Hoc mode**: In this kind of network, a peer-to-peer network is formed where two clients are connected to each other. The packets sent and received by the wireless clients are not relayed to the access point. The clients taking part in this communication now handle the process of sending beacons and processing authentication that a WAP handles in normal scenarios.

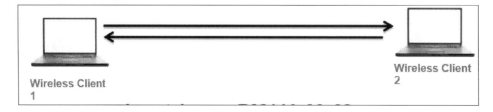

- **Master mode**: When the NIC card in your machine lets you become an AP, this is what the master mode is all about. Higher-end devices have a capability to act like access points, and this is possible when NIC cards start working together with a special driver.

- **Monitor mode**: For the purpose of this chapter, this mode is very important. This mode is used to listen to the packets that are flying around; when the monitor mode is activated, your device will stop transmitting and receiving any packets and it will just sit silently and sniff live traffic. If you want to capture packets from the wireless network concerning 802.11 protocols, then your NIC and the driver that is being used must support the monitor mode. It is quite easy to activate the monitor mode on an OS, such as Linux and MAC; however, with Windows, it becomes quite troublesome to activate the monitor mode. This mode is often termed as the **Radio Frequency Monitor Mode (RFMON)**.

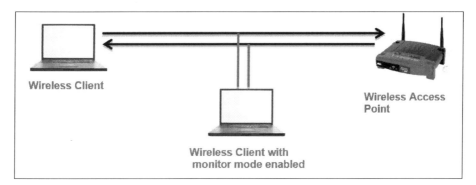

After learning the basics of different forms of wireless networking infrastructures that you might note in a production environment very casually, it would definitely become a bit easier for you to choose between the various modes available as per your requirements.

Wireless interference and strength

To better understand the normal traffic pattern, we should be aware of the various usual factors that govern the performance of a wireless network. For example, data packets, associations, and disassociations, signal strength with/without interferences. Our objective while analyzing preceding parameters is to form a baseline that can prove worthy when comparing the traffic patterns with unusual ones. The factor that affects the network performance the most is a different form of interference, which is caused due to various factors such as physical obstructions such as thick walls, roofs; and electronic appliances, such as microwave, cordless phones, and so on.

While dealing with wireless networks, the integrity of data becomes more important because the packets are simply traveling in the air, and anyone with some basic hardware and knowledge of how wireless networks work can sniff and capture these packets easily. Wireless networks don't have any rescue options to protect the integrity, so using them, you cannot be 100% assured regarding the security of data.

Let's say, for example, you are listening to a particular channel in the spectrum. Normally, you can sniff only one channel at a time, but if the channels start overlapping each other, than it is quite possible that you will see other channel packets in the list pane. As per the normal functioning of a wireless spectrum, the networks that operate close to each other are supposed to choose non-overlapping channels such as 1,6,11,14 to avoid any issues. Refer to the following figure that best illustrates channel overlapping (I used from the same from Wikipedia):

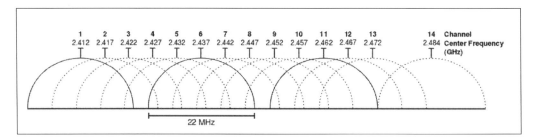

The strength of the wireless network is totally dependent on **Radio Frequency** (**RF**) signals that carry the traffic. Once the wireless signal starts traveling, the strength is supposed to lessen eventually, as it travels farther because of the obstructions that come in between. The device that works over the same RF energy is also responsible for reducing the wireless signal strength. If you are also dealing with such issues, then just using Wireshark to listen on an interface in the monitor mode won't solve the purpose. You need a spectrum analyzer, such as Wi-Spy+Channelyzer, that is paired with a USB (refer to `http://metageek.com`) adapter and gives you an extra eye over the RF energy form; otherwise, you won't be able to see them. Most of the time, the device emitting high RF energy can be the cause of poor network performance.

To inspect the environment for RF energy, you need to walk down the office on your own with your laptop running a spectrum analyzer, which would be able to detect the RF anomalies that can affect your wireless network performance. The placement of these analyzers does play an important role in solving the problem. If a host in your office is not able to connect then the best option is to place your analyzer as close to the host as possible in order to perceive the situation from the host's perspective. If various hosts in your office experience a similar problem, then the best option would be to place the analyzer near the access point they are trying to connect to. Depending on the scenario you are dealing with, you can dynamically decide and even manually scan through the office premises to get to know whether there is any RF energy interfering.

I don't have any special hardware to show you RF energy, but I will use an inbuilt tool from the Kali Linux OS, which will help us fetch various granular details regarding different WLANs available around my premises and all the devices that are connected to Wi-Fi (if paired with a hardware used for spectrum analysis, this can prove really useful). The name of the tool is Kismet, and it is quite efficient in representing details in graphical and various available statistical formats, thus enabling us to know more about the neighborhood (use it for ethical purposes). Follow these steps to use the Kismet tool on Kali Linux:

1. First I enable the monitor mode using the `airmon-ng start wlan0` command (`wlan0` is my wireless interface).

2. Open the terminal and type `Kismet`. You will be asked to set various customization options—do not change any default settings.

3. Once you're asked for the source (interface name) for the Kismet server to capture the packets, specify your interface running on the monitor mode (in my case, this is `mon0`. You can check your interface using the `iwconfig` command).

4. Now, let the tool run on its own for a few minutes; gradually, you will start noticing that a graph is getting plotted for the live traffic captured. You will see various wireless networks around you and most of the associated devices connected with it.

5. In the network section, you will see specific details for the wireless network, such as BSSID, SSID, encryption algorithm used, and so on.

6. The clients' section will show various devices associated with the network. Refer to the following figure of the tool that lists my network and various clients connected to it:

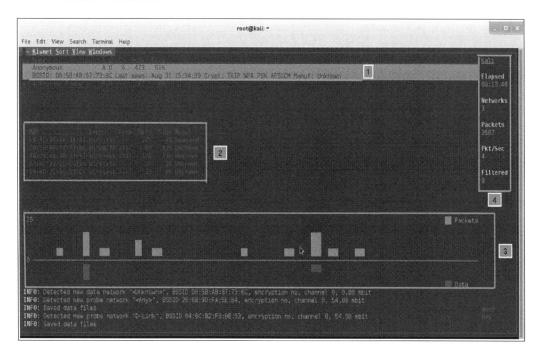

Now, let's see what does each pointer in the preceding screenshot signifies:

*   In this part, just below the menu bar, the number of networks that my Wi-Fi adapter is able to scan is shown. The first row shows my home network **Anonymous** and its BSSID, when the network was last seen, the algorithm used, and the manufacturer of the device.

*   In this second section, Kismet lists out various devices that are currently associated with the **Anonymous** network, their type (is it an access point or a wireless client), the frequency that the devices are using for transmission, the total number of packets a particular device has transmitted, the size of all packets, and the manufacturer of the device (interestingly, Kismet was able to identify one device manufacturer that is currently associated with my network, as shown in the first row). Refer to the following screenshot that shows the device section separately:

- In the third section, there is a graph that shows the current rate at which the packets are traveling around and the total amount of data packets that are shown with red bars.

- In the fourth section, we can see a lot of details that are listed, such as the hostname (Kali), total number of networks my NIC is able to see, for how long Kismet is running, the total number of packets captured, and an average rate of packets seen per second. Using such simple tools without any special configuration, we were able to collect a good amount of specific details.

In the bottom-right corner of the window, the interface used to capture details is shown: mon0 (a monitor mode activated interface). Through this tool, we are not able to capture any RF energy that can distort the traffic shape, which lessens our network performance. But the same tool, when paired with Wi-Spy or Ubertooth hardware, will show the RF energy spectrum. If you are one of those professionals who needs to deal with Wi-Fi troubleshooting in day-to-day working, then you should use this—if not now, then someday you will.

The RF energy emitted from the devices won't be the problem every time; sometimes, you would be required to look at the packet level like checking authentication and association packets, that is, you can match your normal traffic pattern with the anomaly you might be facing.

The IEEE 802.11 packet structure

The medium used by the packets to travel from one host to another is changed for now, but the basic protocols that work on the preceding layers are still the same. As we already discussed, layer 2 (data link) is of great importance here. Understanding packets traveling in detail is obviously a good thing; we will discuss various types of frames, header structures, and information an 802.11 packet contains.

There are basically three types of frames that you will see while analyzing wireless packets. All the packets listed are almost similar to the one we saw earlier; the only difference here is the extra information that is appended because of the 802.11 header. The following are the header types that you will see:

- **Management**: To form a connection between the hosts at the data link layer, these frames are used. These frames are used to join or leave a network, associations/disassociation/reassociation and to broadcast beacon packets and a few administrative tasks. Management frames are responsible for a lot of activities that take place while the connection between the hosts is established.

  ○ **The beacon frame**: The AP sends beacon frames every 10th of a second to let the STA know that the AP is available for connection.

  ○ **The authentication frame**: This type of frame is sent by the STA to the AP containing its identity. If the AP follows an open system authentication, then STA would send just one authentication frame that AP acknowledges to understand whether the connection is accepted or rejected. If the AP follows shared key authentication, then the STA sends a request to the AP to get connected. Now, AP sends a challenge text to the STA. After this, STA completes the challenge and encrypts the challenge text requested using the same algorithm that the AP is using, and then it sends it to the AP. AP receives and decrypts the text using it's own key value, and no matter what the result is, it determines the status of the connection request.

  ○ **The association request frame**: This frame is sent from the STA to the AP to provide details of the allocation of resources and for syncing purpose.

  ○ **The associate response frame**: This frame is sent in response to the AP for the STA request that is sent.

  ○ **The deauthentication frame**: This is sent by the STA to terminate the connection with the AP/STA.

  ○ **The disassociation frame**: This frame is a graceful way of terminating the connection so that the AP can free up the resources allocated for the STA.

  ○ **The probe request frame**: This frame is sent by the STA to another STA/AP to request for its details; this is basically used to find nearby APs.

- **The probe response frame**: This frame is sent in response to the request that AP/STS might have received from another device in the network.

- **The reassociation (request/response) frame**: This frame is sent to the new AP when an STA's association with the current AP gets dropped. In response, the AP acknowledges the acceptance/rejection for the reassociation request.

Monitoring the time gap between each beacon frame sent from the hosts can be useful when dealing with high latencies. Due to these beacon packets broadcasted from the AP, the devices know that they are available to connect to.

- **Control**: This is to ensure that the delivery of the packets between the hosts manages the level of congestion in your channel and uses packets such as clear-to-send and request-to-send. In short, we can say that these frames are used for maintenance tasks. These control packets ensure the integrity of the packets that are transmitted. Likewise, the management frame several kinds control frame has just three kinds:

  - **Request-to-send (RTS)**: This frame is sent by the STA to request for gaining the control of the medium for a particular duration.

  - **Clear-to-send (CTS)**: This frame is sent by the AP from where it received the RTS to specify when the medium will be allocated to the STA for transmission. This frame is often used for protection from older stations that want to gain access to the medium again.

  - **Acknowledgement (ACK)**: This frame is sent by the receiving STA to tell the sending station that the data packet was received successfully. If the sending station does not receive this packet, then after a definite period of time, the sending station will resend the data packet to the same recipient to ensure the delivery of the packet.

- **Data**: These frames contain the data that is actually sent between the hosts. These are the only frames that get transmitted between the wireless and the wired domain.

The 802.11 packets are similar to the wired network packets that we saw; the terminologies do differ a little bit, but the basic concept is identical. Let's take a look at a beacon frame. Refer to the following screenshot for that:

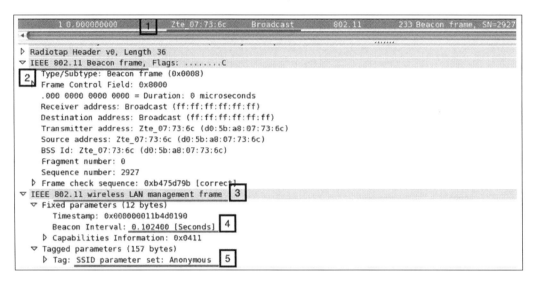

Now, let's see what all the pointers in the preceding figure signify:

- **1**: The packet describes it all; the beacon frame is sent to the broadcast address from the Wi-Fi-enabled device or any device that is currently listening can connect to it using the right credentials.

- **2** and **3**: Here, the type of the frame is management and the subtype is beacon.

- **4**: As we discussed earlier, beacon frames are transmitted every 10 seconds. You can verify the same from the packet itself, to be precise; the next beacon frame was sent after an average time of 0.102385000 seconds (this is just the time gap I calculated between the two packets seen in the list pane).

- **5**: The SSID broadcast is enabled, and hence, the packet is shown with the broadcasted SSID **Anonymous**, which will be visible when you try to scan nearby Wi-Fi hotspots that you wish to connect to (you need to use the monitor mode to capture this packet). Various other details are included in the beacon frame that is part of the header and is quite necessary to know about. Refer to the following frame structure that shows how a layer 2 datagram looks like in theory and in Wireshark:

Frame Control	Duration/ID	Address1	Address2	Address3	Sequence Control	Address4

```
▽ IEEE 802.11 Beacon frame, Flags: ........C
    Type/Subtype: Beacon frame (0x0008)
  ▽ Frame Control Field: 0x8000
      .... ..00 = Version: 0
      .... 00.. = Type: Management frame (0)
      1000 .... = Subtype: 8
    ▽ Flags: 0x00
        .... ..00 = DS status: Not leaving DS or network is operating in AD-HOC mode (To DS: 0 From DS: 0) (0x00)
        .... .0.. = More Fragments: This is the last fragment
        .... 0... = Retry: Frame is not being retransmitted
        ...0 .... = PWR MGT: STA will stay up
        ..0. .... = More Data: No data buffered
        .0.. .... = Protected flag: Data is not protected
        0... .... = Order flag: Not strictly ordered
    .000 0000 0000 0000 = Duration: 0 microseconds
    Receiver address: Broadcast (ff:ff:ff:ff:ff:ff)
    Destination address: Broadcast (ff:ff:ff:ff:ff:ff)
    Transmitter address: Zte_07:73:6c (d0:5b:a8:07:73:6c)
    Source address: Zte_07:73:6c (d0:5b:a8:07:73:6c)
    BSS Id: Zte_07:73:6c (d0:5b:a8:07:73:6c)
    Fragment number: 0
    Sequence number: 2928
  ▽ Frame check sequence: 0xea046565 [correct]
      [Good: True]
      [Bad: False]
```

Let's take a look at the fields present in the frame in detail:

This is the first section in the frame header that lists out quite a good amount of info in it.

- **Frame Control:**
- `Protocol Version`: This represents a 2-bit value that is used to verify the version of the protocol in use; the current version is 0 at the time of writing.
- `Type`: This identifies the type of the frame; in our case, we are dealing with a management frame (beacon).
- `Subtype`: This represents the subtype of the header; for us, it is a beacon frame for which we are seeing a numerical code 8.
- `DS Status`: This represents whether a data frame is heading to a **distribution system (DS)** or working in which mode. If the bit is set to 1, then this must be a data frame; if this is set to 0, then this frame is probably a management/control frame.
- `More Fragments`: If this bit is set to 1, this means that the frame has been distributed into couple of parts and is being sent one by one.
- `Retry`: This bit is set to 1 when there is a requirement upon retransmission of the frame.
- `PWR Management`: If this is set to 1, it represents the current power management state of the STA whether it is `active:0` or in the `power-save:1` mode.

- `More Data`: This bit is set to 1 if the AP is trying to tell the STA in the power-save mode that it has more frames to send. In case of control frames, this will always be 0.

- `Order`: If this bit is set to 1, this means that the frame is forcefully lined up and would be sent in a sequence. Usually, this bit is not set because it might cost transmission performance.

- `Duration ID`: This denotes the time the sender might require for frame exchange; this is usually seen in an **request-to-send** (**RTS**) frame, which requests to occupy the medium for a certain amount of time.

- `Address 1/2/3`: This is the physical address of the communicating device (receiver, transmitter, and destination address).

- `Sequence Control`: This is composed of two subfields: a 12-bit sequence number and a fragment number of 4 bit. A sequence number field is used to identify the sequence of the frames that arrive and for their proper reassembly (this ranges between 0-4,095). The fragment number field is used to denote the number of fragments for each frame (this ranges between 0-15).

- `Address 4`: This represents the sender's physical address and would only be present in a wireless distribution mode.

- `Data/Payload`: This field is not part of the header, but at the end, it will be appended when data is being sent across. The size of this field can be up to 2,324 bytes.

- `FCS`: The frame check sequence field is used to perform a data integrity test; you must have heard about the **cyclic redundancy check** (**CRC**), which helps in calculating a value related to the data we received. If the FCS value is identical to the one we calculated, then the packet is received without errors.

RTS/CTS

These are one of those essential components of WLAN data transfers that avoid collisions from happening and ensure the integrity of the data that is sent. The following illustration determines the four-step process that takes place to follow a 100% fail-proof delivery:

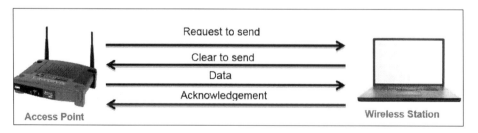

First, the AP sends a request to the STA to gain medium access; once the STA approves the AP's request, the AP starts sending data. As soon as the data transfer is completed, the STA sends an ACK packet to acknowledge error-free delivery. If the ACK is not sent, then then the AP will start retransmission after some time.

Usual and unusual WEP – open/shared key communication

Here, we will discuss two types of **Wired Equivalent Privacy (WEP)** authentication procedures: open and shared keys. As a matter of fact, discussing WEP is really unnecessary, but we should be aware of how it works because you never know when you might be asked to troubleshoot an old router whose firmware is still not upgraded and just supports WEP as an authentication mechanism.

WEP-open is way better than WEP-shared because even when the password that you provide turns out to be wrong, you will get connected to the network; here, it reduces the chance of getting the router brute forced. If you are using WEP-shared communication, then an experienced hacker won't take more than 2 minutes to crack your strongest key, and because of the small pool of keys that WEP supports, your password won't last long.

So, to begin with, we need the infrastructure to capture packets that are required for WEP-open. A key point to note here is that the infrastructure I am using consists of three different machines: the access point on the 192.168.1.1 IP, the station on the 192.168.1.105 IP, and Kali Linux running Wireshark on the 192.168.1.104 IP. Refer to the following illustration to understand this:

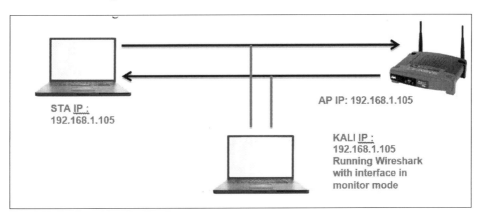

1. First, let's activate the monitor mode over my interface:

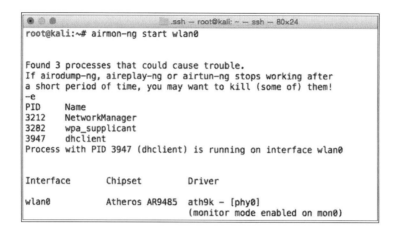

In the bottom-right corner of the preceding screenshot, you can see the message that the monitor mode is enabled over the mon0 interface. This is the same interface that we will use to capture 802.11 packets from our AP and STA.

2. Next, to confirm the channel over which my channel is working, I used the airodump-ng mon0 command.

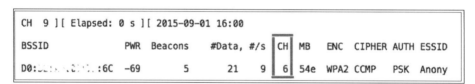

3. Now, once we have figured out that the channel is 6, we can go ahead and make our interface listen specifically to this channel, thus avoiding any noise from other channels. To do so, I used the iwconfig mon0 channel 6 command.

Figure 1: Configuring mon0 interface to channel 6

4. Once you have completed all these steps, go ahead and launch Wireshark. If the output of the commands you issued gives any error, then please rectify it before you proceed.

WEP-open key

Once the interface starts working fine and you are able to see the beacon frames broadcasted from your access point and probe request or response to and from your station, then you can simply launch a WEP-open authentication session. When asked for a password, just give any random password which will let you get connected to the network, but it might be possible that you won't be able to access the Internet connection shared by the AP with other STAs. Refer to the following screenshot depicting a WEP-open authentication session.

To capture the normal traffic pattern, I will use a Linux distribution (Kali) running on an independent machine that has a feature to activate the monitor mode (without the monitor mode, you can not capture 802.11 packets.) First, activate the monitor mode on our WLAN adapter using a basic set of commands, and we will also configure the same adapter to listen to a specific channel.

After launching Wireshark, make sure that you choose the mono interface only; then, you will be able to capture relevant traffic (keep the promiscuous mode on as well).

As clearly visible in the details pane of the first authentication frame selected in the list pane, the authentication system is Open-System (numeric code 0) and the connection attempt is successful as well. Following this, we can see an association request/response and then some QOS and Null function data frames.

An **association request/response** is sent and received by the STA/AP to associate a dropped connection, which the client was already a part of before, and to allocate the resources STA might require for communication over the channel.

A **QOS data** packet is a subtype of the control frame types, which depicts the quality of service and the over all performance.

Null Function packets are used to inform AP that the STA is going in the power-save mode. This packet does not carry any data, just some flag information.

And for every kind of information being shared between hosts, there are **ACK** packets that are sent across to determine the delivery of every packet in the communication.

The shared key

Before we start configuring, I want you to understand the process of WEP-shared key authentication, that is, the steps involved in the whole session. Refer to the following illustration to understand this:

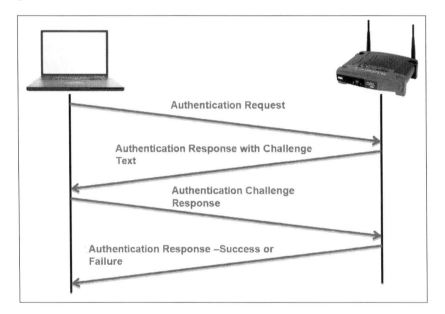

In short, the STA tries to connect to the AP by sending an authentication request, which the AP acknowledges by sending a text challenge that the STA is supposed to complete and before sending an encrypt using the key algorithm AP knows about. Once STA has completed the challenge process over his end, STA sends the challenge response which is being evaluated by the AP and determines the success or failure of the connection and the same is acknowledged to the STA in another authentication frame.

So, for a normal WEP authentication session, you will observe at least four authentication frames. If the authentication is successful, then the authentication frames will be followed by an association request/response along with some data transfer. And if the authentication is not successful, then after four authentication frames, the session between the STA and the AP will end. Follow the next steps to capture WEP management, control and data frames from your WLAN.

As discussed, you will note that the same pattern of packets is captured. Refer to the following screenshot depicting a successful WEP authentication session that was captured by Wireshark:

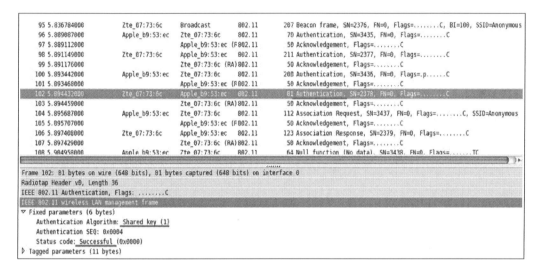

- For the fourth authentication frame, I have expanded the details section to confirm whether the connection attempt was successful or not. And from the preceding screenshot, we can verify that it was successful. The authentication type used for the communication can also be seen here.

- As we know, now if the connection attempt between the STA and AP fails, the whole session will be terminated after the fourth authentication frame and we will see a failure message. To verify the same, I tried duplicating the scenario while Wireshark was listening through an interface in the monitor mode on an individual system.

- • Refer to the following figure that illustrates a failed WEP connection attempt. In the list pane, we can see the same authentication frame pattern (just four authentication frames), but the last frame that the STA received from the AP acknowledges the connection status. As is clearly visible in the details pane, the connection attempt failed due to an incorrect challenge response text sent by the STA.

We witnessed two types of authentication procedures that WEP supports, but what is really important to know is that WEP is now obsolete, so I would never recommend to any of you to use this as an authentication protocol. If you have any old devices that only support WEP, then kindly upgrade to the latest hardware.

WPA-Personal

We talked about a crappy authentication algorithm that has been used since the birth of wireless networking, but when we have a better option, why not use it. I am talking about the **Wi-Fi Protected Access** (**WPA**) security algorithm that is stronger than WEP when we add the corrective measures required. In 2003 when WPA was launched by Wi-Fi Alliance as a measure to make WLAN communication stronger than the previous protocol, WEP. Nowadays, almost every WNIC supports WPA authentication mechanism, thus enabling you to take advantage of using a better security protocol. The **Temporal Key Integrity Protocol** (**TKIP**) lets the existing legacy hardware upgrade easily to implement WPA. The key size used by WEP was 40/104 bits, whereas WPA uses a key size of 256 bits, and the interesting thing to know is that every packet transmitted between the AP and STA is encrypted using the 256-bit key, which makes the situation quite tight for malicious users. One more advance was done in WPA that let the devices communicate with more assurance about the integrity of the message.

In WEP, the traditional CRC was implemented, but here, the popular Michael 64-bit **Message Integrity Check (MIC)** was introduced to address the issue. WPA also uses the RC4 algorithm to build a session based on dynamic encryption keys (you would never end up using the same key pair between two hosts). If compared to WEP, it has a larger IV size of 48 bits. Refer to the following illustration of how the cipher text is formed that is transmitted over the medium:

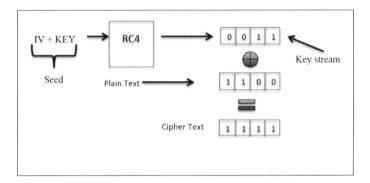

The preceding illustration depicts how the whole process starts by appending the IV and the dynamically generated 256-bit key. Then, is passed on to the RC4 algorithm, which encrypts the packets with keys, and then the resulting encrypted key stream is appended with the data and voila! We have the cipher text. Now, I will introduce you to the normal authentication session between an AP and an STA. Refer to the following figure for the same:

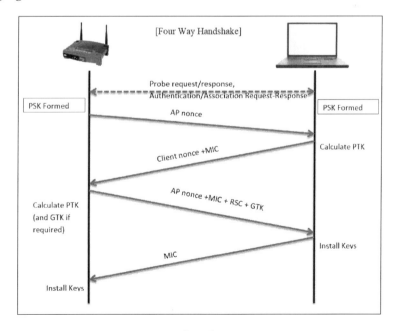

In the case of the Enterprise WPA configuration, first, the *Master Key Exchange* takes place. I will later give you a brief about it. As of now, we have an AP that sends its nonce (random value) to the STA (initiation of connection) that will use the AP's nonce value and its own nonce to calculate the **Pairwise Transient Key** (**PTK**) along with the **Pre Shared Key** (**PSK**), which was established during the initial connection process. The resulting value will be sent to the AP. Then, the AP will calculate the PTK over its end and append the MIC with the **receive sequence counter** (**RSC**) that helps in identifying the replayed messages. The resulting value will be passed on to the STA. Now, the STA will first verify the MIC in the message to ensure the integrity and install the keys. Then, a response will be sent to the AP regarding the status. If the status shows success, the AP then installs the same keys (dynamic keys) that will be used in further communication between the hosts.

After configuring WPA-Personal on my AP, I had sent an authentication request from my client and the corresponding communication was captured by Wireshark, which is shown in the following screenshot:

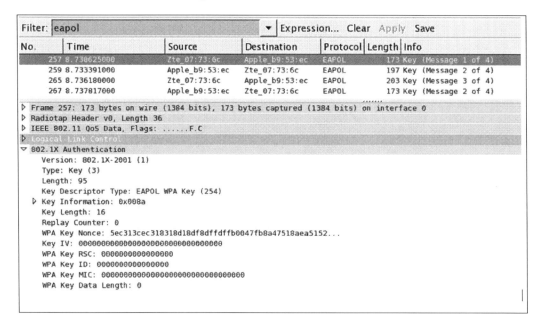

 You need the same infrastructure that we used while capturing WEP communication that is an interface in the monitor mode that is listening on a separate machine.

This is what a normal WPA successful handshake (authentication) process looks like, that is, four EAPOL packets. To analyze the session specifically between the AP and STA, I applied a display filter to see only EAPOL packets (authentication frames). Before the authentication frames, AP's beacon frame, and STA's probe, we looked at authentication and association request/response packets that led to the authentication session, following which PSK was used to generate the dynamic keys. Because of a software package error that I installed on my machine, the fourth packet says `Message 2 of 4`, whereas it should be `Message 4 of 4`.

Getting into more detail, I would like to show you the flags marked in all of these four authentication packets that will definitely clear your thoughts regarding the WPA handshake process. Refer to the following screenshot that illustrates this:

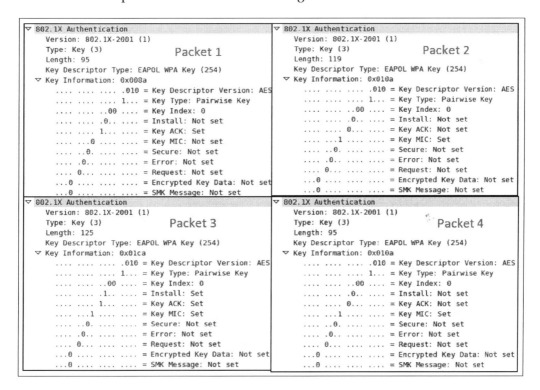

Here is the description of the preceding authentication packets:

- **Packet 1**: The pairwise master key (pre-shared key) and the `ACK` bit are set (probably because of the association request/response exchanged earlier), which was sent by the AP to STA to initiate the connection along with the nonce value that was chosen randomly.

- **Packet 2**: The pairwise master key and the MIC flag is set, which STA sent to the AP to for acknowledging the request received, along with its own nonce value appended to the AP's nonce and the MIC for integrity check.

- **Packet 3**: The pairwise master key, `install`, key ACK, and MIC flags are set, which the AP tries to send to the STA. The STA will fulfill the challenge text values received and will confirm to the AP along with the encrypted challenge text which AP is going to be crosschecked.

- **Packet 4**: Here, the pairwise master key and the MIC flag are set, which the STA sends to the AP to make the connection complete. Now, the AP is mutually ready to perform data transfer with the STA.

I hope these flags help you understand the four-way handshake process in an easy and realistic manner.

Next, we are going to see what happens when the AP receives an incorrect challenge text from the STA, what the packets look like in the list pane, and whether there would there be any difference in the pattern of packets that are captured.

The STA will try to connect to the AP and the AP will request the challenge text. The STA this time is not aware of the secret keys used by other clients in the network, so ending with an incorrect pass key which won't be accepted by the AP, or please check acknowledged by the STA. The STA will try again to send the challenge text and the same process goes on. After this, you will notice a couple of similar packets in the list pane. Refer to the following figure for the same:

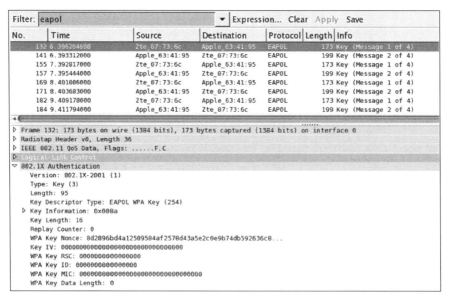

Figure 2: WPA Failed authentication

As you can see in the preceding screenshot, **EAPOL Message 1 and 2** can only be seen because when the STA provides the challenge text response, the AP rejects it and again the process starts from beginning. The same thing will continue for a couple of times, but a packets pattern of such kind denotes unsuccessful connection attempts (may be a brute force attack). The packets listed can be associated with each other using the replay counter listed that we saw earlier in the key nonce in details section.

WPA-Enterprise

I promised we would be discussing the enterprise mode in brief, so here it is. In the corporate infrastructure, the key and passwords are not kept with the AP, and even the AP is not responsible for authentication with the **STA**. There is an extra entity, the **RADIUS** server, that takes care of authentication here. Before the four-way handshake takes place, the **RADIUS** server and the access point are supposed to go through a **Master Key Exchange**, which gives an assurance to both the communicating devices that the other part is legitimate. Let's have a look at the following figure:

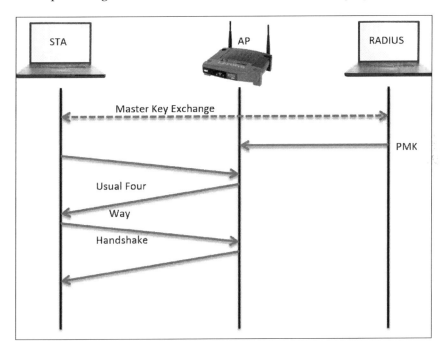

Afterwards, the pairwise master key is created and passed on to the AP, which will lead on and complete the four-way handshake process and complete the authentication session.

I've scrolled down the packet list and look what I found for you: **Disassociation** and **Deauthentication** packets in action captured by our sniffer. So, before we wrap up, you should take a look at them.

The wireless stations/access points use disassociation packets in order to notify the access point that the client is now going offline and the resources that have been allocated by the AP to wireless clients can now be released. Refer to the following figure that illustrates the same:

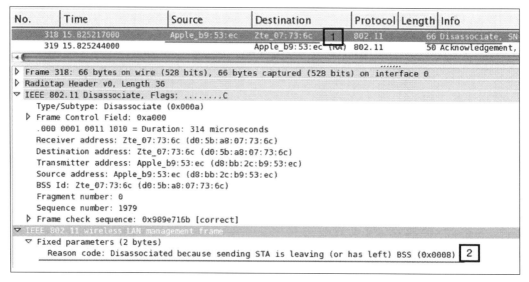

Figure 3: The disassociation packet

As you can observe, at first, the STA sends a `disassociation` frame and receives `ACK` (318,319) for the same. Now, for better understanding of the packets, we can take a look at the details pane (select the disassociation packet first), where the `Reason Code` parameter states that the STA is leaving or has already left. This gives us a feature through which we can view and understand packet behavior efficiently.

The wireless stations or the access points use the `deauthentication` frames to notify the other side of the communication that the other device is leaving. There can be several reasons for it. Refer to the following figure to understand this:

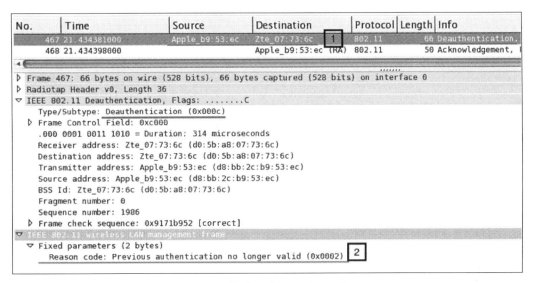

Figure 4: The deauthentication packet

First, the STA sends a `deauthentication` frame to the access point, which gets acknowledged in the next packets (`467,468`). After expanding the details section for the deauthentication packet, we can easily note that the `Type/Subtype` field is verifying the same. And at the bottom, we get to understand why the deauthentication packet was generated. In our case, it is `Previous authentication no longer valid`, which the STA tried to notify the AP about, and if they wish to communicate again in the future, then the process of authentication has to start over, from the probe and association frame, following the four-way handshake.

Decrypting WEP and WPA traffic

The technique to decrypt WEP and WPA traffic is available with the use of Wireshark. As we know, WEP is the weakest security encryption protocol and it has been exploited for a long time. Once you have the key for the wireless network, it becomes a matter of a few clicks to decrypt the traffic.

To demonstrate the same, I have sanitized the wireless traffic between my access point and a client that is connected to it. Refer to the following screenshot where the normal IEEE802.11 traffic is captured using Wireshark:

No.	Time	Source	Destination	Protocol	Length	Info
1	0.000000	MS-NLB-PhysServer-10_Tp-LinkT_2a:84:4v		802.11	117	QoS Data, SN=344, FN=0, Flags=.p.....T
2	0.000004	Tp-LinkT_2a:84:4e	MS-NLB-PhysServer-10_al	802.11	145	QoS Data, SN=197, FN=0, Flags=.p....F.
3	0.101892	MS-NLB-PhysServer-10_	Tp-LinkT_2a:84:4e	802.11	26	QoS Null function (No data), SN=2641, FN=0, Flags=...P...T
4	4.038400	MS-NLB-PhysServer-10_	Tp-LinkT_2a:84:4e	802.11	111	QoS Data, SN=345, FN=0, Flags=.p.....T
5	4.039428	Tp-LinkT_2a:84:4e	MS-NLB-PhysServer-10_al	802.11	139	QoS Data, SN=198, FN=0, Flags=.p....F.
6	4.141316	MS-NLB-PhysServer-10_	Tp-LinkT_2a:84:4e	802.11	26	QoS Null function (No data), SN=2642, FN=0, Flags=...P...T
7	5.038400	MS-NLB-PhysServer-10_	Tp-LinkT_2a:84:4e	802.11	111	QoS Data, SN=346, FN=0, Flags=.p.....T
8	5.039430	Tp-LinkT_2a:84:4e	MS-NLB-PhysServer-10_al	802.11	139	QoS Data, SN=199, FN=0, Flags=.p....F.
9	5.141316	MS-NLB-PhysServer-10_	Tp-LinkT_2a:84:4e	802.11	26	QoS Null function (No data), SN=2643, FN=0, Flags=...P...T
10	6.039426	MS-NLB-PhysServer-10_	Tp-LinkT_2a:84:4e	802.11	111	QoS Data, SN=347, FN=0, Flags=.p.....T
11	6.040452	Tp-LinkT_2a:84:4e	MS-NLB-PhysServer-10_al	802.11	139	QoS Data, SN=200, FN=0, Flags=.p....F.
12	6.142340	MS-NLB-PhysServer-10_	Tp-LinkT_2a:84:4e	802.11	26	QoS Null function (No data), SN=2644, FN=0, Flags=...P...T
13	8.039426	MS-NLB-PhysServer-10_	Tp-LinkT_2a:84:4e	802.11	111	QoS Data, SN=348, FN=0, Flags=.p.....T
14	8.040964	Tp-LinkT_2a:84:4e	MS-NLB-PhysServer-10_al	802.11	139	QoS Data, SN=201, FN=0, Flags=.p....F.
15	8.143876	MS-NLB-PhysServer-10_	Tp-LinkT_2a:84:4e	802.11	26	QoS Null function (No data), SN=2645, FN=0, Flags=...P...T
16	12.042496	MS-NLB-PhysServer-10_	Tp-LinkT_2a:84:4e	802.11	111	QoS Data, SN=349, FN=0, Flags=.p.....T

Figure 5: WLAN traffic before decryption

I hope that by now you must be aware of the kind of packets that we see in the list pane, but still, it does not make much sense in terms of network-activity-related traffic. This is why you need to learn the technique to make the entire traffic more readable. Before you proceed, you need to make some changes in the preferences section of the IEEE 802.11 protocol.

Go to **Edit | Preferences**, expand **protocol** section and select **IEEE 802.11** and make the changes. Refer to the following screenshot and make the changes that are highlighted:

Reassemble fragmented 802.11 datagrams: ☑
Ignore vendor-specific HT elements: ☐
Call subdissector for retransmitted 802.11 frames: ☑
Assume packets have FCS: ☐
Ignore the Protection bit: ● No   ○ Yes – without IV   ○ Yes – with IV
Enable decryption: ☑
Key examples: 01:02:03:04:05 (40/64–bit WEP),
010203040506070809101111213 (104/128–bit WEP),
MyPassword[:MyAP] (WPA + plaintext password [+ SSID]),
0102030405...6061626364 (WPA + 256–bit key). Invalid keys will be ignored.
Decryption Keys: 🔑 Edit...

Once you have set the configuration as shown in the preceding screenshot, click on the **Edit** button next to **Decryption Keys** (to add the **WEP/WPA** key). Refer to the following screenshot:

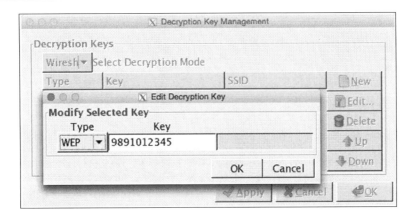

Click on **New** and you will be presented with the same dialog where you can add the **WEP/WPA** key in order to decrypt the preceding communication that we saw. After all the changes have been made, click on **OK** under **Apply**. Now, you will be shown the decrypted traffic similar to the one shown here:

No.	Time	Source	Destination	Protocol	Length	Info
1	0.000000	192.168.0.100	192.168.0.1	DNS	115	Standard query 0x7730 A www.cltest.com
2	0.000004	192.168.0.1	192.168.0.100	ICMP	145	Destination unreachable (Network unreachable)
3	0.101892	MS-NLB-PhysServer-10_Tp-LinkT_2a:84:4e		802.11	26	QoS Null function (No data), SN=2641, FN=0, Flags=...P...T
4	4.038400	192.168.0.100	192.168.0.1	DNS	111	Standard query 0xeed6 A ctldl.windowsupdate.com
5	4.039428	192.168.0.1	192.168.0.100	ICMP	139	Destination unreachable (Network unreachable)
6	4.141316	MS-NLB-PhysServer-10_Tp-LinkT_2a:84:4e		802.11	26	QoS Null function (No data), SN=2642, FN=0, Flags=...P...T
7	5.038400	192.168.0.100	192.168.0.1	DNS	111	Standard query 0xeed6 A ctldl.windowsupdate.com
8	5.039430	192.168.0.1	192.168.0.100	ICMP	136	Destination unreachable (Network unreachable)
9	5.141316	MS-NLB-PhysServer-10_Tp-LinkT_2a:84:4e		802.11	26	QoS Null function (No data), SN=2643, FN=0, Flags=...P...T
10	6.039426	192.168.0.100	192.168.0.1	DNS	111	Standard query 0xeed6 A ctldl.windowsupdate.com
11	6.040452	192.168.0.1	192.168.0.100	ICMP	139	Destination unreachable (Network unreachable)
12	6.142340	MS-NLB-PhysServer-10_Tp-LinkT_2a:84:4e		802.11	26	QoS Null function (No data), SN=2644, FN=0, Flags=...P...T
13	8.039426	192.168.0.100	192.168.0.1	DNS	111	Standard query 0xeed6 A ctldl.windowsupdate.com
14	8.040964	192.168.0.1	192.168.0.100	ICMP	139	Destination unreachable (Network unreachable)
15	8.143876	MS-NLB-PhysServer-10_Tp-LinkT_2a:84:4e		802.11	26	QoS Null function (No data), SN=2645, FN=0, Flags=...P...T
16	12.042496	192.168.0.100	192.168.0.1	DNS	111	Standard query 0xeed6 A ctldl.windowsupdate.com

Figure 6: WLAN traffic after decryption

The same list pane that we saw in the beginning of this section for this capture file is shown in a decrypted format now. Here, we are able to see the **ICMP** and **DNS** packets (normal network traffic); this is the normal traffic I was talking about. To manage the keys, there is a more effective way where you are not required to open the **Decryption keys** dialog from the **Preferences** section under **IEEE 802.11**. Just navigate to **View | Wireless toolbar**; this will add a new toolbar just below the display filter area.

Once added, you can easily mage the WEP/WPA keys. The dropdown showing **Wireshark** is really helpful and will enable you to toggle encryption on/off. If you choose **None** from the list, the decryption will be disabled and your traffic will be back to normal from just 802.11 wireless traffic. If you choose **Wireshark**, as in the preceding screenshot, then the decryption will be applied.

Summary

What we discussed here is not going to facilitate you with every scenario that can be seen in wireless communication, but definitely, it will give you a jump start.

The IEEE 802.11 standard works over radio frequencies for communication purpose. The protocol that works behind WLANS is CSMA/CD, which facilitates a collision-free environment that is required for a wireless infrastructure. Under 802.11, there are multiple standards that have been developed, and this provides a robust solution for different infrastructure-based requirements.

Sometimes, you need to look at the RF energy level too, which can really play a big role in performance upgrade. Due to various devices that work over the same spectrum of 2.4 Ghz, it is possible that your WLAN signals may get distorted. What you need in such cases is a spectrum analyzer, which lets you analyze and monitor the RF energy flowing around you. To do so, you need special hardware that can be purchased from an online tech store, and you need to pair the same hardware with software that lets you use the same, for example, Metageek's Wi-SPY hardware paired with Channelyzer.

Kismet is a graphical tool available in Kali Linux that lets you collect various advanced details about the wireless networks that are available around you and the devices connected to those networks. Kismet comes with various customization options that can be really helpful while you look for specific information. Kismet also facilitates users with several graphical features to plot live traffic over a graph for a particular duration.

In a conventional WLAN environment, there is an AP and an STA that communicate with each other. Before the actual data transfer takes place, both the devices are supposed to negotiate the session over a key (password and encryption algorithm), which will be used by both the devices that are communicating to maintain the integrity of the data that is sent.

There are commonly three types of frames that you will see while working with Wireshark: management, control, and data frames. These are the packets that you can see in the details pane once a packet is selected. Management frames control the establishment of the connection, control frames control the transfer of management, and data frames simply consist of the actual data that is sent.

Authentication protocols such as WEP and WPA take care of how an AP and STA negotiate to start communicating.

EAP is used to let the exchange of master keys take place. As defined in RFC 3748, EAP is an authentication framework that supports multiple kinds of authentication methods, and to execute EAP, you do not require an IP because it runs over data-link layer.

EAP with LAN becomes EAPOL, which is used in 802.11 infrastructures (RADIUS/AAA) for the exchange of master keys. As per the normal pattern, an AP broadcasts beacon frames that STAs listen for. If not, then the STAs will send a probe request to get connected by themselves. Then, the AP and STA conduct an authentication session and negotiate until both the hosts are convinced with each other. Once this is done, the AP would send a success message to the STA.

Using Wireshark, it is possible to decrypt WEP communications by simply adding wireless network keys with the protocol in use and modifying the preferences for the IEEE 802.11 protocol.

The monitor mode used to capture the relevant packets can be configured easily over a Linux-based system, and it is essential for Wireshark 802.11 analysis.

RTS/CTS are used in contrast to CSMA/CA in 802.11, which keeps the medium collision free and easy to work with.

Using the hash function, **Password-based key derivation function (PBKDF2)**, the 256-bit preshared key is evaluated using the passphrase.

Practice questions

Q.1 After reading the IEEE 802.11 section in this chapter, make an extensive note regarding this protocol and whatever you have understood—take help from the respective RFC if you want to.

Q.2 Install any Linux-based system live on an individual machine and try to enable the monitor mode using the commands mentioned in this chapter.

Q.3 Capture the packets with the monitor mode off and the promiscuous mode on first, and then capture with the monitor mode on and the Promiscuous mode on. Analyze the difference.

Q.4 Install the Aircrack tool on your Windows machine and try capturing the 802.11 traffic around you.

Q.5 What is the difference between the various standards available in 802.11 (b/a/g/n/i.)?

Q.6 Suppose you have a router, and over to one end of the router you have a switch connected, which further connects to multiple wired clients. Over the other end of the router, you have a wireless access point connect, which serves as a medium to let various wireless devices connect to the corporate network. Now, send a packet from the wireless domain to the wired domain and analyze the packets while they transit between the domains. What difference would it make in the 802.11 header?

Q.7 What can be happen when your wireless NIC does not support the monitor mode or the promiscuous mode? Explain the importance of each.

Q.8 To view the availability of the probe requests that your device has sent to the access point, which display filter would you use?

Q.9 Configure your AP with the WEP-Open authentication and then try to connect to it using the AP while capturing the traffic, and do the same with WEP-Shared and analyze the difference in the pattern of the packets that appear.

Q.10 Which one is better: WEP-Open or WEP-Shared key and why?

Q.11 Use a capture filter to capture traffic only from your host, access point, and the broadcast address. Does this help you to decrease the noise?

Q.12 Configure your wireless interface in the monitor mode to a specific channel and capture the WLAN traffic then.

Q.13 What is the difference between the WPA-Shared key and WPA-Enterprise authentication protocols? Elaborate the same.

Q.14 Duplicate the scenario where you have a WEP-Shared key configured access point capture, with quite a good amount of traffic for the same, and try to decrypt the traffic you have using the WEP key.

Q.15 Why is WEP-Open better than the WEP-Shared key authentication mechanism?

Q.16 Can you figure out a way that you can forcefully disassociate a wireless client from it's own currently connected network?

Q.17 For deauthentication packets, how many types you do think exist? Modify the coloring rule for the same to view the packets uniquely. In what way are they different from the disassociation packets?

Q.18 While analyzing the WPA handshake, do you observe any open-system-based authentication before the actual handshake? If it is there, then analyze the traffic and explain what is it for?

Q.19 Configure your access point with the WEP protocol encryption capture normal 802.11 wireless frames. Then, using the same approach that we discussed, try to decrypt your traffic using the key for your network.

Q.20 Is it possible to decrypt the traffic using the ASCII format key or you can you also mention the key in HEX format? If yes, in which case can writing the key in HEX format prove worthy?

7

Network Security Analysis

This chapter will teach you how to use Wireshark to analyze network security issues, such as analyzing malware traffic and foot printing attempts. You will learn how to use Wireshark for network security analysis. This chapter will cover the following topics:

- Analyzing port scanning, foot printing, and attack activities
- Lab up—port scanning with Nmap
- Analyzing brute force attacks
- Lab up—analyzing brute force attacks
- Inspecting malicious traffic
- Lab up—inspecting malicious traffic
- Solving real-world CTF challenges
- Practice questions

Up to this chapter, I have tried to make you aware of how one should use Wireshark to analyze the packets flowing around. We have just focused on how to use this sniffing tool for basic analysis purposes. However, what I am about to tell you is that in most of the places, Wireshark is used for security-analysis purpose, ranging from basic footprinting attacks to advanced Trojan-based attacks.

Using a couple of scenarios in my virtual lab, I will try to duplicate the most common one, along with capturing the live traffic between the attacker and the victim. Later on, we will dissect the trace file to get an idea of how malicious traffic looks like. We will use this knowledge base to create IDS/IPS or firewall signatures in an attempt to protect our internal critical infrastructure by analyzing the traffic shown in Wireshark.

To achieve all this, you need to change your perspective a little bit. In other words, you need to act and think like a security professional who is in charge of the corporate network and constantly working to tighten the perimeter that will make the attack process more complex for bad users. We can start all of this by analyzing the packets captured for our daily usual traffic and also duplicate certain scenarios.

Information gathering

The primary step in the exploitation process is to collect as much information as you can. In today's world, gathering specific and relevant information about a person or an organization is not so difficult (using search engines), and this is where everything begins. A lot of security professionals will start launching attacks directly on the targets, which is not appropriate in the beginning. Let's say, for example, there is an ABC Corp. Ltd. located in the next block, and an XYZ attacker is planning to exploit it in terms of physical security (to get entry to the server rooms or any high-valued target available inside). To do so, the first thing the attacker should know is the working hours and the non-working hours. Then, they should know about the working days in the targeted company. The attacker should also know about the physical layout of the building the company is located in, and they should have some basic knowledge about the security policy. With all this information, the attacker should be able to identify the weak points inside the premises that might be an easy target and can give access to what they are looking for. Did you notice what just happened in the preceding scenario? We assumed that the attacker is collecting useful information and then planning and figuring out the easy targets to attack, because following this approach will improve the chances of success. Footprinting and reconnaissance are synonyms for the term *information gathering*. The chances of success would be higher if you are following the planned approach.

Let's use the same approach in targeting an organization using networks. The first step would be to identify the public IP address of the organization, the subnet it belongs to, and the range of IP addresses allocated to the organization. This basic information can be passively (without directly interacting with the company's network) collected through the use of DNS lookup services available online. We can try to check whether zone transfer is available, which can give some juicy and granular details regarding the organization's infrastructure we are targeting. After you have collected the basic information and have mapped the basic layout, you are ready to perform a **port scan**. I would prefer that you do a **ping sweep** first, which will tell you about the live machines over the network, and from where you will get to know more about the network (while performing a ping sweep, you can modify the TTL value to figure out the internal LAN architecture).

Before we go ahead and try duplicating the most common scenarios, I want you to visualize the local virtual computer infrastructure I have created for practice purpose. Refer to the following figure:

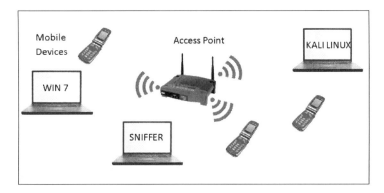

Hopefully, now you have a rough idea about my internal network that I'll be working with. The access point located at 192.168.1.1 assigns the IP address to all these devices using DHCP (the DHCP range starts from 192.168.1.100 and continues up to 192.168.1.110; it means I can have a maximum of 10 DHCP clients at one instance). For this chapter, the IP address for our attacking machine is static assigned to 192.168.1.106.

PING sweep

Let's begin with our first scenario where an attacker would try to perform a ping sweep attack over the subnet, and the traffic generated is captured by our sniffer listening through its interface in the promiscuous mode Refer to the following figure that displays the traffic pattern that was generated after running a bash script the script pings each IP starting from 100 to 110):

No.	Time	Source	Destination	Protocol	Length	Info
1	0.000000000	Apple_b9:53:ec	Broadcast	ARP	42	Who has 192.168.1.110? Tell 192.168.1.106
2	0.004128000	Apple_b9:53:ec	Broadcast	ARP	42	Who has 192.168.1.109? Tell 192.168.1.106
3	0.008476000	Apple_b9:53:ec	Broadcast	ARP	42	Who has 192.168.1.108? Tell 192.168.1.106
4	0.012705000	Apple_b9:53:ec	Broadcast	ARP	42	Who has 192.168.1.107? Tell 192.168.1.106
5	0.023785000	192.168.1.106	192.168.1.105	ICMP	98	Echo (ping) request id=0x11a8, seq=1/256, ttl=64
6	0.027774000	192.168.1.104	192.168.1.106	ICMP	98	Echo (ping) reply id=0x11a3, seq=1/256, ttl=64
7	0.031652000	Apple_b9:53:ec	Broadcast	ARP	42	Who has 192.168.1.103? Tell 192.168.1.106
8	0.035462000	192.168.1.106	192.168.1.102	ICMP	98	Echo (ping) request id=0x1199, seq=1/256, ttl=64
9	0.040423000	192.168.1.106	192.168.1.101	ICMP	98	Echo (ping) request id=0x1194, seq=1/256, ttl=64
10	0.047374000	192.168.1.106	192.168.1.100	ICMP	98	Echo (ping) request id=0x118f, seq=1/256, ttl=64
11	0.122601000	LiteonTe_fa:5e:b4	Broadcast	ARP	42	Who has 192.168.1.106? Tell 192.168.1.105
12	0.124979000	Apple_b9:53:ec	LiteonTe_fa:5e:b4	ARP	42	192.168.1.106 is at d8:bb:2c:b9:53:ec
13	0.125118000	192.168.1.100	192.168.1.106	ICMP	98	Echo (ping) reply id=0x118f, seq=1/256, ttl=64
14	0.126606000	192.168.1.105	192.168.1.106	ICMP	98	Echo (ping) reply id=0x11a8, seq=1/256, ttl=64
15	0.131304000	192.168.1.101	192.168.1.106	ICMP	98	Echo (ping) reply id=0x1194, seq=1/256, ttl=64
16	0.438404000	Apple_b9:53:ec	Zte_07:73:6c	ARP	42	Who has 192.168.1.1? Tell 192.168.1.106
17	0.528177000	Zte_07:73:6c	Apple_b9:53:ec	ARP	42	192.168.1.1 is at d0:5b:a8:07:73:6c

Figure 7.1: Ping sweep

Starting from packet 1–4, the Kali box started generating an ARP request because of the ICMP `ping` command issued, but none of those IP's are allocated. Hence, we did not receive any replies. In packet 5, Kali box sent a `ping` request to 105, and the reply for it was received in packet 14, which means the device is on. Then, in packet 7, an ARP request was sent to 103, but this IP might also be unallocated for the instance, so no reply again. In packets 8–10, Kali box sent an ICMP request packet to IP's 102, 101, and 100. The reply for the same can be seen in packets 13 and 15 from IP's 101 and 100. For 102, we did not receive any reply. It might be any device blocking our ping probes or some mobile device not responding to the ping probes. Finally, in packet number 17, we can see that the access point is informing the Kali Machine about its physical address. If you scroll down through your trace file, you would see various replies from online devices describing their physical addresses.

Half-open scan (SYN)

The next step in the process would be to scan any specific device that you would like to target. Let's suppose I want to target my Win7 machine running at IP `192.168.1.105`. My next step should be to check for available services running on that box. By services, I mean HTTP daemons, mail server daemons, FTP server, and so on. You might be wondering what a half-open scan is? Look at the process of a TCP three-way handshake we discussed, where the client initiates the connection by sending a `SYN` packet if the server is available. Then, the client receives the `SYN`, `ACK` packet, and in return, the client sends an `ACK` packet to the server for completing the handshake process.

Now, what would happen if the `ACK` packet sent in the last step of the TCP handshake is never sent to the server? The server will wait for a specific period before terminating the handshake process initiated by the client, and the connection to the specific TCP service would never be completed. That's why this type of scan is called half-open scan. This is a very common scanning technique used by the majority of users who are involved in malicious activities, being aware of such traffic pattern could help us in identifying future risks. I initiated the half-open scan from Kali box to target Win7 box. I am using Nmap, which is an open source tool available for every platform and can be downloaded for free from `http://nmap.org` (to use the tool, you can refer to various tutorials available online). The traffic generated because of the `SYN` scan is captured and shown in the following screenshot:

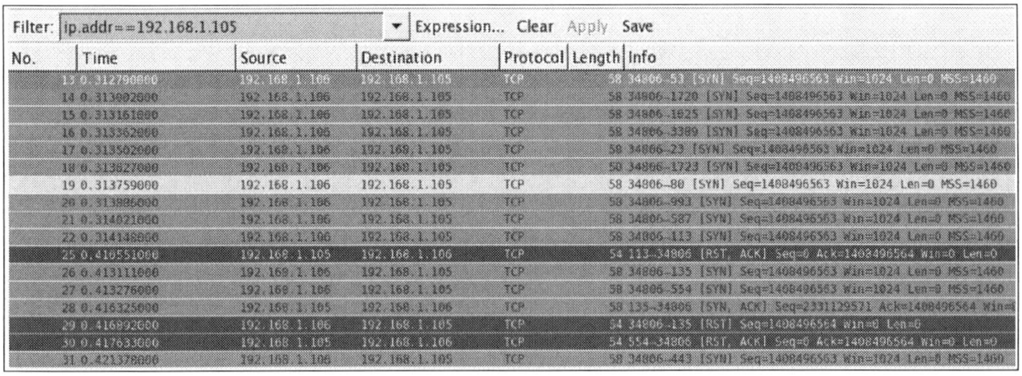

Figure 7.2: Half-open scan

There are three kinds of replies that you can see after the scanning is completed: Open, Closed, and Filtered. Now, the point to discuss is what these states mean and what relation do these states have with the packet shown in the preceding screenshot. Let's look at the states in more detail here:

- **Open**: If a service is open, then a SYN, ACK packet will be sent back to your machine for taking the TCP handshake process to the next step of completion. In packet 26, Kali sent an SYN request to port 135 and received a SYN, ACK reply in packet 28.

- **Closed**: If a service is not available to respond, then you would receive an RST packet that confirms that the service/daemon is currently not running. In packet 22, a SYN request was sent destined to port 113. In packet 25, the RST packet for the same is received. It states that the service is not available at this moment.

- **Filtered**: Sometimes, a firewall might be configured between you and your target that might be intercepting your requests and would be dropping them without forwarding them to the target. In such scenarios, you might be seeing port states such as open|filtered, closed|filtered, or just filtered.

- Let's suppose you are trying to scan an HTTP webserver that is outside your VLAN and is restricted by the firewall from your machine. Then, the handshake process would never move to the second step, that is, you will never receive a reply of any kind. You will not receive any SYN, ACK or RST packet.

Using this scan type, you can identify the state of the services running. However, using this kind of scan type will generate a hefty amount of traffic too. The scan I initiated was completed in 1.76 seconds, and in such a short time, it generated 2024 packets between the two machines. Now, this proves disadvantageous. Any well-configured IDS/IPS can figure out such activity very easily, which will in turn trigger an alert to notify the security admins. Nmap has configurable switches that can help you out in these situations too.

OS fingerprinting

Being aware of the operating system running on the target takes the scanning process to the next step in the methodology. If the attacker knows about the OS you are running, the patch level of your OS, and the version of your OS, then it would be quite simple to structure the attack process and will increase the chances of success.

There are a couple of tools available in Kali that will let you identify the target's OS. It is not 100 percent accurate, and it is correct most of the times. Now, how do you think a simple tool is available to identify the remote machine's OS? I will tell you the secret. Every OS has a different way of implementing the TCP stack. So, a packet received from the remote machine will have certain fields in it such as TTL, fragment offset, and most importantly window size. By comparing the values in the packet with the database we have, it will tell you the OS. For example, if you try to ping a Windows machine, the TTL value returned would be 128, and if you ping a Linux machine, the TTL value would be 64 most of the time. Simple, isn't?

There are two types of fingerprinting: active and passive. They are described here:

- **Active fingerprinting**: When you are directly interacting with the system, the requests and responses are directly shared between you and the target. This kind of scan can be really dangerous and is not stealthy. The captured packets will give you values that can be matched with the signature we have to identify the OS running on the remote machine.

- **Passive fingerprinting**: When you are just listening for the packets originated or destined to the target, the values in the packets can be examined in order to identify the OS running. A disadvantage off passive type scan is that it is not as accurate as active fingerprinting. But the process would be stealthier than active scans.

Using the `nmap` scan, I will try to fingerprint a machine at IP `192.168.1.109` and `192.168.1.104` and see what kind of traffic is generated due to such requests. The type of scan we will witness is active scanning, and we will be directly interacting with the systems. We won't just rely on Nmap's output to confirm the OS. The packet that would be returned to our attacking machine is the base of all necessary information, which I will try to dissect for your better understanding.

I will use the `nmap -O 192.168.1.109,192.168.1.104` command for active OS fingerprinting, where the `-O` switch is for checking the OS and its version. Refer to the following two screenshots to compare the outputs they present to us:

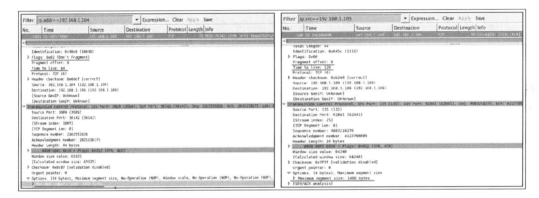

Using just the TTL field, we can verify that the first traffic we captured is from some Linux/Macintosh-based machine, as the TTL value is `64`. The second traffic screenshot belongs to a Windows machine as the TTL value is set to `128`.

Secondly, the maximum segment size highlighted at the bottom can also be a deciding factor for OS fingerprinting. In both cases, it is `1460`. The value is correct if you are talking about a Linux-based machine, but if it is a Windows machine, then you might observe that the value is `1440` most of the time.

For both Linux and Windows platforms, the Fragment Offset field should be 0 (not set). See how, simply by observing basic fields in the TCP header and IP header, we were able to fingerprint on our own. Now let's see what `nmap` has to say.

Refer to the following screenshots for illustration:

```
Running: Apple Mac OS X 10.7.X|10.9.X|10.8.X, Apple iOS 4.X|5.X|6.X
OS CPE: cpe:/o:apple:mac_os_x:10.7 cpe:/o:apple:mac_os_x:10.9 cpe:/o:apple:mac_
s_x:10.8 cpe:/o:apple:iphone_os:4 cpe:/a:apple:apple_tv:4 cpe:/o:apple:iphone_o
:5 cpe:/o:apple:iphone_os:6
OS details: Apple Mac OS X 10.7.0 (Lion) - 10.9.2 (Mavericks) or iOS 4.1 - 7.1
Darwin 10.0.0 - 14.0.0)
Network Distance: 1 hop
```

Figure 7.3: nmap output for 192.168.1.104

The nmap output for the machine IP 192.168.1.104 detects that the machine might be one of these OSes running (in the red box). I think what we figured out and it is quite close. OS detection by nmap is done by analyzing the requests and responses traffic that the target machine generates.

```
Running: Microsoft Windows 2003
OS CPE: cpe:/o:microsoft:windows_server_2003::sp1 cpe:/o:microsoft:windows_serve
r_2003::sp2
OS details: Microsoft Windows Server 2003 SP1 or SP2
Network Distance: 1 hop
```

The nmap output for the machine at 192.168.1.109 says that it is a Windows server machine, may be SP1 or SP2. This time, the result is more accurate than the previous one. We also presumed that it would be a Windows OS, and it is.

The traffic generated from both these scans would be quite similar to the SYN scan traffic where the TCP handshake request and ICMP request/replies can be seen. Once the attacker's machine running nmap receives the replies for the requests made, it will start analyzing and comparing the results with the database of the results it already has. Thus, in the end, after comparing the values, Nmap will present you with the most accurate results.

So, if you are seeing a lot of RST or RST, ACK packets sent from one of your internal LAN machines, then it is something that you should be worried about. Better create signatures for such traffic in your firewall so that they can alert you.

ARP poisoning

As we all know, the function of the ARP protocol is to translate an IP address to its corresponding MAC address. By doing so, the devices are able to communicate effectively in a LAN-based network. Any device that wishes to get connected with the other device on the same network requires the MAC address of the other hosts. Every OS maintains a list of communicating devices that can be populated in the terminal window using the arp -a command. The same command is used on every platform. We have also seen the ARP requests and reply packets that are used by the devices connected to the local network to gain the MAC addresses of other devices.

For instance, I have a local network too, which is being governed by the router (gateway) located at `192.168.1.1`, and there are 3 devices connected to it. The following table lists all the required information specific to the devices connected, which we will use later:

Device	IP Address	MAC Address
Router (default gateway)	192.168.1.1	D0:5B:A8:07:73:6C
Apple (victim)	192.168.1.103	D8:BB:2C:B9:53:EC
Windows server (victim)	192.168.1.109	00:0C:29:B3:CB:B6
Kali Linux (attacker)	192.168.1.106	00:0C:29:5D:A7:F7

This preceding information is listed in the ARP cache of every host connected to the local network. You must be thinking exactly how this is being populated in the local cache. Whenever any device intends to communicate with the other device, the requesting device sends a broadcast to the whole subnet. Then, the device to which the IP address belongs replies with it's MAC address using a unicast packet. For example, if the Apple machine wishes to communicate with the Windows machine located at `192.168.1.109`, Apple will send a broadcast asking for the Windows MAC address stating `Who has 192.168.1.109? Tell 192.168.1.103`. Then, as soon as the Windows machine gets to know about the request, the ARP reply unicast packet stating `192.168.1.109 is at 00:0C:29:B3:CB:B6` will be broadcasted. This is how the process works.

The preceding packets transfer will only happen if the Apple machine has the Windows MAC address in it's local cache. After searching in the local cache, the request is sent to the default gateway. If the default gateway knows about it, an ARP reply packet is sent by the gateway itself. If not, then the request will be forwarded to the subnet from where the destination PC will reply with the physical address using a unicast packet. After this, the conversation can happen using TCP/IP.

ARP poisoning is used to poison the local cache of the victim that enables the attacker to sniff the data that is travelling between the two victims. The attacker intercepts the traffic and then forwards it to the other side. Refer to the following illustration:

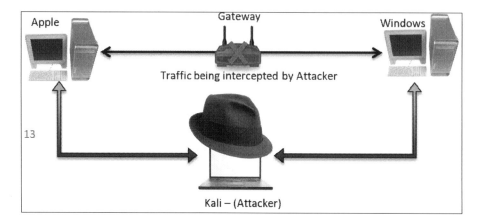

We can poison the local ARP cache of both the victims and can achieve the same. There is one more thing you need to configure: IP forwarding on Kali so that your attacking machine would be able to transfer the traffic back and forth without any loss or without letting the victims get suspicious. Follow these steps to achieve ARP poisoning:

- First, configure IP forwarding using the `echo '1' > /proc/sys/net/ipv4/ip_forward` command.

- Once this is configured, you can go ahead and send unsolicited ARP reply packets to both the victims for poisoning the cache. Before we poison it, let's take a look at how they look in normal form, for both the victim machines:

Figure 7.4: Windows server cache

To populate entries in `linux arp` cache use similar commands; refer to the following screenshot for reference.

```
Anonymous:~ NotFound$ arp -a
? (172.16.136.1) at 0:50:56:c0:0:1 on vmnet1 ifscope permanent [ethernet]
? (172.16.158.1) at 0:50:56:c0:0:8 on vmnet8 ifscope permanent [ethernet]
? (192.168.1.1) at d0:5b:a8:7:73:6c on en1 ifscope [ethernet]
? (192.168.1.100) at f0:c1:f1:63:41:95 on en1 ifscope [ethernet]
? (192.168.1.106) at 0:c:29:5d:a7:f7 on en1 ifscope [ethernet]
? (192.168.1.109) at 0:c:29:b3:cb:b6 on en1 ifscope [ethernet]
```

Figure 7.5: Apple cache

- Now, let's start sending unsolicited ARP reply packets to the Windows server machine that Apple machine is located at `00:0C:29:5D:A7:F7`. The same packet would be sent to the Apple machine that the Windows server machine is located at `00:0C:29:5D:A7:F7`. If you notice, the MAC address specified in the packets sent to the Windows and Apple machines belongs to Kali (the attacker). Refer to the following screenshot to check out the command I used for the spoofing fake MAC addresses:

```
root@kali:~/Desktop/         # arpspoof -i eth0 -t 192.168.1.109 192.168.1.103
0:c:29:5d:a7:f7 d8:bb:2c:b9:53:ec 0806 42: arp reply 192.168.1.103 is-at 0:c:29:5d:a7:f7
0:c:29:5d:a7:f7 d8:bb:2c:b9:53:ec 0806 42: arp reply 192.168.1.103 is-at 0:c:29:5d:a7:f7
0:c:29:5d:a7:f7 d8:bb:2c:b9:53:ec 0806 42: arp reply 192.168.1.103 is-at 0:c:29:5d:a7:f7
0:c:29:5d:a7:f7 d8:bb:2c:b9:53:ec 0806 42: arp reply 192.168.1.103 is-at 0:c:29:5d:a7:f7
0:c:29:5d:a7:f7 d8:bb:2c:b9:53:ec 0806 42: arp reply 192.168.1.103 is-at 0:c:29:5d:a7:f7
0:c:29:5d:a7:f7 d8:bb:2c:b9:53:ec 0806 42: arp reply 192.168.1.103 is-at 0:c:29:5d:a7:f7
```

Figure 7.6: ARP reply packets sent to the Windows server on behalf of the Apple device

```
root@kali:~/Desktop/         # arpspoof -i eth0 -t 192.168.1.103 192.168.1.109
0:c:29:5d:a7:f7 d8:bb:2c:b9:53:ec 0806 42: arp reply 192.168.1.109 is-at 0:c:29:5d:a7:f7
0:c:29:5d:a7:f7 d8:bb:2c:b9:53:ec 0806 42: arp reply 192.168.1.109 is-at 0:c:29:5d:a7:f7
0:c:29:5d:a7:f7 d8:bb:2c:b9:53:ec 0806 42: arp reply 192.168.1.109 is-at 0:c:29:5d:a7:f7
0:c:29:5d:a7:f7 d8:bb:2c:b9:53:ec 0806 42: arp reply 192.168.1.109 is-at 0:c:29:5d:a7:f7
0:c:29:5d:a7:f7 d8:bb:2c:b9:53:ec 0806 42: arp reply 192.168.1.109 is-at 0:c:29:5d:a7:f7
0:c:29:5d:a7:f7 d8:bb:2c:b9:53:ec 0806 42: arp reply 192.168.1.109 is-at 0:c:29:5d:a7:f7
0:c:29:5d:a7:f7 d8:bb:2c:b9:53:ec 0806 42: arp reply 192.168.1.109 is-at 0:c:29:5d:a7:f7
```

Figure 7.7: ARP reply packets sent to Apple device on behalf of the Windows server

Using a one-liner command with few parameters, we were able to poison the victim's cache by sending numerous ARP reply packets.

- The traffic generated due to the preceding command was also captured at the same time. Let's see how it looks. Refer to the following screenshot:

```
23 3.015821000 Vmware_5d:a7:f7      Vmware_b3:cb:b6       ARP      42 192.168.1.103 is at 00:0c:29:5d:a7:f7
24 5.016999000 Vmware_5d:a7:f7      Vmware_b3:cb:b6       ARP      42 192.168.1.103 is at 00:0c:29:5d:a7:f7

5 2.001262000 Vmware_5d:a7:f7       d8:bb:2c:b9:53:ec     ARP      42 192.168.1.109 is at 00:0c:29:5d:a7:f7
6 4.001992000 Vmware_5d:a7:f7       d8:bb:2c:b9:53:ec     ARP      42 192.168.1.109 is at 00:0c:29:5d:a7:f7
```

- Once multiple number of such packets are received by both of the victims, they will start believing it and accordingly will update the cache. Let's have a look at both the machine caches to verify this. Refer to the following screenshots:

```
Command Prompt                                              _ □ ×
^C
C:\Documents and Settings\Administrator>arp -a

Interface: 192.168.1.109 --- 0x10003
  Internet Address        Physical Address        Type
  192.168.1.103           00-0c-29-5d-a7-f7        dynamic
  192.168.1.106           00-0c-29-5d-a7-f7        dynamic

C:\Documents and Settings\Administrator>
```

Figure 7.8: Poisoned window's cache

```
Anonymous:~ NotFound$ arp -a
? (172.16.136.1) at 0:50:56:c0:0:1 on vmnet1 ifscope permanent [ethernet]
? (172.16.158.1) at 0:50:56:c0:0:8 on vmnet8 ifscope permanent [ethernet]
? (192.168.1.1) at d0:5b:a8:7:73:6c on en1 ifscope [ethernet]
? (192.168.1.100) at f0:c1:f1:63:41:95 on en1 ifscope [ethernet]
? (192.168.1.106) at 0:c:29:5d:a7:f7 on en1 ifscope [ethernet]
? (192.168.1.109) at 0:c:29:5d:a7:f7 on en1 ifscope [ethernet]
```

Figure 7.9: Poisoned Apple's cache

- Now, whatever traffic is sent between these two devices will be forwarded through the attacking box. For verification purposes, I turned off the Windows server machine and tried sending ICMP packets from the Apple machine. Refer to the following output shown for the ICMP destination host unreachable replies coming from 192.168.1.106 (Kali):

```
Anonymous:~ NotFound$ ping 192.168.1.109
PING 192.168.1.109 (192.168.1.109): 56 data bytes
92 bytes from 192.168.1.106: Redirect Host(New addr: 192.168.1.109)
Vr HL TOS  Len   ID Flg  off TTL Pro  cks      Src         Dst
 4  5 00 0054 8554    0 0000  3f  01 7230 192.168.1.103  192.168.1.109
```

The preceding output assures that the packets are being forwarded through 192.168.1.106, hence making our ARP poisoning attack a success.

- Now, the question is how to secure yourself from such attacks. The best thing I would suggest is to make manual entries for the device's MAC address in the local cache of the communicating client. This will definitely ignore unsolicited ARP reply packets while modifying the local cache. Refer to the following screenshot:

```
C:\Documents and Settings\Administrator>arp -s 192.168.1.103 d8-bb-2c-b9-53-ec

C:\Documents and Settings\Administrator>arp -a

Interface: 192.168.1.109 --- 0x10003
  Internet Address      Physical Address      Type
  192.168.1.103         d8-bb-2c-b9-53-ec     static
```

Figure 7.10: Adding a static entry to local ARP cache

Once you add a static entry in every possible host in your network, it won't be possible then to modify the local cache using the `arp` spoof tool. Similarly, for HTTPS traffic, you can use the SSL strip tool available online in order to sniff secure traffic.

Analyzing brute force attacks

Most of you must be aware of the popularity of brute force attacks. The chances of success are not high. Yet, many security professionals and malicious users implement their password-guessing ability with the help of modern tools. Brute force attack is just a way in which you try to log on to a particular service/application using the password dictionary that might have been created on the basis of the target's profile. Tools such as Cewl, Crunch, and John let you create dictionary files. Even you can salt the passwords. Discussing how to create one for yourself is out of the scope of this book, but I would recommend that you have a look at these tools (all of them come preinstalled with Kali Linux).

To analyze these common and malicious attacks, I will attempt to brute force two important services: Telnet and FTP. You might be aware of these two services and how much they are being used in corporate networking infrastructure. Telnet is used to perform administration of devices such as routers, switches, and different kinds of web servers remotely. FTP is used to transfer files efficiently with the assurance of integrity and confirmed delivery of the data.

First, take a look at most widely used protocol for remote administration that is often overlooked from a security standpoint. Using simple brute force techniques, any script kiddie can gain access to your network, and the consequences of such acts can be really destructive in terms of money and availability of the service. If dealing with consumers, then their records that might be worth millions, leading to full remote code execution of the administrative systems.

For this illustration, I have a Windows server machine running at `192.168.1.109` and an attacker at `192.168.1.106`. The attacker will first prepare its dictionary file and then will proceed to use an automated tool to attack over the Telnet administration service running under the Windows server machine. The traffic generated for such activities will be logged in through our wonderful sniffer for our analysis. I tried connecting to the Telnet service like a normal user using these steps:

- Using the Telnet command followed by the IP address, I was able to get connected to the service. In return, it printed a banner for me: `Welcome to Microsoft Telnet service.`

- Then, I supplied the wrong user credentials, which was not accepted by the server. Hence, it showed a login error, which stated `bad username or password.`

- Then, I supplied a legitimate set of credentials, which were identified and accepted by the service.

- Once the user is authorized, the Windows command prompt with certain authorization is presented along with a banner. `Welcome to Microsoft Telnet Server.`

- After I got connected, I was able to issue remote commands (Windows) from my machine itself.

- Then, at the end, to terminate the connection gracefully and to free up all resources that were allocated to use for smooth functioning, I issued the `exit` command that gave a message `connection closed by foreign host.`

Here is the screenshot illustrates the normal functioning of a Microsoft Telnet server:

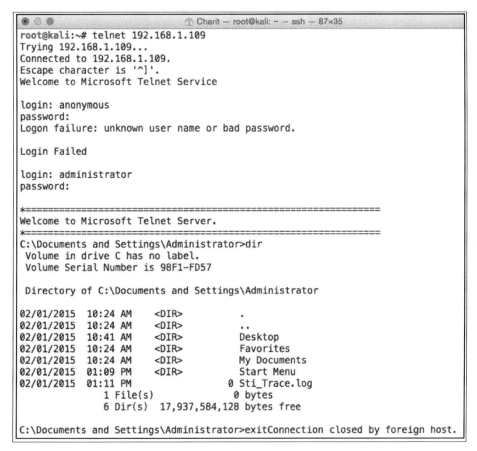

Figure 7.11: Telnet normal session

The traffic generated was also captured by Wireshark. Instead of showing the traffic, I decided to show you the whole communication in plain text format that you can achieve by assembling the TCP stream by right-clicking on the list pane and choosing **show TCP stream** (the Telnet server is configured with an echo option, so there is a chance we might see some characters echoed back from the server to the client). Refer to the following screenshot:

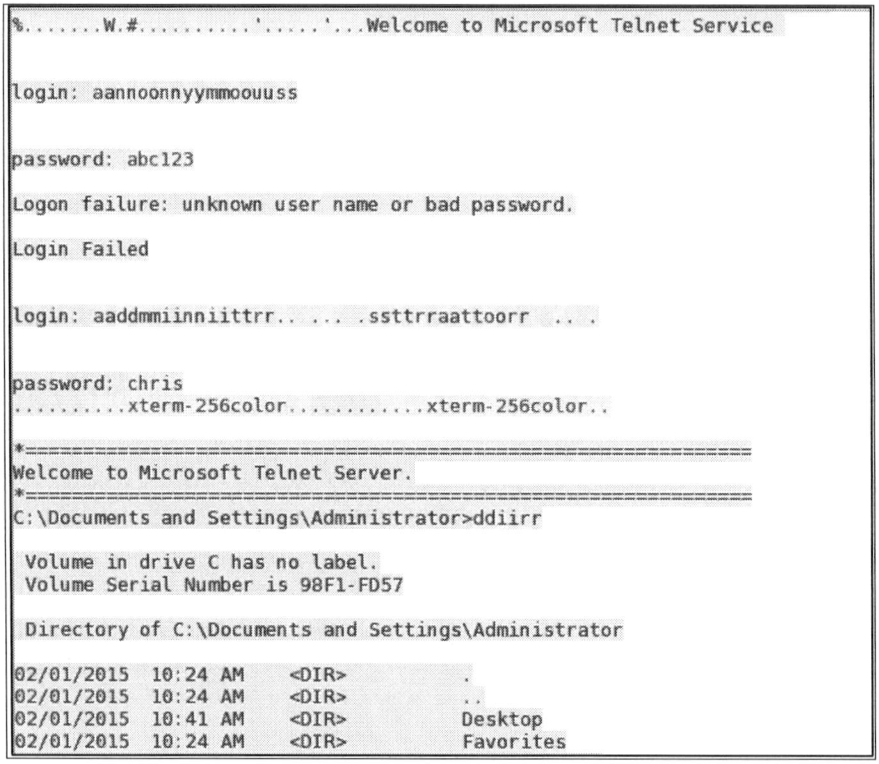

```
%.......W.#..........'.....'...Welcome to Microsoft Telnet Service


login: aannoonnyymmoouuss

password: abc123

Logon failure: unknown user name or bad password.

Login Failed


login: aaddmmiinniittrr.. ... .ssttrraattoorr .. .


password: chris
.........xterm-256color...........xterm-256color..

*===================================================
Welcome to Microsoft Telnet Server.
*===================================================
C:\Documents and Settings\Administrator>ddiirr

 Volume in drive C has no label.
 Volume Serial Number is 98F1-FD57

 Directory of C:\Documents and Settings\Administrator

02/01/2015  10:24 AM    <DIR>          .
02/01/2015  10:24 AM    <DIR>          ..
02/01/2015  10:41 AM    <DIR>          Desktop
02/01/2015  10:24 AM    <DIR>          Favorites
```

Figure 7.12: Telnet follow TCP stream

Everything we typed and received in response from the server is being shown in simple plain text readable form by just following the TCP stream.

Now, after seeing how a normal session looks, if you want to learn how to perform a brute force attack, follow these steps:

- Create a virtual pen-testing lab that consists of at least two machines: one will be an attacker (Kali) and the other machine can be of your choice (make sure you can install Telnet on it).

- Try pinging the target to test the connectivity. Issue the Telnet command to create a normal session and test whether everything is working fine.

- Now, open Kali and issue the `medusa -h <target ip> -U <usernames file> -P <password file> -M telnet` command. Refer to the following screenshot:

```
root@Kali:~# medusa -h 192.168.1.109 -U user.txt -P pass.txt -M telnet
Medusa v2.0 [http://www.foofus.net] (C) JoMo-Kun / Foofus Networks <jmk@foofus.net>

ACCOUNT CHECK: [telnet] Host: 192.168.1.109 (1 of 1, 0 complete) User: Alice (1 of 8, 0 complete) Password: abc (1 of 4 complete)
ACCOUNT CHECK: [telnet] Host: 192.168.1.109 (1 of 1, 0 complete) User: Alice (1 of 8, 0 complete) Password: efg (2 of 4 complete)
ACCOUNT CHECK: [telnet] Host: 192.168.1.109 (1 of 1, 0 complete) User: Alice (1 of 8, 0 complete) Password: chris (3 of 4 complete)
ACCOUNT CHECK: [telnet] Host: 192.168.1.109 (1 of 1, 0 complete) User: Alice (1 of 8, 0 complete) Password: mno (4 of 4 complete)
ACCOUNT CHECK: [telnet] Host: 192.168.1.109 (1 of 1, 0 complete) User: Admin (2 of 8, 1 complete) Password: abc (1 of 4 complete)
ACCOUNT CHECK: [telnet] Host: 192.168.1.109 (1 of 1, 0 complete) User: Admin (2 of 8, 1 complete) Password: efg (2 of 4 complete)
ACCOUNT CHECK: [telnet] Host: 192.168.1.109 (1 of 1, 0 complete) User: Admin (2 of 8, 1 complete) Password: chris (3 of 4 complete)
ACCOUNT CHECK: [telnet] Host: 192.168.1.109 (1 of 1, 0 complete) User: Admin (2 of 8, 1 complete) Password: mno (4 of 4 complete)
ACCOUNT CHECK: [telnet] Host: 192.168.1.109 (1 of 1, 0 complete) User: root (3 of 8, 2 complete) Password: abc (1 of 4 complete)
ACCOUNT CHECK: [telnet] Host: 192.168.1.109 (1 of 1, 0 complete) User: root (3 of 8, 2 complete) Password: efg (2 of 4 complete)
ACCOUNT CHECK: [telnet] Host: 192.168.1.109 (1 of 1, 0 complete) User: root (3 of 8, 2 complete) Password: chris (3 of 4 complete)
ACCOUNT CHECK: [telnet] Host: 192.168.1.109 (1 of 1, 0 complete) User: root (3 of 8, 2 complete) Password: mno (4 of 4 complete)
```

Figure 7.13: Brute force—Telnet

At last, using a different set of combinations, we were able to brute force the server. The traffic generated because of all these attempts made one after another is of special interest to us.

- There is a lot of TCP and TELNET traffic generated in the file, which include traffic patterns such as the three-way handshake and transfer of data between the server and client through Telnet. However, not everything is of interest to us. Refer to the following screenshot:

Time	Source	Destination	Protocol	Length	Info
40 16.336439000	192.168.1.106	192.168.1.109	TCP	66	43702→23 [ACK] Seq=3010083708 Ack=57989536
41 16.336554000	192.168.1.106	192.168.1.109	TCP	66	[TCP Dup ACK 40#1] 43702→23 [ACK] Seq=3010
53 20.908945000	192.168.1.109	192.168.1.106	TELNET	87	Telnet Data ...
54 20.909263000	192.168.1.106	192.168.1.109	TCP	66	43702→23 [ACK] Seq=3010083708 Ack=57989557
55 20.909334000	192.168.1.106	192.168.1.109	TCP	78	[TCP Dup ACK 54#1] 43702→23 [ACK] Seq=3010
56 21.411738000	192.168.1.106	192.168.1.109	TELNET	69	Telnet Data ...
57 21.412049000	192.168.1.109	192.168.1.106	TCP	66	23→43702 [ACK] Seq=57989557 Ack=3010083711
58 21.412169000	192.168.1.109	192.168.1.106	TELNET	104	Telnet Data ...
59 21.412294000	192.168.1.109	192.168.1.106	TELNET	84	Telnet Data ...
60 21.412410000	192.168.1.106	192.168.1.109	TCP	66	43702→23 [ACK] Seq=3010083729 Ack=57989595
61 21.412410000	192.168.1.109	192.168.1.106	TCP	66	23→43702 [ACK] Seq=57989595 Ack=3010083729
62 21.412515000	192.168.1.106	192.168.1.109	TCP	78	[TCP Dup ACK 60#1] 43702→23 [ACK] Seq=3010
63 21.412630000	192.168.1.109	192.168.1.106	TELNET	75	Telnet Data ...
64 21.412757000	192.168.1.106	192.168.1.109	TCP	66	43702→23 [ACK] Seq=3010083729 Ack=57989604
65 21.412805000	192.168.1.106	192.168.1.109	TCP	78	[TCP Dup ACK 64#1] 43702→23 [ACK] Seq=3010
66 21.915442000	192.168.1.106	192.168.1.109	TELNET	73	Telnet Data ...
67 21.915638000	192.168.1.109	192.168.1.106	TCP	66	23→43702 [ACK] Seq=57989604 Ack=3010083736
68 21.916603000	192.168.1.109	192.168.1.106	TELNET	83	Telnet Data ...

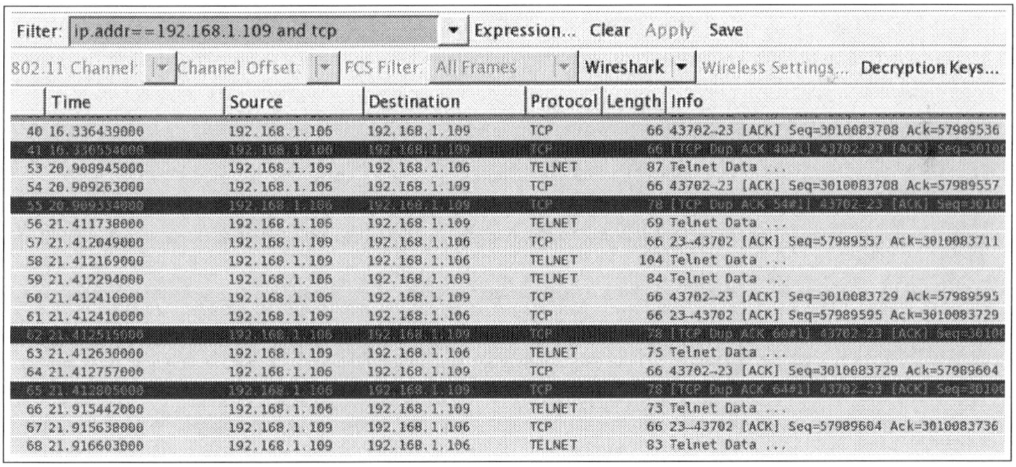

Figure 7.14: Telnet and TCP traffic between the server and our client

- To view only the malicious traffic, I applied another display filter that will show only the various connection attempts between the two hosts. Refer to the following screenshot:

No.	Time	Source	Destination	Protocol	Length	Info
58	21.412169000	192.168.1.109	192.168.1.106	TELNET	104	Telnet Data ...
100	29.029568000	192.168.1.109	192.168.1.106	TELNET	104	Telnet Data ...
150	36.661261000	192.168.1.109	192.168.1.106	TELNET	104	Telnet Data ...
197	44.413837000	192.168.1.109	192.168.1.106	TELNET	104	Telnet Data ...
242	52.032871000	192.168.1.109	192.168.1.106	TELNET	104	Telnet Data ...
295	59.571317000	192.168.1.109	192.168.1.106	TELNET	104	Telnet Data ...
348	67.125144000	192.168.1.109	192.168.1.106	TELNET	104	Telnet Data ...
427	74.695691000	192.168.1.109	192.168.1.106	TELNET	104	Telnet Data ...
517	82.307902000	192.168.1.109	192.168.1.106	TELNET	104	Telnet Data ...
572	89.889223000	192.168.1.109	192.168.1.106	TELNET	104	Telnet Data ...
622	97.457400000	192.168.1.109	192.168.1.106	TELNET	104	Telnet Data ...
683	105.004159000	192.168.1.109	192.168.1.106	TELNET	104	Telnet Data ...
695	112.538637000	192.168.1.109	192.168.1.106	TELNET	104	Telnet Data ...
708	120.257229000	192.168.1.109	192.168.1.106	TELNET	104	Telnet Data ...
720	127.819544000	192.168.1.109	192.168.1.106	TELNET	104	Telnet Data ...

Filter: `telnet.data == "Welcome to Microsoft Telnet` ▼ Expression... Clear Apply Save

```
▷ Frame 58: 104 bytes on wire (832 bits), 104 bytes captured (832 bits) on interface 0
▷ Ethernet II, Src: Apple_b9:53:ec (d8:bb:2c:b9:53:ec), Dst: Vmware_5d:a7:f7 (00:0c:29:5d:a7:f7)
▷ Internet Protocol Version 4, Src: 192.168.1.109 (192.168.1.109), Dst: 192.168.1.106 (192.168.1.106)
▷ Transmission Control Protocol, Src Port: 23 (23), Dst Port: 43702 (43702), Seq: 57989557, Ack: 3010083711, Len: 38
▽ Telnet
    Data: Welcome to Microsoft Telnet Service \r\n
```

- Now, observe the display filter `telnet.data==Welcome to Microsoft Telnet Service` along with the Time column. The string I applied in as the filter is the same as the one we received as a banner while connecting to the service. The banner is printed approximately 15 times in a span of 100 seconds (less than a minute).

- Does this now seem suspicious to you now? If it is, then you can take preventive measures to protect your infrastructure by creating useful signatures for the same traffic pattern that will help you in getting alarmed.

Next, it's time to look at another popular service, FTP, that we discussed in earlier chapters in detail. Let's look at how a brute force attack would look like against the FTP service. FTP is a very crucial service. If attacked by any means, the service will crash or become unusable for the legitimate users. It can cause big trouble to the network admins with serious downtime. To deal with such activity that happens in day-to-day operations, you need to be prepared by being aware of the malicious traffic patterns that you can compare with the baseline traffic pattern we created earlier.

For testing and analysis purpose, I configured one FTP server at 192.168.1.108 over a Windows 7 machine and the attacker is at the same place over IP 192.168.1.106. I used a Kali Linux operating system to duplicate the attack and normal traffic pattern scenario. Follow these steps if you want to duplicate it for educational purpose only:

- Configure the client and the server using whatever platform suits your needs best and make sure the connection between the FTP server and the client works freely without a single glitch.

- Now, first, we will try to visit the server using a legitimate user and will record the traffic. Later, we will use the **Follow TCP stream** option in Wireshark to view the traffic details in easy to understand plain text format.

- Refer to the following screenshot where I initiated the connection between the server and the client using the netcat client available over the Kali platform. I then logged in using the wrong credentials in the first attempt, and then used the correct ones in the second attempt:

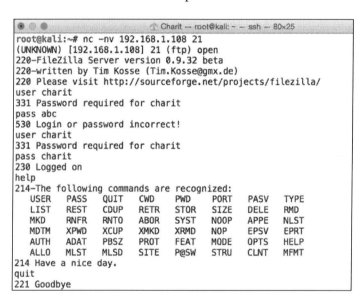

- After I successfully logged in, I issued the help command to view the commands available for execution. Then, I issued the quit command to terminate the connection gracefully. Refer to the preceding screenshot.

- Our sniffer captured the whole conversation. Instead of viewing the traffic in the list pane, we are again seeing the assembled TCP stream. Refer to the following screenshot:

```
Stream Content
220-FileZilla Server version 0.9.32 beta
220-written by Tim Kosse (Tim.Kosse@gmx.de)
220 Please visit http://sourceforge.net/projects/filezilla/
user charit
331 Password required for charit
pass abc
530 Login or password incorrect!
user charit
331 Password required for charit
pass charit
230 Logged on
help
214-The following commands are recognized:
   USER    PASS    QUIT    CWD     PWD     PORT    PASV    TYPE
   LIST    REST    CDUP    RETR    STOR    SIZE    DELE    RMD
   MKD     RNFR    RNTO    ABOR    SYST    NOOP    APPE    NLST
   MDTM    XPWD    XCUP    XMKD    XRMD    NOP     EPSV    EPRT
   AUTH    ADAT    PBSZ    PROT    FEAT    MODE    OPTS    HELP
   ALLO    MLST    MLSD    SITE    P@SW    STRU    CLNT    MFMT
214 Have a nice day.
quit
221 Goodbye
```

Figure 7.15: FTP assembled stream

- Now, as we have seen the normal traffic patterns that you would witness in every day operations, it's time to look at something malicious, such as the brute force attack attempts executed against your FTP servers. I used a different brute force tool that is it also popular among the category THC-hydra.

- Before you issue the command, make sure you have you own custom-made dictionary file that suits you well for your target (refer to the openwall website at http://www.openwall.com/wordlists/ to get the best dictionary files available).

- Once you have the dictionary file and the target up and running, issue the hydra -l <username> -P <password file> ftp://<you target's IP address> command. Refer to the following screenshot:

```
root@kali:~# hydra -l charit -P pass.txt ftp://192.168.1.103
Hydra v7.6 (c)2013 by van Hauser/THC & David Maciejak - for legal purposes only

Hydra (http://www.thc.org/thc-hydra) starting at 2015-09-12 18:16:00
[DATA] 11 tasks, 1 server, 11 login tries (l:1/p:11), ~1 try per task
[DATA] attacking service ftp on port 21
[21][ftp] host: 192.168.1.103   login: charit   password: charit
1 of 1 target successfully completed, 1 valid password found
Hydra (http://www.thc.org/thc-hydra) finished at 2015-09-12 18:16:04
```

- The traffic generated was also captured by our sniffer. Instead of displaying all the traffic, I used a display filter `ftp.request.command==PASS` in order to view only traffic that might be malicious. The following screenshot shows what display filter I used to query malicious repetitive packets.

No.	Time	Source	Destination	Protocol	Length	Info
59	1.169167000	192.168.1.106	192.168.1.103	FTP	76	Request: PASS xyz
60	1.169458000	192.168.1.106	192.168.1.103	FTP	76	Request: PASS 007
61	1.169645000	192.168.1.106	192.168.1.103	FTP	76	Request: PASS mno
62	1.169830000	192.168.1.106	192.168.1.103	FTP	79	Request: PASS charit
63	1.170013000	192.168.1.106	192.168.1.103	FTP	77	Request: PASS root
128	3.500600000	192.168.1.106	192.168.1.103	FTP	76	Request: PASS 123
131	3.501315000	192.168.1.106	192.168.1.103	FTP	76	Request: PASS efg
132	3.501529000	192.168.1.106	192.168.1.103	FTP	76	Request: PASS abc
133	3.502078000	192.168.1.106	192.168.1.103	FTP	78	Request: PASS admin
134	3.502479000	192.168.1.106	192.168.1.103	FTP	78	Request: PASS chris
136	3.503548000	192.168.1.106	192.168.1.103	FTP	76	Request: PASS mno

Filter: ftp.request.command == "PASS"   ▼ Expression... Clear Apply Save

Figure 7.16: FTP Brute Force attack traffic pattern

- It is easily identifiable that the traffic is malicious because, in a span of maximum 85 seconds (calculated using the time column), there were approximately 10 password attempts made. This does look dangerous, and activities of such kind should be monitored closely in order to protect your resources facing the Internet.

There is one more way through which you can point out such traffic patterns. The best advisable option using Wireshark is to create a different coloring scheme using the same display filter expression that we used in order to point out the malicious traffic even faster. Refer to the following screenshot where I did the same and created a different coloring scheme for both TELNET and FTP traffic:

Filter	
List is processed in order until match is found	
Name	**String**
FTP-bruteforce	ftp.request.command == "PASS"
Telnet Brute force	telnet.data == "Welcome to Microsoft Telnet Service \x0d\x0a"

Figure 7.17: Coloring scheme for malicious traffic

There are various other application layer protocols (HTTP, SSH, SMTP, and so on) that fall prey to these brute forcing techniques and might result in heavy losses for corporate infrastructures. In order to make these services secure, you can force encryption over the service that you are configuring and use strong password policies, such as an alphanumeric password with minimum length. You can also enforce a password change policy at a regular intervals, such as 30 days or something. Last but not least, you can make the employees aware of such activities. Any form of social engineering attacks executed against an employee can leverage the attacker to gain access to the infrastructure more easily.

Inspecting malicious traffic

In some previously mentioned topics, we have witnessed a few scenarios that generated malicious traffic. Some of the common protocols, such as HTTP, DNS, ARP, IRC, that are seen in the list pane can carry malicious traffic. So, knowing about the malware traffic analysis is definitely an important skill every network and security professional should be well versed with. In today's digital world, various advance have been made. Yet, threats including malware infection persist. Every organization should consider threats of such nature to be critical. For illustrating the threats that are caused due to various malicious traffic, I have configured a few things in my virtual lab. The traffic generated because of the activities between the client and the server would be captured in parallel, which we will use to analyze later. Refer to the following screenshot:

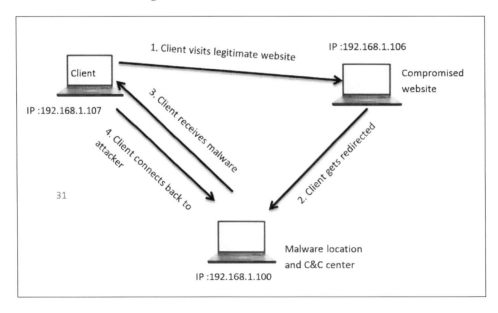

Malwares are supposed to perform a couple of tasks once installed on the victim's machine, such as passing on the secret content to the person in command, receiving commands from the server, and infecting and corrupting systems. Even if you have the best security solutions installed in your infrastructure, you are still open to wide attack vectors, including malware infections.

Now, we have understood the basics of how malicious traffic is being generated, and we also have a clear image of the infrastructure that we will work with. So, without wasting even a second more, let's go ahead and start the process. Follow these steps if you want to replicate the scenario in your own virtual lab:

- You require three machines connected to the same LAN. Make sure they are able to talk to each other, that is, verify the connectivity.

- On the IP address 192.168.1.106 stays a legitimate website, which the client is habituated to visit. However, this time, the client is not aware of the infection that causes redirection to another webserver. Refer to the following screenshot of the legitimate server:

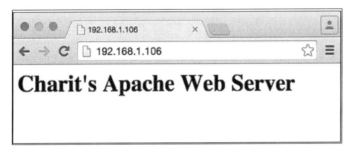

Figure 7.18: Legitimate website

- To simulate the redirection, I have configured my Apache server running on 106 to redirect every request coming to IP 192.168.1.100 and download the efg.exe malware from there.

- So, next time the client visits the website running at `192.168.1.106`, it gets redirected to a new webserver address, which directly asks the client to run a file named `efg.exe`. Refer to the following screenshot:

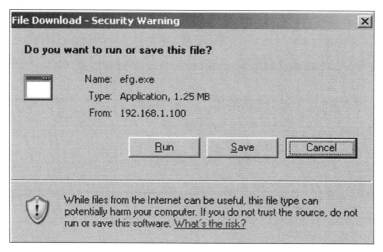

Figure 7.19: Client gets redirected to IP 192.168.1.100 and is asked to run the application.

- If the client clicks on **Run** they might not be aware of the dangerous effects the malware can pose to the client's machine and the network client is a part of. The publisher of the application is not verified, so the browser is not able to verify it. This results in giving an unknown publisher error. If the client still proceeds and clicks on **Run**, the malware will be installed. Refer to the following screenshot:

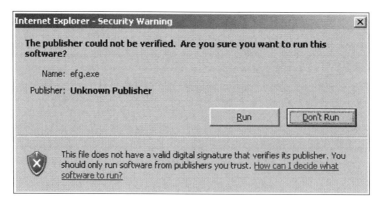

Figure 7.20: Unknown publisher error

- Now, let's suppose that, if the client hits run, then the malware will be downloaded to the client's machine. It will be executed later on, thus creating a connection back to the command and control center.

- If the connection back to the attacker was successful, then without the knowledge of the client, the attacker can copy files, delete files, take screenshots, take webcam snaps, record voice through the mic, corrupt system files, and so on. You might have heard of various malwares such as ransom wares, spywares, and adwares.

- The whole traffic generated because of all these activities is being captured. Let's take a look at it. Instead of showing you the traffic, I assembled the TCP stream first between the client and the legitimate server.

- To understand the way our malware works, we need to look at more details, which can be presented to us by Wireshark. Refer to the following screenshot that shows the assembled TCP stream:

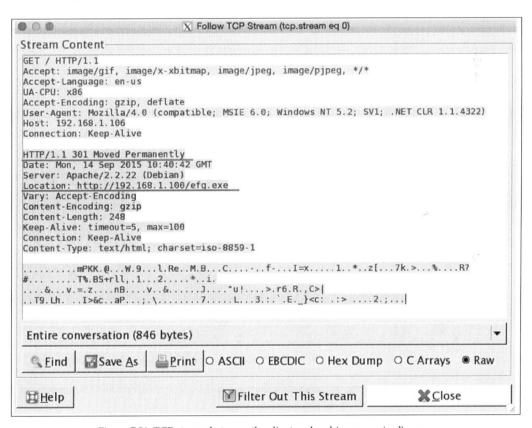

Figure 7.21: TCP stream between the client and real (compromised) server

As you can clearly see, the client is trying to visit the webserver, and the request is being forwarded with HTTP redirection to the new address `192.168.1.100`, trying to download the malicious file.

- Once the client gets a redirection response, the client again initiates a three-way handshake with the new server and tries to download the file. After a couple of packets were exchanged between the hosts in the later frames, the clients received a `200 OK` status message, suggesting successful download of the malware.

1255 36.428063(192.168.1.100   192.168.1.107   HTTP   1458 HTTP/1.1 200 OK (application/x-msdownload)

In the following screenshot, you can see that the malware signature can be easily recognized by any `IDS`/`IPS` in place:

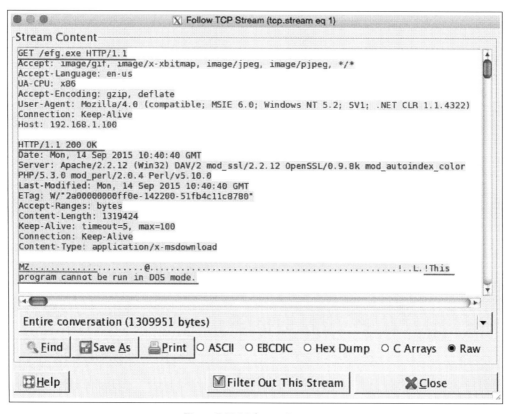

Figure 7.22: Malware signature

The GET request was initiated by the client in search of efg.exe, to which the server responded with a 200 OK status message. Later, you can see the known malware signature starting with the characters MZ followed by some random character. A quick Google search regarding the same will reveal its behavior and pattern. Our search also reveals that it is an executable file, as Wikipedia states 16/32 bit DOS executable files can be identified by the letters MZ at the beginning of the file in ASCII. Refer to the following screenshot:

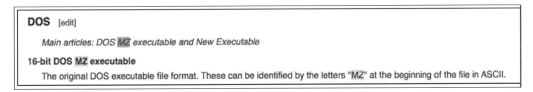

Until this point, its clear that the is a Windows executable file is clear which might be malicious.

Moving on with our investigation regarding the malicious file, I would like to export the efg.exe file using Wireshark.

1. Go to **File | Export Objects | HTTP**. You will see a dialog similar to the one shown here:

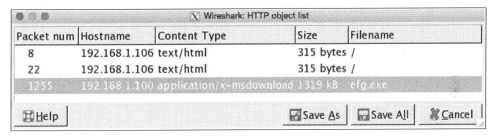

Figure 7.23: Exporting HTTP objects

2. Now, to export the file, you need to select the conversation that states the name of the file along with it. Then click on **Save As** and save the file at a location of your choice.

3. The best option would be to upload this file to websites such as `http://www.virustotal.com`, which will cross examine the PE-executable file with numerous antivirus software online and will show you a detailed analytical report. Refer to the following screenshot:

Figure 7.24: Uploading `efg.exe` to virustotal.com

4. Now, click on **Scan it!** to let the website examine the file and wait for the results:

Figure 7.25: `efg.exe` examination completed

31 out of 56 antivirus software detected the executable file as malicious, which is quite alarming.

5. Further, I manually examine the conversation between the infected machine and the command and control center by looking at the hex dump in the following TCP stream window. I observe something. Refer to the following screenshot:

```
Stream Content
000A1978  46 69 6c 65 54 69 6d 65   54 6f 4c 6f 63 61 6c 46   FileTime ToLocalF
000A1988  69 6c 65 54 69 6d 65 00   ec 01 47 65 74 46 69 6c   ileTime. ..GetFil
000A1998  65 49 6e 66 6f 72 6d 61   74 69 6f 6e 42 79 48 61   eInforma tionByHa
000A19A8  6e 64 6c 65 00 00 8d 03   50 65 65 6b 4e 61 6d 65   ndle.... PeekName
000A19B8  64 50 69 70 65 00 fb 01   47 65 74 46 75 6c 6c 50   dPipe... GetFullP
000A19C8  61 74 68 4e 61 6d 65 57   00 00 bf 01 47 65 74 43   athNameW ....GetC
000A19D8  75 72 72 65 6e 74 44 69   72 65 63 74 6f 72 79 57   urrentDi rectoryW
000A19E8  00 00 d4 02 48 65 61 70   53 69 7a 65 00 00 53 04   ....Heap Size..S.
000A19F8  53 65 74 45 6e 64 4f 66   46 69 6c 65 00 00 73 01   SetEndOf File..s.
000A1A08  49 6d 70 65 72 73 6f 6e   61 74 65 4c 6f 67 67 65   Imperson ateLogge
000A1A18  64 4f 6e 55 73 65 72 00   1f 00 41 64 6a 75 73 74   dOnUser. ..Adjust
000A1A28  54 6f 6b 65 6e 50 72 69   76 69 6c 65 67 65 73 00   TokenPri vileges.
000A1A38  96 01 4c 6f 6f 6b 75 70   50 72 69 76 69 6c 65 67   ..Lookup Privileg
000A1A48  65 56 61 6c 75 65 41 00   00 00 00 00 00 00 00 00   eValueA. ........
000A1A58  00 00 00 00 00 00 00 00   00 00 00 00 00 00 00 00   ........ ........
```

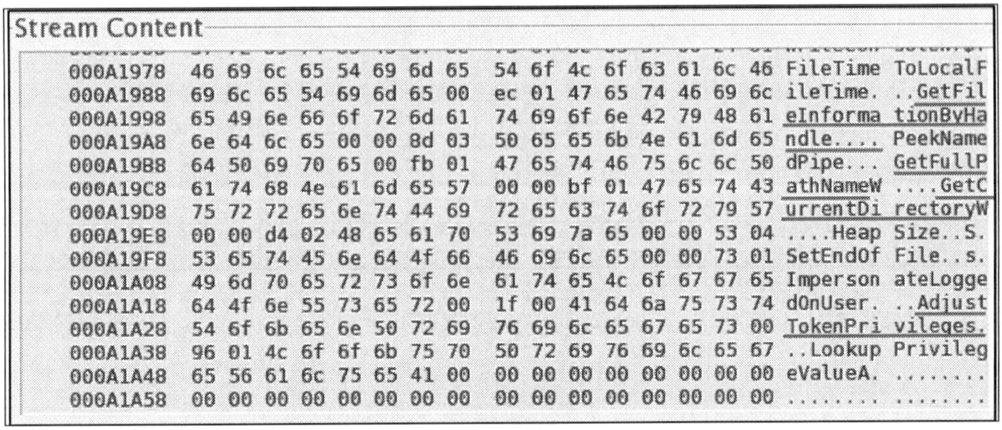

Figure 7.26: Hexdump in TCP stream dialog

It seems that the server machine that has taken the control of the victim issues some command to gather quick information regarding the machine. The highlighted content on the right-hand side of the window states strings such as Get File Information, Get full PC name, Get Current directory, Adjust token Privileges, and so on.

As per my analysis, the file that got installed to the windows box is definitely malicious. It might have caused some serious damage to the individual machine as well as the network. The best advisable solution is to isolate the machine from the network, unless it is being disinfected using specialized tools.

To conclude this section, I have one more thing to depict using the list pane in Wireshark. Refer to the following screenshot:

```
 1 0.000000(Apple_b9:53:ec     Broadcast          ARP    42 Who has 192.168.1.106? Tell 192.168.1.107
 2 0.000237(Apple_b9:53:ec     Vmware_b3:cb:b6    ARP    42 192.168.1.106 is at d8:bb:2c:b9:53:ec (dupl
 3 0.000410(192.168.1.107      192.168.1.106      TCP    62 1339-80 [SYN] Seq=2857922741 Win=64240 Len=
 4 0.000512(192.168.1.106      192.168.1.107      TCP    62 80-1339 [SYN, ACK] Seq=2114108500 Ack=28579
 5 0.000660(192.168.1.107      192.168.1.106      TCP    54 1339-80 [ACK] Seq=2857922742 Ack=2114108501
 6 0.001145(192.168.1.107      192.168.1.106      HTTP  340 GET / HTTP/1.1
 7 0.001346(192.168.1.106      192.168.1.107      TCP    54 80-1339 [ACK] Seq=2114108501 Ack=2857923028
 8 0.002089(192.168.1.106      192.168.1.107      HTTP  614 HTTP/1.1 301 Moved Permanently (text/html)
 9 0.003459(192.168.1.107      192.168.1.100      TCP    62 1340-80 [SYN] Seq=3060050075 Win=64240 Len=
10 0.140452(LiteonTe_fa:5e:b4  Broadcast          ARP    42 Who has 192.168.1.107? Tell 192.168.1.100
11 0.140998(Apple_b9:53:ec     LiteonTe_fa:5e:b4  ARP    42 192.168.1.107 is at d8:bb:2c:b9:53:ec
12 0.162001(192.168.1.100      192.168.1.107      TCP    62 80-1340 [SYN, ACK] Seq=2258050522 Ack=30600
13 0.162267(192.168.1.107      192.168.1.100      TCP    54 1340-80 [ACK] Seq=3060050076 Ack=2258050523
14 0.162779(192.168.1.107      192.168.1.100      HTTP  347 GET /efg.exe HTTP/1.1
```

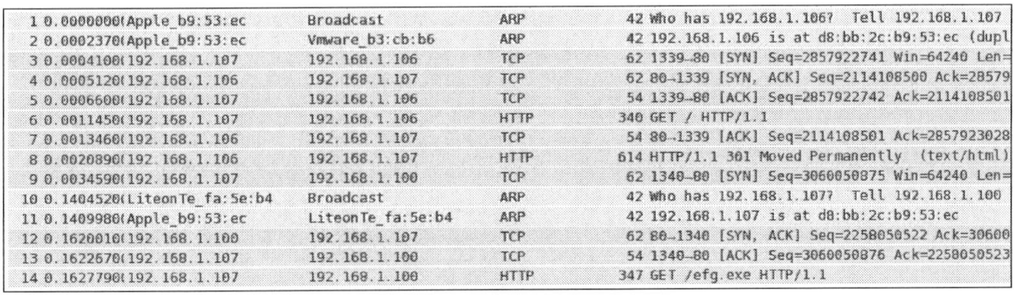

Figure 7.27: Unusual behavior noticed in list pane

Observe the behavior of the packets from the beginning, as it started with the ARP request sent by the Windows machine because it was trying to look for a legitimate web server locally configured. Followed by the three-way handshake, the client initiates a GET request in frame 6, which the server acknowledged in the following packet. Then, the server states that the resource the client is looking for has been moved to another location, and the client is required to go there. After this, the client generates an SYN request in frame 9. Then, the command and control center generates the ARP packets asking for the client's physical address in order to get in touch with it and to transfer the file. Then, at last, in frames 12 and 13, the three-way handshake is completed, which ends in generating a GET request from the victim's machine in order to start the transfer of the exploit as seen in frame 13. The consequences of such traffic patterns can be highly devastating. A good network/security admin should be aware of such traffic patterns and can use such traffic behavior to create firewall/IDS-IPS signatures that can generate quick alerts. They can help in avoiding and making their infrastructures ready to fight with these malicious traffic.

Solving real-world CTF challenges

Capturing the flag events is the most common thing that happens in security conferences. The objective is to learn and play with the challenges based on real-world scenarios that can assist you quite well in learning the methodology. Popular conferences such as DEF Con, PlaidCTF, CSAW, and Codegate can be searched for if you are interested in cracking flags. Basic programming, networking, forensics, and common sense are the skills required to take part in these challenges.

I have made a couple of challenges for you and we will be solving them as well in a step-by-step approach. I have made all of them pretty simple in order to give you an idea of how the CTF thing works and definitely the approach you are supposed to follow. So, let's begin and capture some flags.

First CTF: Leverage the weakness in remote administration services

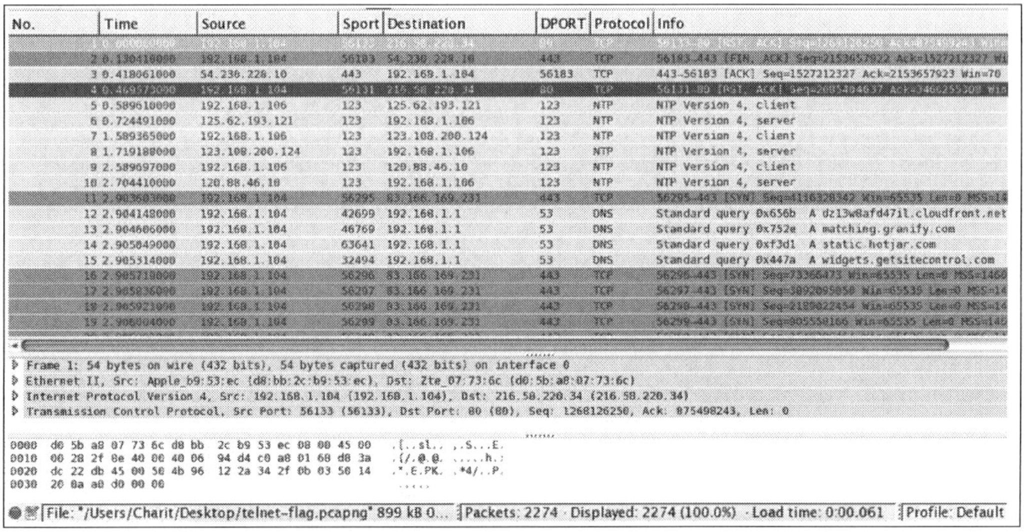

Figure 7.28: CTF1 trace file

- **Solution**: We have a `telnet-flag.pcap` file that lists multiple packets in the list pane. The question is asking us to take advantage of remote administration services. How many services do we know which are used for remote administration RDP, Telnet, and SSH? To better understand the scenario, let's open our trace file in Wireshark first. Refer to the following screenshot:

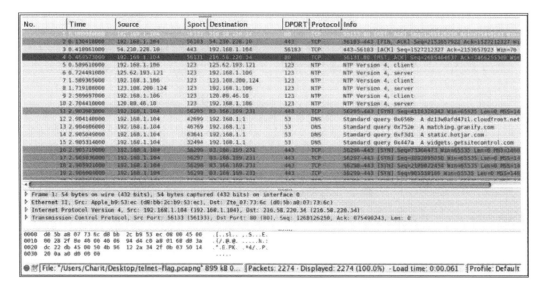

As you can see, there are more than two thousand packets in our trace file. It would be practically impossible to scroll to the bottom to see each packet. The best option would be to look into the protocol hierarchy window, which will give us a brief regarding all protocols involved in the whole trace file. From here, it would be easy for us to identify the remote administration services. The protocol hierarchy window can be accessed from the Statistics menu. Refer to the following screenshot:

Protocol	% Packets	Packets	% Bytes	Bytes	Mbit/s
▽ Frame	100.00 %	2274	100.00 %	823058	0.146
▽ Ethernet	100.00 %	2274	100.00 %	823058	0.146
▽ Internet Protocol Version 4	99.65 %	2266	99.96 %	822722	0.146
▽ Transmission Control Protocol	95.73 %	2177	97.16 %	799706	0.142
▽ Secure Sockets Layer	27.92 %	635	42.44 %	349318	0.062
Secure Sockets Layer	0.48 %	11	0.87 %	7149	0.001
Malformed Packet	1.10 %	25	0.17 %	1375	0.000
File Transfer Protocol (FTP)	0.44 %	10	0.09 %	756	0.000
Telnet	3.43 %	78	0.73 %	6000	0.001
Hypertext Transfer Protocol	0.09 %	2	0.20 %	1636	0.000
▽ User Datagram Protocol	3.78 %	86	2.75 %	22656	0.004
Network Time Protocol	0.26 %	6	0.07 %	540	0.000
Domain Name Service	2.95 %	67	2.43 %	19972	0.004
NetBIOS Name Service	0.31 %	7	0.09 %	716	0.000
▽ NetBIOS Datagram Service	0.26 %	6	0.17 %	1428	0.000
▽ SMB (Server Message Block Protocol)	0.26 %	6	0.17 %	1428	0.000
▽ SMB MailSlot Protocol	0.26 %	6	0.17 %	1428	0.000
Microsoft Windows Browser Protocol	0.26 %	6	0.17 %	1428	0.000
Internet Control Message Protocol	0.13 %	3	0.04 %	360	0.000
Address Resolution Protocol	0.31 %	7	0.04 %	294	0.000
▽ Text item	0.04 %	1	0.01 %	42	0.000
Address Resolution Protocol	0.04 %	1	0.01 %	42	0.000

Figure 7.29: Protocol hierarchy CTF1

Among all the protocols listed, I can see only one that is used for remote administration, and we can use it to move on with our CTF process. So, I applied the display filter `telnet` in order to see only relevant traffic. Refer to the following screenshot:

| Filter: | telnet | | | | ▼ Expression... Clear Apply Save | | | |

No.	Time	Source	Sport	Destination	DPORT	Protocol	Info
391	6.797840000	192.168.1.106	45932	192.168.1.108	23	TELNET	Telnet Data ...
404	6.895186000	192.168.1.108	23	192.168.1.106	45932	TELNET	Telnet Data ...
407	6.964431000	192.168.1.106	45932	192.168.1.108	23	TELNET	Telnet Data ...
409	7.066463000	192.168.1.108	23	192.168.1.106	45932	TELNET	Telnet Data ...
419	7.108133000	192.168.1.106	45932	192.168.1.108	23	TELNET	Telnet Data ...
421	7.207867000	192.168.1.108	23	192.168.1.106	45932	TELNET	Telnet Data ...
423	7.268273000	192.168.1.106	45932	192.168.1.108	23	TELNET	Telnet Data ...
424	7.364004000	192.168.1.108	23	192.168.1.106	45932	TELNET	Telnet Data ...
428	7.500046000	192.168.1.106	45932	192.168.1.108	23	TELNET	Telnet Data ...
457	11.207799000	192.168.1.106	45933	192.168.1.108	23	TELNET	Telnet Data ...
494	15.754880000	192.168.1.108	23	192.168.1.106	45933	TELNET	Telnet Data ...
496	15.755366000	192.168.1.108	23	192.168.1.106	45933	TELNET	Telnet Data ...
498	15.755873000	192.168.1.106	45933	192.168.1.108	23	TELNET	Telnet Data ...
499	15.756022000	192.168.1.108	23	192.168.1.106	45933	TELNET	Telnet Data ...
501	16.564974000	192.168.1.106	45933	192.168.1.108	23	TELNET	Telnet Data ...
502	16.565218000	192.168.1.108	23	192.168.1.106	45933	TELNET	Telnet Data ...

Figure 7.30: Telnet traffic CTF1

Now, the next step would be to follow the TCP stream of these packets, which will reveal more information regarding the Telnet session.

This is what the question was about: leveraging the weakness in a remote administration service. Telnet sessions can be viewed in plain text format, and we finally leveraged the weakness to take advantage of viewing the session's information in plain text format. The flag is the password used by the user to log in to the Windows machine to perform maintenance activities.

FLAG : Sup3rs3cr3t

The following screenshot illustrates how the TCP stream windows will look after the packets are assembled. Also, the Telnet session's password can be seen clearly.

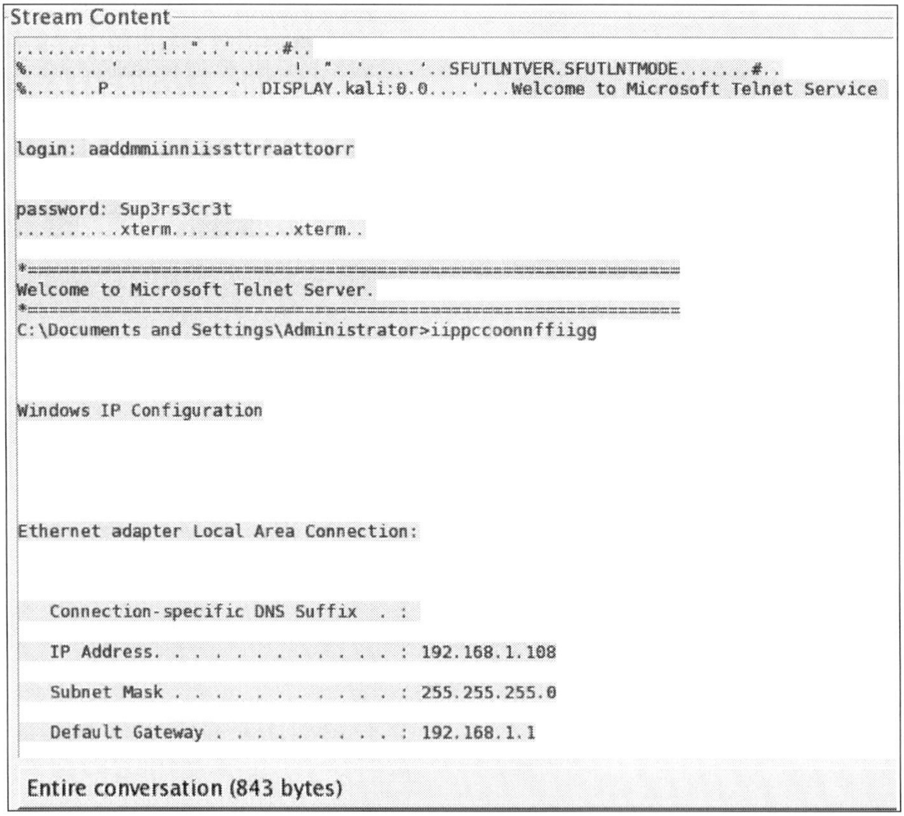

```
Stream Content
.......... ..!..".. '.....#..
%.......',............. ..!.."..'.....'..SFUTLNTVER.SFUTLNTMODE.......#..
%.......P............'..DISPLAY.kali:0.0....'...Welcome to Microsoft Telnet Service


login: aaddmmiinniissttrraattoorr


password: Sup3rs3cr3t
..........xterm...........xterm..

*=========================================================================
Welcome to Microsoft Telnet Server.
*=========================================================================
C:\Documents and Settings\Administrator>iippccoonnffiigg


Windows IP Configuration



Ethernet adapter Local Area Connection:


   Connection-specific DNS Suffix  . :

   IP Address. . . . . . . . . . . . : 192.168.1.108

   Subnet Mask . . . . . . . . . . . : 255.255.255.0

   Default Gateway . . . . . . . . . : 192.168.1.1

Entire conversation (843 bytes)
```

Figure 7.31: TCP stream dialog CTF1

I hope you have understood the basic approach of CTF solving. We would follow similar approach in solving further CTF challenges.

This time I have designed a CTF that utilizes another common protocol and will let you learn the basics of the CTF challenge approach.

Second CTF: Image magic

Solution is in the title of this CTF and it is pretty small and attractive, though we have no idea what we are looking for, but for sure there is something related to images. Wireshark performs magic every time; this is what my perspective tells me about the challenge.

Following an approach similar to the one we talked about first, we would open the trace file in order to learn basic stats related to the traffic capture that will give us an overview of the protocols used during the session. Refer to the following screenshot:

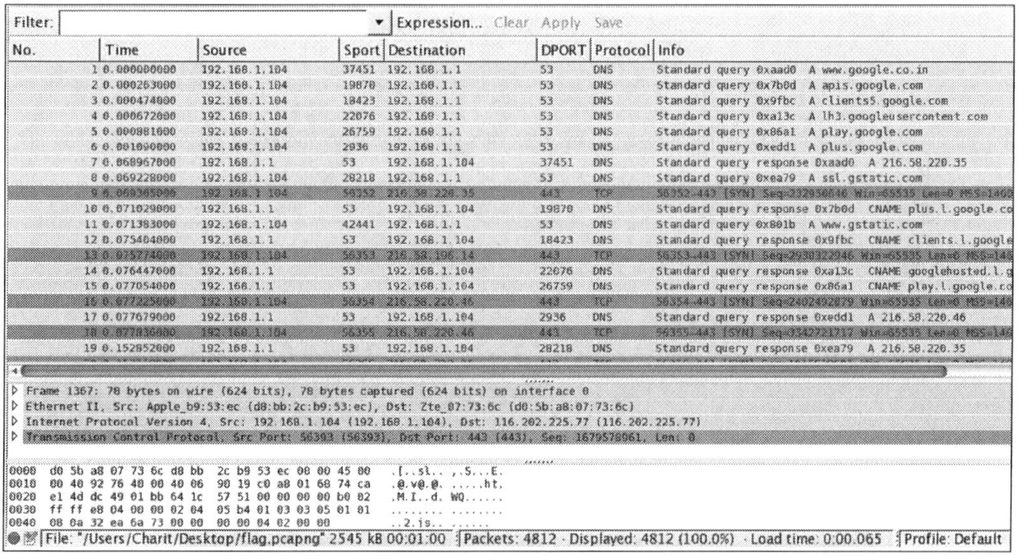

Figure 7.32: Trace file CTF2

The trace file starts with a lot of DNS packets, which don't look very useful for our analysis. Looking at the following status bar in Wireshark, we can say that there are around 4,800 frames definitely captured. This one is not something that we can inspect element by element, so we need the help of our best guy: protocol hierarchy dialog (now I hope, without any specific instruction, that you can open the dialog):

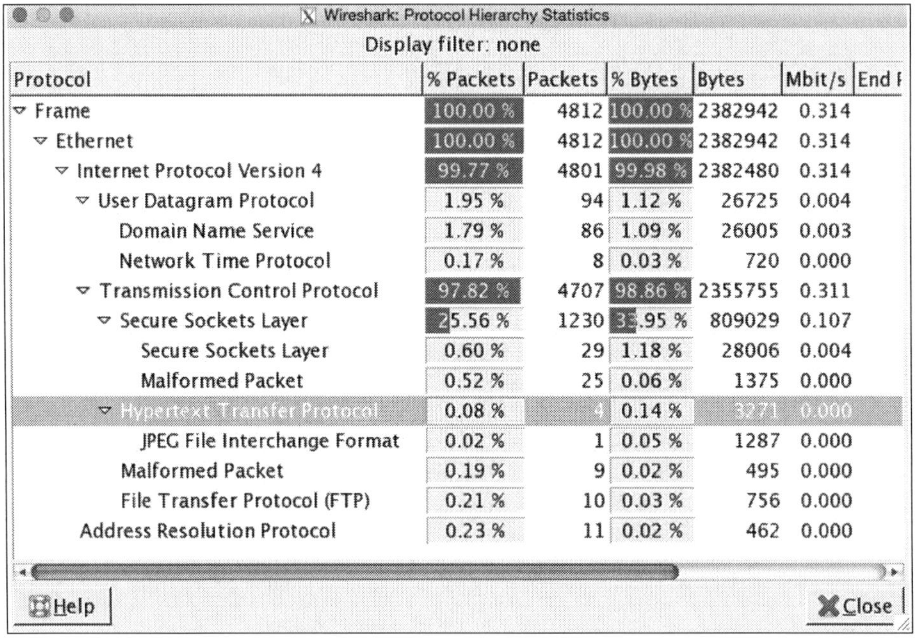

Protocol	% Packets	Packets	% Bytes	Bytes	Mbit/s	End F
▽ Frame	100.00 %	4812	100.00 %	2382942	0.314	
▽ Ethernet	100.00 %	4812	100.00 %	2382942	0.314	
▽ Internet Protocol Version 4	99.77 %	4801	99.98 %	2382480	0.314	
▽ User Datagram Protocol	1.95 %	94	1.12 %	26725	0.004	
Domain Name Service	1.79 %	86	1.09 %	26005	0.003	
Network Time Protocol	0.17 %	8	0.03 %	720	0.000	
▽ Transmission Control Protocol	97.82 %	4707	98.86 %	2355755	0.311	
▽ Secure Sockets Layer	25.56 %	1230	35.95 %	809029	0.107	
Secure Sockets Layer	0.60 %	29	1.18 %	28006	0.004	
Malformed Packet	0.52 %	25	0.06 %	1375	0.000	
▽ Hypertext Transfer Protocol	0.08 %	4	0.14 %	3271	0.000	
JPEG File Interchange Format	0.02 %	1	0.05 %	1287	0.000	
Malformed Packet	0.19 %	9	0.02 %	495	0.000	
File Transfer Protocol (FTP)	0.21 %	10	0.03 %	756	0.000	
Address Resolution Protocol	0.23 %	11	0.02 %	462	0.000	

Figure 7.33: Protocol hierarchy CTF2

In the list of various protocols, I spotted JPEG, which is an image extension, and is listed under the HTTP section in the dialog. We can conclude from this that there is some relation between these two ,so our display filter could become HTTP, which will keep us moving in the right direction.

As soon as I type HTTP in the display filter box and press enter, I am presented with just four packets. One of those listed is a `.jpg` file with the name flag. Refer to the following screenshot:

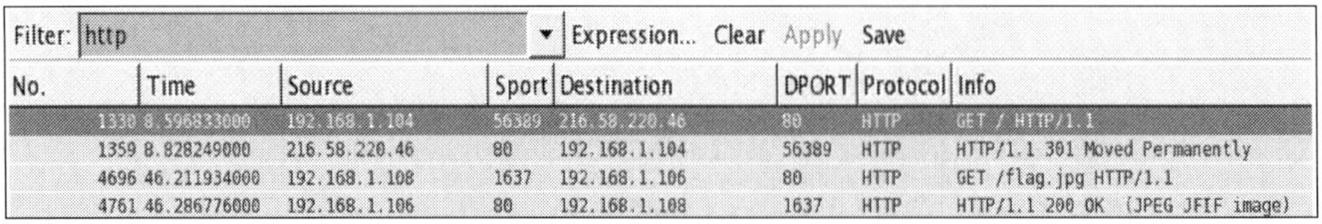

No.	Time	Source	Sport	Destination	DPORT	Protocol	Info
1330	8.596833000	192.168.1.104	56389	216.58.220.46	80	HTTP	GET / HTTP/1.1
1359	8.828249000	216.58.220.46	80	192.168.1.104	56389	HTTP	HTTP/1.1 301 Moved Permanently
4696	46.211934000	192.168.1.108	1637	192.168.1.106	80	HTTP	GET /flag.jpg HTTP/1.1
4761	46.286776000	192.168.1.106	80	192.168.1.108	1637	HTTP	HTTP/1.1 200 OK (JPEG JFIF image)

Figure 7.34: Display filter HTTP—CTF2

Frame number 4,696 lists a GET request for a `alg.jpg` file. Investigating, further by looking at the TCP stream of this packet, confirms that there was a `.jpg` file requested by the client at `192.168.1.108`. Refer to the following screenshot:

```
Stream Content
GET /flag.jpg HTTP/1.1
Accept: image/gif, image/x-xbitmap, image/jpeg, image/pjpeg, */*
Accept-Language: en-us
UA-CPU: x86
Accept-Encoding: gzip, deflate
User-Agent: Mozilla/4.0 (compatible; MSIE 6.0; Windows NT 5.2; SV1; .NET CLR 1.1.432:
Host: 192.168.1.106
Connection: Keep-Alive

HTTP/1.1 200 OK
Date: Thu, 17 Sep 2015 09:05:24 GMT
Server: Apache/2.2.22 (Debian)
Last-Modified: Thu, 17 Sep 2015 08:10:02 GMT
ETag: "154002-12ef5-51fecf132d262"
Accept-Ranges: bytes
Content-Length: 77557
Keep-Alive: timeout=5, max=100
Connection: Keep-Alive
Content-Type: image/jpeg

......JFIF.....`.`.....
C................................................................
C.........................................................9....
"............................................

Entire conversation (78148 bytes)
```

Figure 7.35: TCP stream—CTF2

The request made by the client is now confirmed and verified. The next step would be to export this object from the stream. Go to **File** | **Export Objets** | **HTTP**.

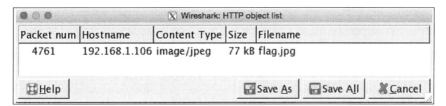

Packet num	Hostname	Content Type	Size	Filename
4761	192.168.1.106	image/jpeg	77 kB	flag.jpg

Help · Save As · Save All · Cancel

The window just lists one `flag.jpg` file. Follow the mentioned steps in order to export the image object. First select the row one showing the images object then click on **save as** and save the file at any desired location. When finished, open the file to view the flag content. Refer to the following screenshot to see the content of the exported object.

Figure 7.36: CTF2

This challenge was pretty interesting, because you learned about a different idea behind CTF challenges.

Our final challenge also introduces us to a new idea behind CTF's.

Third CTF: Are you Pro Enough!!

Title of the challenge is pretty challenging in itself. However, we will solve this together. So, let's open the trace file first.

At first glance, it looks like other trace files we have seen with numerous useless packets filled in. Without getting ourselves confused with the overwhelming amount of information there, let's follow the approach that we have been following so far. Refer to the following screenshot:

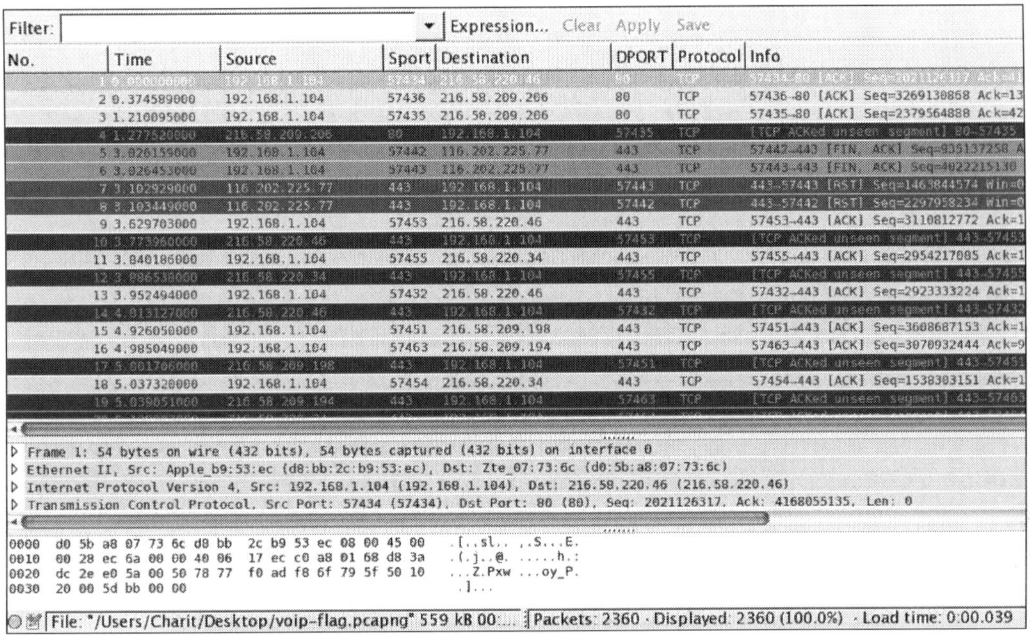
Filter:
Expression... Clear Apply Save
No. Time Source Sport Destination DPORT Protocol Info
Frame 1: 54 bytes on wire (432 bits), 54 bytes captured (432 bits) on interface 0
Ethernet II, Src: Apple_b9:53:ec (d8:bb:2c:b9:53:ec), Dst: Zte_07:73:6c (d0:5b:a8:07:73:6c)
Internet Protocol Version 4, Src: 192.168.1.104 (192.168.1.104), Dst: 216.58.220.46 (216.58.220.46)
Transmission Control Protocol, Src Port: 57434 (57434), Dst Port: 80 (80), Seq: 2021126317, Ack: 4168055135, Len: 0
File: "/Users/Charit/Desktop/voip-flag.pcapng" 559 kB 00:...
Packets: 2360 · Displayed: 2360 (100.0%) · Load time: 0:00.039

Figure 7.37: Packet list pane—CTF3

Look at the protocol hierarchy window that can help us in revealing more about the CTF challenge we are dealing with. Refer to the following screenshot:

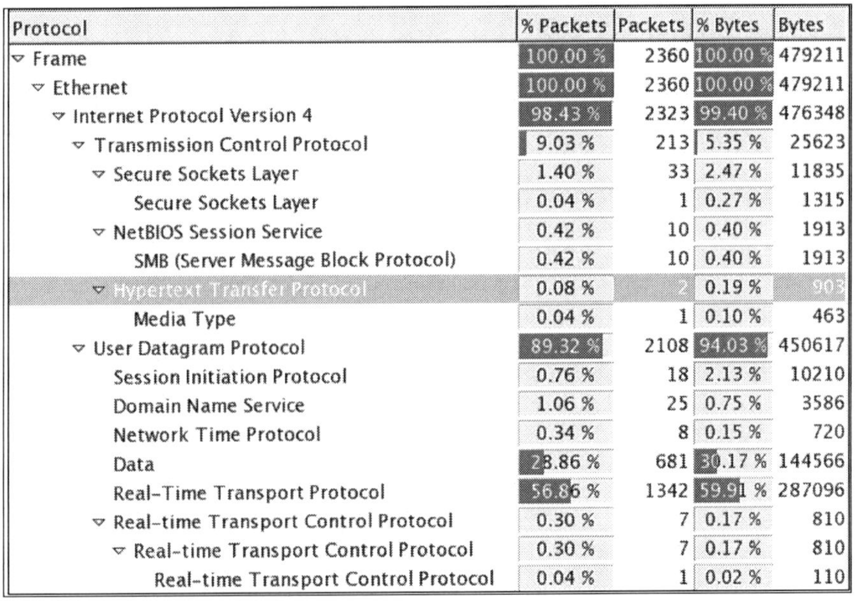
Protocol | % Packets | Packets | % Bytes | Bytes
Frame 100.00 % 2360 100.00 % 479211
Ethernet 100.00 % 2360 100.00 % 479211
Internet Protocol Version 4 98.43 % 2323 99.40 % 476348
Transmission Control Protocol 9.03 % 213 5.35 % 25623
Secure Sockets Layer 1.40 % 33 2.47 % 11835
Secure Sockets Layer 0.04 % 1 0.27 % 1315
NetBIOS Session Service 0.42 % 10 0.40 % 1913
SMB (Server Message Block Protocol) 0.42 % 10 0.40 % 1913
Hypertext Transfer Protocol 0.08 % 2 0.19 % 903
Media Type 0.04 % 1 0.10 % 463
User Datagram Protocol 89.32 % 2108 94.03 % 450617
Session Initiation Protocol 0.76 % 18 2.13 % 10210
Domain Name Service 1.06 % 25 0.75 % 3586
Network Time Protocol 0.34 % 8 0.15 % 720
Data 28.86 % 681 30.17 % 144566
Real-Time Transport Protocol 56.86 % 1342 59.91 % 287096
Real-time Transport Control Protocol 0.30 % 7 0.17 % 810
Real-time Transport Control Protocol 0.30 % 7 0.17 % 810
Real-time Transport Control Protocol 0.04 % 1 0.02 % 110

Figure 7.38: Protocol hierarchy—CTF3

As expected, we get a new insight about the trace file, and we can observe that the UDP traffic percentage is about 89 percent, which is quite a big number. It lists Real Time Protocol under it. So, let's go ahead and create a display filter for RTP traffic, which can take us to the next step in solving the riddle. Refer to the following screenshot:

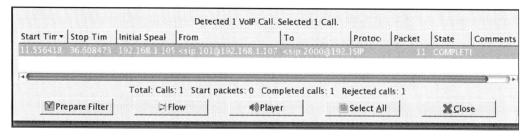

Figure 7.39: RTP display filter—CTF3

It seems like a call session is in progress between the two hosts at `192.168.1.107` and `192.168.1.105`. Next, using the playback feature in Wireshark, I will reassemble the stream and will try to play back. Go to **Telephony menu** | **VoIP Calls** and select the SIP call in row 1 and click on **Player**. Refer to the following screenshot:

Figure 7.40: VoIP calls dialog—CTF3

Once the call session is visible, select it and click on the player where you will be asked to give the jitter value. Specify `200` as the value and click on **Decode**:

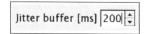

Now, you should be able to see the assembled VoIP stream available for playback. Select the first part of the communication and click on Play. The person communicating from Side A side says, *Start the transfer of the rabbit* and playing Side B's part we can observe that it is just an echo of Side's A message. Refer to the following screenshot:

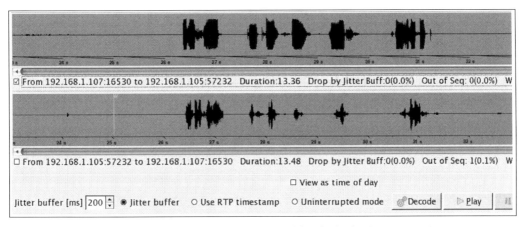

Figure 7.41: Reassembled VoIP call for playback—CTF3

We did not get many clues from this message. Let's look at the protocol hierarchy dialog once again and see what we have in the TCP section. Other than the HTTP protocol, there isn't much useful information. Under the HTTP tree, there is a media type, which means something got transferred between the hosts on the network (as the person on VOIP call said `start the transfer`). We applied HTTP as a display filter, we got the following screenshot:

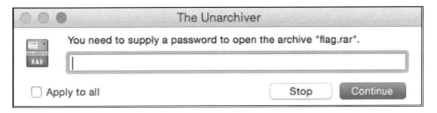

As is clearly visible, a `flag.rar` file got transferred. Let's export this to a `.rar` file for extraction. Go to **File** | **Export Objects** | **HTTP**, select the first row, and click on **Save as** to save the `.rar` file. The file got successfully saved, but when we tried opening the file, it asked for a password, which we don't know have:

Figure 7.42: `Flag.rar` ask password

Did you notice what the person said over the call "start the transfer of the rabbit", so why don't we check `therabbit` as password to this archive file.

Luckily, our first guess worked. This might not happen every time we solve CTF challenges. There is a file inside it called `flag.txt` that reads **You Gotcha!!** Refer to the following screenshot:

This section was particularly real fun! I enjoyed solving it for you. I hope the approach and flow we followed would prove useful for other CTFs that you might start solving after reading this chapter. Best of luck to you for your independent analysis, and remember that using out-of-the-box thinking and a bit of common sense is also required.

Summary

Use Wireshark to keep your network secure by defending against the most common form of infiltration attempts. Analyzing the packets with security perspective will give you a new insight into how to deal with malicious users.

Activities such as port scanning, footprinting, and various active information-gathering attempts are the basis of attacking methodologies that can be taken advantage of to bypass your security infrastructure.

Guessing passwords for a legitimate service is called a brute force attack. If the same form of attack is combined with dictionaries, which consist of millions of passwords, the chances to break in get higher. Through Wireshark, you can view such attempts made against a service in your network.

Using a legitimate looking piece of software, a malicious user can gain entry into your network. These days, the most common form through which malwares are being distributed is emails. Another attack form, such as phishing, when combined with malwares, becomes seriously dangerous.

Wireshark can help you in analyzing malware behaviors, and using the behavior analyzed, you would be able to create the necessary signatures for your IDS/IPS firewalls in place.

Capture the flag events are commonly conducted at security conferences. Multiple educational exercises are provided to the participants to experience real-world scenarios. The real CTF is where a TEAM A tries to penetrate into TEAM B's network and vice versa at the same time. Both the teams are responsible for securing against the malicious attacks sent in. There are multiple categories in CTF events, such as reverse engineering, protocol analysis, programming, cryptanalysis, and so on. Mastering Wireshark can ease your way while dealing with protocol analysis related CTFs.

Observing things scattered around with a security professional's perspective will let you see things differently. From a person inside the corporate infrastructure, things might feel OK. However, from outside, you might be very vulnerable. Security professionals are like immunity to the IT industry, and analyzing the packets using Wireshark is one of their weapons in the arsenal.

Practice questions

Q.1 What is the difference between the active and passive information gathering techniques?

Q.2 Which information-gathering technique is stealthier and why?

Q.3 What do you understand by the term banner grabbing?

Q.4 Use the netcat utility in Linux to connect to a running HTTP service.

Q.5 What is the difference between the -sT and -sS switches used in nmap scans? Can you use both at the same time?

Q.6 Use nmap to perform OS fingerprinting on a machine and then redirect the output of the scan to a file for later use.

Q.7 Without using nmap, can you fingerprint an OS using Wireshark?

Q.8 How OS fingerprinting attempts made against you can lead to serious damage?

Q.9 Figure out the techniques to evade firewalls deployed in corporate environments using nmap.

Q.9 Is it possible to combine two attacking methodologies, ARP spoofing and DNS poisoning, in order to achieve bigger and better results?

Q.10 Try brute forcing a service in you lab environment and analyze the traffic pattern using your own custom-made dictionary files.

Q.11 Try leaning about brute forcing tools already installed in Kali Linux and figure out which tool is more suitable for RDP brute force attacks.

Q.12 What other filter expression can be useful while analyzing the malicious FTP traffic patterns?

Q.13 Is it possible to force encryption over the FTP session so that the following TCP stream won't show the traffic in normal text form?

Q.14 Why is it important to isolate an infected PC that emits unusual traffic from your network, and what traffic patterns related to it make it malicious?

Q.15 Visit various online CTF challenge websites and try solving a few of them. Do you still find it difficult to understand the challenge, or does it seem a bit easier now?

8

Troubleshooting

This chapter will teach you how to configure and use Wireshark to perform network troubleshooting. You will also master the art of troubleshooting network issues using Wireshark. The following are the topics that we will cover in this chapter:

- Using Wireshark to troubleshoot slow Internet issues
- Lab up
- Troubleshooting network latencies
- Lab up
- Troubleshooting bottleneck issues
- Lab up
- Troubleshooting application-based issues
- Lab up
- Practice questions

The loss of packets during transmissions is one of the most common problems that all network administrators deal with in their day-to-day lives. However, thankfully, we have various built-in error recovery features in the transmission protocol that come to our rescue to deal with the problems. However, it is essential to understand how these error recovery features work in order to troubleshoot the problems by just looking at the packets flow in the list pane if and when human intelligence is required. Troubleshooting latencies or any application-based issues in your network requires you to have an understanding of the traffic flow and the way packets interact with each other. Before we start getting our hands dirty with a troublesome network, we need to understand some basics of the recovery features that would help you diagnose and figure out the root of such problems. Consider yourself blessed that you have the privilege of using Wireshark—the most popular and well-versed tool for network packet analysis—which is an open source tool. This won't state the problems for you, but the time required to troubleshoot network-related issues is drastically reduced.

Now, you might feel like asking the question: "how does it looks like or how you can identify such happenings?" Just as every coin has two sides, the network communication has two ends: a sender and a receiver. On the sender side, recovery features are handled by the **Retransmission Timeout** (**RTO**) values, which are a sum of **Round Trip Time** (**RTT**) and mean of standard deviation. On the receiver side, recovery mechanism is handled by keeping a track of SEQ and ACK values that are shared between the communicating hosts.

You definitely have heard about flow control features, we discussed the same in previous chapters while dissecting TCP-based communications. Flow control features are used in order to keep the transmission more reliable by taking help of dynamic functionalities such as sliding window and zero window notifications. Now that you have the basic understanding of, I want you to understand things in detail. Note that we will talk about TCP-based communication most of the time in this chapter.

Recovery features

TCP retransmissions and duplicate ACKs are the tactics that are used while recovering from a failed packet transmission or an out-of-order packets transmission scenario. Commonly, network latencies (the total time it takes for a packet to be sent along with the time its ACK is received) are observed, due to which the performance of networks are significantly disturbed. When the amount of retransmissions and duplicate ACK packets are seen very often in the list pane, most probably, there is a chance that your network is facing high latencies; if not, then just sit back and relax. My point is that you should be concerned about such activities, and if possible, mix some network management techniques with your protocol analysis that can keep you updated all the time with what's happening inside

The devices use TCP retransmission in order to send data reliably. Values such as RTT and RTO are maintained by the sender of the data in order to facilitate a reliable form of communication. The sender initiates the retransmission timer as soon as the packet leaves the ACK, and when the same is received, the sender stops the retransmission timer. The timer value here determines the timeout value. Now, if the sender does not receive the ACK, after a certain amount of time, the sender initializes the retransmission of the same packet. If the sender still does not receive any ACK, the timeout value will be doubled and the sender will retransmit the same packet again. The same cycle is followed until the ACK is received or the sender reaches maximum retransmission attempts. The sender, based on the operating system maintains a number of retransmission attempts, which are triggered when a certain timeout value is reached.

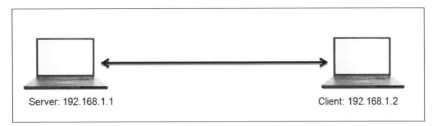

Figure 8.1: TCP duplicate ACK and retransmission

For instance, in the preceding figure, a client is located at `192.168.1.2` and the server is located at `192.168.1.1`. Here, the client is requesting some resource that the server holds, following which the transmission between the two hosts starts after the three-way handshake is successfully completed. For every data packet received, the client sends a `ACK` for the same. Now, suppose that for some random packet in the stream, the server did not receive the ACK even after the timeout value for the data packet expired. The server initiates the retransmission of the similar data packet again. The same process is followed unless and until the server receives an `ACK` for every packet, or the server at `192.168.1.1` reaches the maximum number of default attempts, five, in a row. Refer to the following figure that shows this retransmission process:

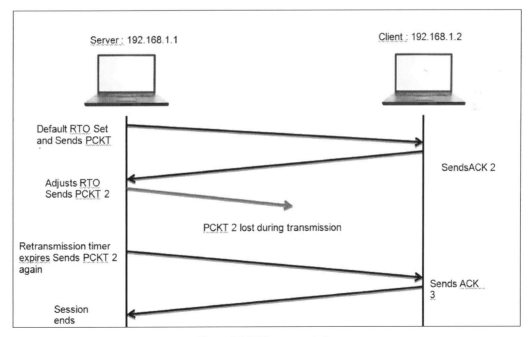

Figure 8.2: TCP retransmission

On the basis of the preceding simplified scenario, I suppose now that you have understood the gist of the retransmission process.

Now, we will discuss duplicate ACKs and fast retransmission, which is another recovery feature that the clients take care of. In the previous chapter, we discussed the SEQ and ACK numbers that are used in order to keep track of TCP-based communication. You might also remember how the ACK values were incremented using the data payload size, where we added the received packet SEQ value and data payload size value and the resulting sum became the ACK value. We sent this value with our ACK packet, and we expect to receive the next data packet marked with the same SEQ value. Suppose that the server starts sending data packets, and the first data packet is marked with a SEQ value of 100 with a data payload size equals 10. Once the client receives the ACK packet, it prepares to send to the server with value set to 110 (remember the formula: *SEQ number received + Data payload size = ACK value*).

As soon as the server receives the ACK packet with the value 110, it prepares for another data packet to be sent with SEQ 110 with a payload size of 10. After receiving this, the client will respond with ACK 120. The same process goes on till the end of the session. Now, suppose that instead of sending the next packet with SEQ set to 10, the server sends a packet with SEQ 130, which is out of order, and after receiving this, the client would send a duplicate ACK set to 120 to the server to recheck and send the missing packet again from the data stream.

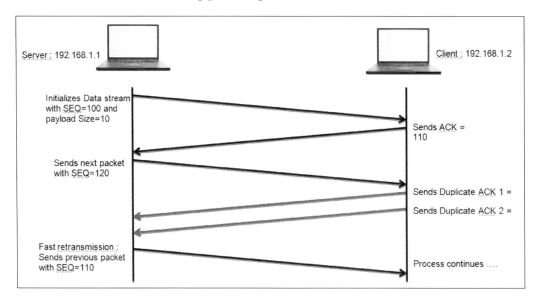

From the preceding scenario, I hope you have understood the process of duplicate ACKs and fast retransmission, which you can use while troubleshooting your real-time network for related anomalies. Before we go ahead and discuss flow control, I would like you to see real packets in my network that are related to both cases of error recovery that we discussed. Refer to the following *Figure 8.3* and *Figure 8.4*:

No.	RTO	Source	Destination	Protocol	Info
18036		192.168.1.103	216.58.220.36	TCP	58915→80 [FIN, ACK]
18038	0.472696	192.168.1.103	216.58.220.36	TCP	[TCP Retransmission]
18044	1.220221	192.168.1.103	216.58.220.36	TCP	[TCP Retransmission]
18056	2.515162	192.168.1.103	216.58.220.36	TCP	[TCP Retransmission]
18067	4.904210	192.168.1.103	216.58.220.36	TCP	[TCP Retransmission]
18075	9.476266	192.168.1.103	216.58.220.36	TCP	[TCP Retransmission]
18082	16.20657	192.168.1.103	216.58.220.36	TCP	[TCP Retransmission]

Figure 8.3: TCP retransmission packets

In the preceding screenshot, a client located at 192.168.1.103 sends FIN and ACK to the server at 216.58.220.36. After this, the client would expect to receive a ACK packet in the next place. However, the client does not receive anything back from the server. Now, after the RTO time expires, the client starts sending the same packet after double the time, and the process of sending TCP retransmission packets after a certain period of time goes on until the client receives an ACK packet or reaches the maximum number of retransmission attempts. Observe the RTO column and how the value starts doubling up until it reaches a maximum limit.

With the next scenario in *Figure 8.4*, I want you to witness the duplicate ACK packet that is being generated because of a malformed packet sent by the server at 216.58.220.46 to the client at 192.168.1.103. As soon as the client receives it, a duplicate ACK packet is sent in response to the malformed packet that is seen out of sequence.

Observe that the 6027 frame with SEQ = 1920 and Data payload size = 46 is being sent across from one host to another. Next, in the response frame 6070, a malformed packet with a random SEQ value was sent in response. Due to this, the host at 192.168.1.103 generates a duplicate ACK packet and sends it to the host on the other side with the SEQ and ACK values similar to the frame 6027. Now, this time in response, the host at 216.58.220.46 sends a valid ACK frame 6115 with ACK incremented to 1966 (1920+46), as expected, and then the communication goes on.

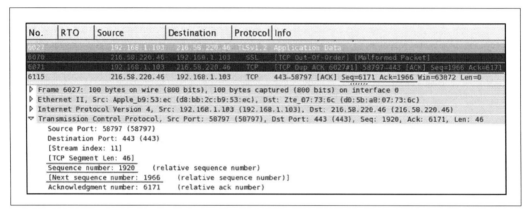

Figure 8.4: Duplicate ACK

With these real-life examples, I expect that you have understood the behavior of TCP error recovery features more precisely.

The flow control mechanism

This is another feature used by the TCP protocol to avoid any data loss during the transmission. Using flow control, the sender syncs the transmission rate with the receiver's buffer space with a motive to avoid any future data loss. Consider a scenario where the recipient has a buffer space of 1,000 bytes available at an instance, and the sender side is capable of sending up to 5,000 bytes per frame. Now, using this information, both the hosts have to sync their window size to 1,000 bytes only to avoid any data loss. Refer to the following figure that shows this feature:

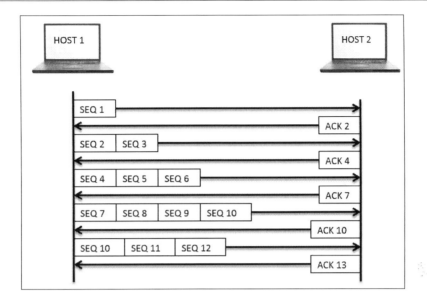

The preceding figure depicts the way both the communicating hosts negotiate the window size for transmission purpose. Observe the behavior, beginning from the frame with **SEQ 1** where **Host 2** responds with **ACK 2** to specify that the frame was successfully received.

Next, **HOST 1** tries to increase the transmission rate to two frames and sends them with **SEQ 2** and 3. **Host 2** responds with **ACK 4**, which denotes that both frames were successfully received. Similarly, we succeed in increasing the rate to three frames.

Next, **HOST 1** increases the rate to 4 and tries sending packets with **SEQ 7**, 8, 9, and 10. This time, **HOST 2** responds with **ACK 10**, which means that **Host 2** receiving the window size can afford maximum 3 frames at an instance, and the sending side should adjust to it.

Next time, when **Host 1** transmits, the windows size would be set to 3 frames, which the recipient can afford to process on his/her end. The window size is not set to a permanent value; it can vary until the whole transmission is completed, and the whole process is called the **TCP sliding window** mechanism and is used to avoid data loss during a transmission.

Think about what would happen if the recipient side is left with no buffer space, that is, 0 bytes. It can handle at some moment during the transmission. What will the TCP do in such case? Will the communication channel drop or the TCP will come up with something more reliable.

Yes, the TCP has another data loss recovery feature called the **Zero window notification**. Here, the recipient side sends a Windows update packet set to 0 bytes and asks the sender to halt the transmission of frames. In response, the sending side will understand the situation and respond with a **Keep Alive** packet that is sent at a particular duration while waiting for the next Window Update packet from the client. Refer to the *Figure 8.6* that illustrates the same.

HOST 1 starts communicating after the three-way handshake process has been completed. After a few packets get transmitted successfully, the receiving side buffer space gets filled up with other resources, so **HOST 2** responds with a Zero Window packet telling **Host 1** to halt sending packets until further notice. Accepting the **Host 2** zero window packet, **Host 1** starts transmitting **Keep Alive** packets in order to keep the connection active and waits for further notice. Once **Host 1** receives the new window size and ACK for the frames that were transmitted, it will start sending the data packets again in accordance with the receiver's buffer space.

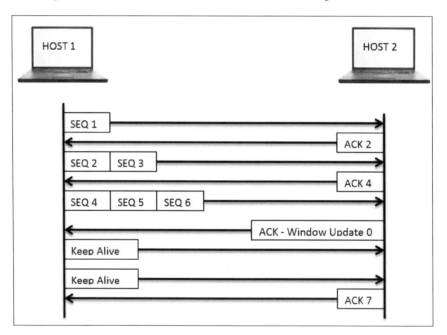

Figure 8.6: The zero window notification

The technique we discussed here is quite efficient in preventing any data loss that might happen during a transmission or due to an overwhelmed sender. The TCP hosts a great mechanism to control the transmission process, thus making it more reliable for any type of communication.

Troubleshooting slow Internet and network latencies

The discussion that we had on delays observed in the list pane can be categorized in two categories: the normal/acceptable delays and the unacceptable delays. Yes, you heard me right, there are some forms of delay that are acceptable, and you should not waste any precious time of yours in troubleshooting any of those cases.

Assign a category to your current scenario on the basis of the test results that you have obtained from the client site (try to put sniff packets from the complaining client's perspective) into one of the following categories: wire latency, client latency, and server latency. Seeing your scenario with the perspective of one of these cases will assist you in solving the problem with a more process-oriented approach, hence making the task less complex, which will end up getting sorted out in lesser time with lesser resources.

Before you start troubleshooting such scenarios, I would highly recommend that you change the default list pane view by customizing the existing time column (customize the time value to `seconds since Previous Displayed Packet`), which would work as a column to figure out latency issues, that is, it will show you the total amount of time between two related packets in a sequence. Refer to the following figure to customize the time column.

To further elaborate the best practices that are followed, I will discuss a step-down approach, which you can use as part of your checklists. Make sure that you understand one thing clearly: tracking an issue can be quite critical on a server side because you may see thousands of packets flying in and out per seconds. This can be really messy and would only end up in making the whole problem more intense. Looking at thousand of packets to figure out the source of slow Internet connection doesn't sound feasible. So, the best option would be to filter out things, prioritize them, and look at the problem from the client's end first.

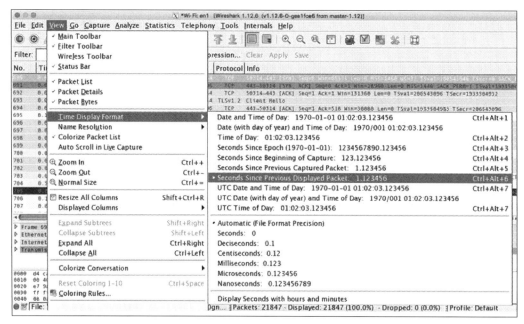

Figure 8.7: Customizing the time column

- Starting your investigation at the client's end makes it much simpler because you won't be dealing with several packets that may not be relevant to your scenario. On the other side, if there is even a hairline chance that you won't be able to see the packets that are relevant to you, this might make the troubleshooting experience a bit challenging.

- Apart from all the challenges that you might face at the client's end, the first thing you should ask your client is to replicate the problem if possible, or if the problem is occurring in a time-based manner, then you should wait at the client's end in order to witness and understand the scenario. The ultimate goal should be to capture the relevant packets and get a crystal clear understanding of the problem that the client is facing from their perspective.

- Now, when you have the trace file in hand, you can look at the process where the client is trying to connect to the server: the whole process where the client issues a DNS query with an objective to attain a server's logical location over the Web. If the local DNS cache already holds the IP address of the server, then you might not observe any DNS packets; instead, a direct SYN packet would be seen in the list pane sent to the server to initiate the independent connection. What you need to make sure here is that if the DNS queries are seen in the list pane, then the round trip time should be low, as expected (approximately less than or equal to 150 ms).

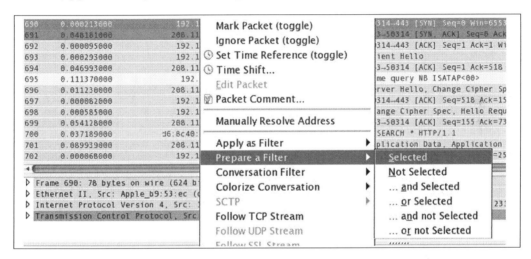

The next would be the three-way handshake packet that you will be observing in the list pane. The best option would be to isolate the communicating hosts that can help you in eliminating any further communication. You can just right-click on the communication and create a filter as illustrated in *Figure 8.8*

- Once you have filtered out the problematic connection between the hosts, the next task would be to observe the total time. The time between duration when the SYN packet was sent and the corresponding SYN/ACK packet was received. This can be compared with the baseline that you already have to come up with a variance that could help you in pointing out whether the connection is slow or is working fine. Refer to the following screenshot that illustrates the same:

Figure 8.8: The time between the SYN and SYN/ACK packets

- As you can see, the time between the SYN and SYN/ACK packets is relatively low, and this seems to be a good working connection. This kind of connections can be helpful while you are designing a baseline for your network. At a later point in time, the same can be used to compare with problematic scenarios. Refer to the following screenshot that show DNS and TCP packets of the same communication:

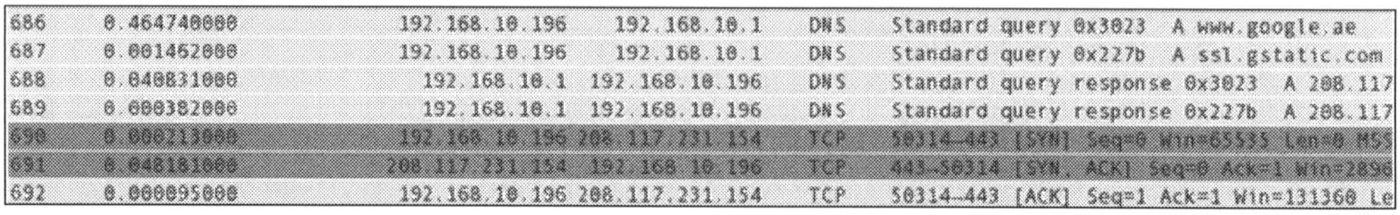

686	0.464740000	192.168.10.196	192.168.10.1	DNS	Standard query 0x3023 A www.google.ae
687	0.001462000	192.168.10.196	192.168.10.1	DNS	Standard query 0x227b A ssl.gstatic.com
688	0.040831000	192.168.10.1	192.168.10.196	DNS	Standard query response 0x3023 A 208.117
689	0.000382000	192.168.10.1	192.168.10.196	DNS	Standard query response 0x227b A 208.117
690	0.000213000	192.168.10.196	208.117.231.154	TCP	50314→443 [SYN] Seq=0 Win=65535 Len=0 MSS
691	0.048181000	208.117.231.154	192.168.10.196	TCP	443→50314 [SYN, ACK] Seq=0 Ack=1 Win=2896
692	0.000095000	192.168.10.196	208.117.231.154	TCP	50314→443 [ACK] Seq=1 Ack=1 Win=131360 Le

Figure 8.9: The ideal baseline trace

- The client issues a request to visit the `google.ae` (frame `686`) website, which the local server acknowledged in order to first look for the IP address in a local cache. Once the local DNS server completes, the search process, the client receives DNS responses including Google's IP address, which can be used to visit the website (frame `688` and `689`).

- As soon as this process completes, the client at `192.168.10.196` issues a SYN request to one of Google's IP address in order to visit the web page. Without any further delay (less than tenth of a second), the server responds with `SYN/ACK`, and the process goes on.

Let's suppose that the total time between the `SYN` and `SYN/ACK` packets is high by approximately 0.90-1.0 seconds. At first glance, you ignore this an move ahead, and you will observe a quick `ACK` packet sent in response from the client followed by a HTTP `GET` request (in case the client is visiting a website). Next, the `ACK` packet acknowledging your `GET` request surprisingly takes more than a second to come. Now, this points to some serious latency issues. The question is, who will be the one you are going to blame—the client or the server? The client did its part by sending the `SYN` packet on time. Then, is it the server who is handling a high load of traffic and is quite busy with other applications, because of which you are handling high round trip time? The answer is neither the client nor the server. Then why is the round trip time high? The probable answer for such cases in my knowledge would be the wire. Yes, you heard it right. The wire can also take part in making your network slower then expected. So, while troubleshooting slow networks, if you observe high round trip times associated with the `SYN/ACK` and `ACK` packets, then you can be sure that your client and server are not the source of the issue.

What you can do is start examining the devices between the hosts, such as the routers, switches, firewalls, proxy servers, and so on. Although the example we talked about doesn't give you the exact source of the problem, it definitely gives you a clear understanding that both the communicating hosts are not promoting any form of latency.

Now, for better understanding, I would like to show you the same in practical terms. Refer to the following screenshot that lists out a few packets shared between two hosts, starting from a three-way handshake:

33	0.000000000	192.168.10.196	128.173.97.169	TCP	50885→80 [SYN] Seq=
36	0.204182000	192.168.10.196	128.173.97.169	TCP	50886→80 [SYN] Seq=
39	0.363438000	128.173.97.169	192.168.10.196	TCP	80→50886 [SYN, ACK]
40	0.000107000	192.168.10.196	128.173.97.169	TCP	50886→80 [ACK] Seq=
41	0.000271000	192.168.10.196	128.173.97.169	HTTP	GET /linux/opensuse
44	0.292131000	128.173.97.169	192.168.10.196	TCP	80→50886 [ACK] Seq=

Figure 8.10: Wire latency

First, the client located at 192.168.10.196 and the server located at 128.173.97.169 start communicating. In the beginning, we see that a three-way handshake takes place between the client and the server, but did you notice the amount of time it took for the SYN/ACK packet to come (more than 0.36 seconds). Look at the frame 39, and it is something that you should take care of. Moving on, we saw one more similar event after the GET request was issued, where the ACK packet took approximately 0.30 seconds to come back. The latency observed is not because of the client or the server, as we discussed earlier. The latency here is promoted by the devices that lie on the wire. The best troubleshooting option in such cases would be to look at the routers, switches, or any firewalls that were implemented without wasting time in troubleshooting the source and the destination.

Client- and server-side latencies

You might think about the scenarios where you would come across or see latency issues that the client/server promotes. Let me explain this to you with some real-life examples; first, we will take a look at the latencies promoted by the clients.

A few days ago, I was just visiting some random websites over the Internet to look for some research material, and meanwhile, Wireshark was running in the background and capturing every packet I was tying to visit. I surfed the Web for approximately 3-4 minutes and then closed the browser as well as stopped Wireshark from sniffing any packets. After the whole thing, I decided to look into the trace file to investigate any client-side latency issues.

Refer to the following screenshot from my trace file, which shows frequent client-side latencies that will eventually affect the performance of my network:

9985	1.002448000	192.168.10.196	149.126.77.16	HTTP	GET /_Inc
10107	0.131159000	149.126.77.16	192.168.10.196	TCP	[TCP segm
10108	0.000558000	149.126.77.16	192.168.10.196	HTTP	HTTP/1.1
10109	0.000064000	192.168.10.196	149.126.77.16	TCP	52043→80
10408	3.540005000	192.168.10.196	149.126.77.16	HTTP	GET /_Inc

Figure 8.11: Client-side latency

As you can see in the frame `9985` and frame `10408`, there are `GET` requests that my machine at `192.168.10.196` had issued, and the amount of time it took was 1 second for the first time and more then 3.5 seconds the next time. I became curious and started thinking about why this happened and what can be the most appropriate reason for such latencies.

Once I started further investigation, I saw that the three-way handshake process happened in a timely manner and there were no signs of latencies. Now, my attention went to my machine. Maybe, there is something that is tampering with my network connectivity. I looked at the resource allocation window in terms of primary memory and CPU utilization. What I saw was that the CPU and memory utilization meter were showing high consumption, which led me to enquire more about the number of applications running. There were three virtual machines running that I forgot to turn off, which were utilizing all the memory. This, in my belief, is one of the strongest reasons, because of which I was experiencing latencies on the client side (my machine). I hope that, with this practical example, you might have understood how client-side latencies can be one of the reasons for low network and Internet performances.

Moving on with this simple example, let's get ourselves introduced with server-side latency issues. I followed the same approach of surfing the Web with random websites while capturing packets with Wireshark for a couple of minutes and then analyzing the cause of any form of latency that can be seen in the list pane. This time, I came across an interesting session between my machine and a website. First, I would like you to have a look at it. Refer to the following screenshot that illustrates this:

498	0.000367000	192.168.10.196	198.41.184.93	TCP	53934→80 [SYN] Seq=0
499	0.006908000	198.41.184.93	192.168.10.196	TCP	80→53934 [SYN, ACK] S
500	0.000101000	192.168.10.196	198.41.184.93	TCP	53934→80 [ACK] Seq=1
501	0.023622000	192.168.10.196	198.41.184.93	HTTP	GET / HTTP/1.1
502	0.007538000	198.41.184.93	192.168.10.196	TCP	80→53934 [ACK] Seq=1
503	0.357595000	198.41.184.93	192.168.10.196	TCP	[TCP segment of a rea

Figure 8.12: Server-side latencies

As you can see, the session between my machine at `192.168.10.96` and the server at `198.41.184.93` begins with a smooth three-way handshake without any sign of latencies. Next, the client issues a web request, following which the server sends an acknowledgement. Uptil here, everything has gone flawlessly, and there were no traces of latencies. However, when the server was about to start the data transfer, the server stopped for a while, as you can see in the frame `503`. The server took around 0.35 seconds to initiate the data transfer. This clearly illustrates that the server might have experienced heavy network traffic, or may be, the server was running several applications that were causing high CPU and memory consumption. There can be several other reasons as well for the latency that we just witnessed. Observing all of it, we can give a conclusion that the server is the reason for the latency; in this case, the server was incapable of processing the client's request in a reasonable amount of time, which ended up as a minor latency issue.

You learned how the devices over the wire, the client side, and the server side can promote high latencies while you surf the Internet or even your internal LAN network can be a victim of the same. We talked about delays before the server's SYN/ACK packet is received. These delays can happen because of the device in between (over the wire) and may be witnessed due to the server's high response time. Let's make things more interesting with a small practical example about identifying high HTTP response time. This will be useful for you to identify high response time. Follow these steps to replicate the same in parallel:

1. Open your browser and visit some websites while Wireshark runs in the background listening to your packets.

2. Once you have visited at least 3-4 websites, you can stop the capture process.

3. Now, switch to Wireshark and make some necessary changes. First, disable **Allow subdissector to reassemble TCP streams**. Select any TCP packet in the list pane, then right-click on the TCP section in the details pane, and then click on the **Allow subdissector to reassemble TCP streams** option to disable it. Look the the following screenshot that illustrates this:

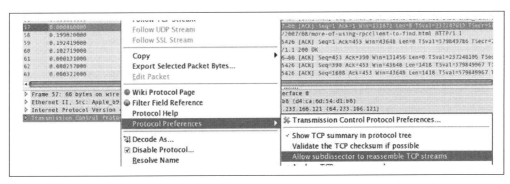

Figure 8.13: Disable the Allow subdissector setting

4. Next, we have to add the `http.time` delta column to the list pane in order to see things more clearly and to easily identify any traces of latencies.

5. Select any HTTP packet from the list pane and then expand the HTTP protocol section in the details pane. Then, right-click on the **Time since request** parameter and click on the **Apply as Column** option. Refer to the following screenshot that illustrates this:

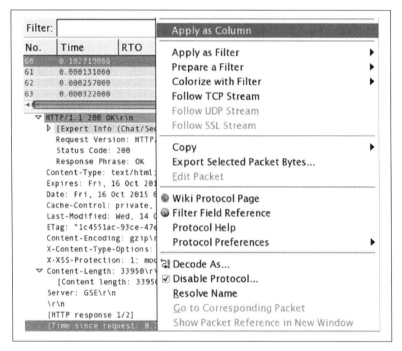

Figure 8.14: Apply Time since request as a column

6. Once this is done, you would be able to see the **Time Since Request** columns just before the info column in the list pane.

7. Now, you are left with just one step: to identify the highest response time from the web servers that you visited. Simply sort the newly added columns in a descending order to the highest response time. Refer to the following screenshot that illustrates this:

Figure 8.15: Sorting the http.time delta column

8. Once this is sorted, you would be able to see the highest response time at the top of the list pane, as shown in the following screenshot:

Figure 8.16: High HTTP response time

9. The session at the top of my list pane between my machine and a web server that I visited denotes quite a high response time of more than a second. See how easy it was to identify the `http` delays in order to make your troubleshooting job easy. I hope it would be easy for you to replicate the same.

You can also achieve this in a visual representation, where you can create an IO graph to identify high latencies. Refer to the following small illustration using which you can replicate the scenario (note that I am using the same trace file that we saw earlier in the previous example):

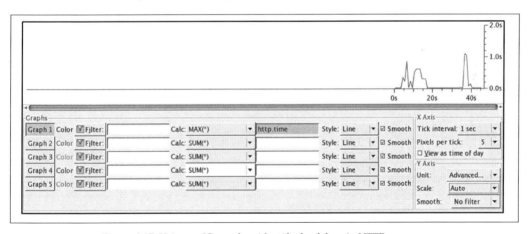

Figure 8.17: Using an IO graph to identify the delays in HTTP response

As you can clearly observe in the graph, the response time for the requests you made took more than a second to complete in a total browsing session of approximately 45 seconds.

There can be multiple situations where you will witness such traffic patterns; this one is definitely because of a web server that makes your web surfing experience bad. The reasons behind such a pattern can vary from a server in a heavy traffic load to a server hosting several applications, or it can be possible that the server you are trying to visit might be consulting some other web server in order to fulfill your request.

Next, let's see an example where DNS queries and their responses are responsible for causing your Internet or local networking experience to suffer. As we saw, other protocols in conjunction with DNS make the whole networking experience better, but at times, the same DNS protocol can cause trouble. Follow the next steps to identify the source of problems using DNS response time:

1. Open your browser and visit at least 3-4 websites. Wireshark should be capturing your web session packets while in the background.

2. Stop the capturing process and apply `dns` as a display filter in your trace file in order to see only `dns` packets.

3. Now, select any `dns` response packet from the list pane and expand the corresponding DNS section in the details pane for the same packet. Right-click on the **Time** parameter and click on **Apply as Column**. Refer to the following screenshot to see this:

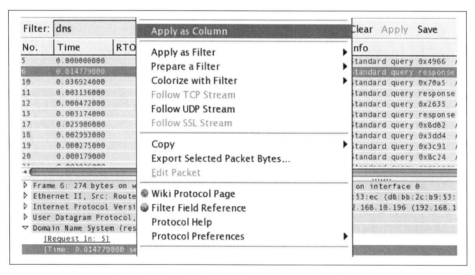

Figure 8.18: Applying DNS Time parameter as column

4. Once you've done this, you will see a time column next to the info column in the list pane.

5. Our next objective is to sort the column in a descending order to figure out the highest DNS response time. Refer to the following screenshot to replicate the same:

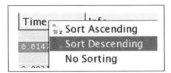

Figure 8.19: Sorting the DNS time column in a descending order

6. Once this is sorted, you would be able to see the session details in the list pane with the highest DNS response time that can be used to investigate further. If the server belongs to your premises, then you are the only one who has to take care of it. Refer to the following screenshot that illustrates this:

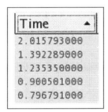

Figure 8.20: High DNS response time

7. Seems like some of the servers are responding really slow, and this badly affects your overall web surfing/networking experience.

8. Similarly, you can create an IO graph to see the whole scenario in a graphical form, and it would be far easier to visualize and understand the case. Refer to this screenshot that illustrates this:

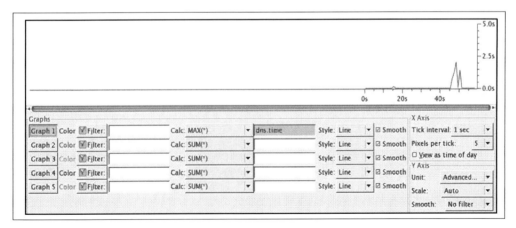

Figure 8.21: DNS high response time depicted with the help of an IO graph

You can easily observe in the preceding graph that the DNS response time was quite high and reached to an approximate of 2.5 seconds, and it is something that should be taken care of.

Through the preceding realistic examples, I hope you have understood the approach that can give you a kickstart in troubleshooting such scenarios in future corporate infrastructures, which you might be asked someday to troubleshoot.

Troubleshooting bottleneck issues

Next, we have a commonly occurring issue in corporate networks. You might have already gone through the harsh suffering of troubleshooting them using various hardware and software tools. The first thing to do is to understand what these issues are and what kind of problems we can we face.

When packets are queued up or there is a delay in the transmission process between the host, which is not expected to happen, you might think "why do such delays happen?" The answer to this depends on many factors such as when your system of the server side is not able to send/receive information with the speed at which it is being processed. These kind of issues severely affect the performance of networks by slowing the rate at which the TCP/IP packets are transmitted, because of which the data between the hosts starts moving back and forth at a comparatively slower rate.

Using my small LAN network, I decided to create an exercise, which you can also replicate on your end easily. For the infrastructure, I have a gateway at `192.168.10.1` and my client at `192.168.10.209`. Refer to the following figure that illustrates this:

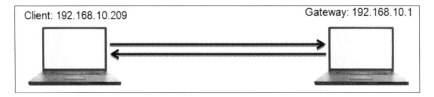

What you need next is a network traffic generator. Research it a bit and try to use anyone that makes you feel comfortable. Lastly, you need a ping utility, which is already installed on every known operating system.

So, here's the scenario. I will start a non-top ping from the client to the server. While the client is pinging, I will launch the traffic generator application, which will try to interrupt the ping process by trying to consume the gateway's resources in order to create a bottleneck scenario for the client.

We will first see a normal traffic pattern in the IO graph so that we would work as our baseline when we would be required to compare with the bottleneck issue. Here is the screenshot for the normal traffic pattern shown in terms of an IO graph:

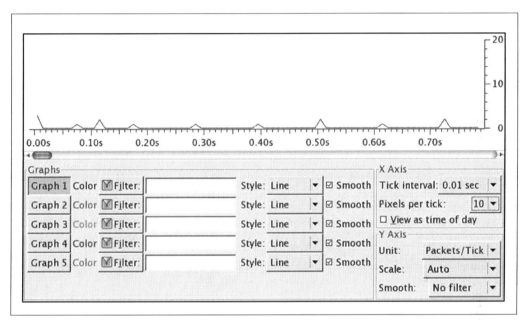

Figure 8.22: Normal traffic in an IO graph

In the preceding graph, no major deviation can be observed; hence, we can include such a traffic pattern while creating a baseline for our network. Just the ICPMP packets are sent from the client to the server without much trouble.

Next, I want you to see and observe the difference between the traffic pattern that we saw and the one below the IO graph, which was captured for the same network infrastructure. However, there was one more application that was involved in the replication of the event, which generated unnecessary traffic. This resulted in network clogging, which is popularly known as a bottleneck.

The application I used is the network traffic generator that can be used to deviate a normal traffic pattern. This results in a network bottleneck scenario and can even result in a denial of service. Refer to the following screenshot for reference:

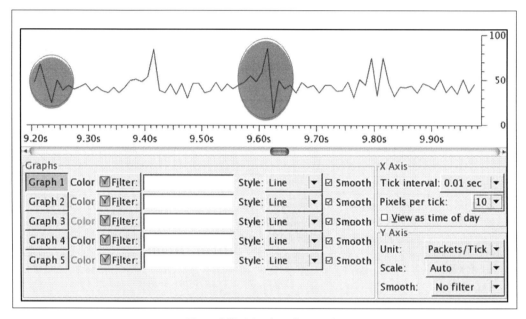

Figure 8.23: A bottleneck scenario

Bottleneck issues are represented by ups and downs, as shown in the preceding graph. The rate at which the throughput drops is the same rate at which it jumps up, and this pattern of deviation in normal traffic denotes that there is a bottleneck being formed.

When every technique you know about troubleshooting fails, then at the end, you can use the network baseline, which can prove worthy while dealing with the slowness of the network. As discussed earlier, a network baseline is just crucial information that you have collected through various points in your network. The sole purpose of the network baseline you have is to compare abnormal traffic with it in order to understand the level of deviation.

We already discussed slow DNS and HTTP responses that make up your web surfing experiences. If you already have a baseline regarding your network, then it would be thousand times easier for you to troubleshoot. You would be able to identify the root cause of the situation you are dealing with, and definitely, this will save a lot of time for other analysis.

Remember one thing that the baseline created for two different networks can vary in vast aspects, so you should not compare them with each another. An interesting and creative way of creating a baseline would be to create separate baselines, that is, one for the network, one for the hosts in your network (how well they coordinate with each other without creating much noise), and one for the applications communicating over a network.

While creating baselines, you can also consider each and every site you are working with separately. In my opinion, the best approach would be break up each site with similar categories. When you are dealing with a WAN, a troubleshooting site baseline can prove useful. Several components can be considered while dealing with WAN sites, such as data transfer rate, several applications in use, the pattern of the broadcast traffic, and various other categories that you may come up with can come handy while making a standardized baseline for a particular site.

Troubleshooting slow networks is definitely a piece of art. I would say, you won't be able to get its real gist unless you get your hands dirty. With experience, you will gradually gain the insight required to solve problems ranging from slow Internet to complex infrastructure-related issues

Troubleshooting application-based issues

There can be scenarios where applications running in your network can be one of the major sources of issues that clients face. You cannot blame the network every time for not working popularly; there can be other reasons as well for the anomalies. When troubleshooting any application-based issue, capturing packets from one end won't be fruitful enough. You should try to move to analyzers all around and capture as many traces of the application's traffic as possible. Capturing from multiple points will give you a much closer insight into network-based applications.

As discussed earlier, you can create baselines by following certain different parameters. Similarly, for network-based applications, there can be a certain defined set of rules, by using which the best baseline for your network can be formed, for example, dependencies applications have another coordinating application, analyzing the startup and shutdown process, the rate at which the application transmits packets, various protocols that coordinate in order to make the application work flawlessly, the way an application interacts with the network once a new installation is in process, and so on.

While creating a baseline for application-based performance issues, it won't be feasible all the time to capture traffic directly from the complaining hosts because it may cause the hosts to suffer high-traffic load and might make it unusable. For your trace file, there might be an unusual number of dropped packets that would get captured and would make your application baseline less appropriate.

As long as dissectors in Wireshark are able to translate the application-based requests and responses in a plain-text format, you are good to go. In the following section, I will take two popular application protocols, HTTP and DNS, to illustrate a few basic scenarios that you can replicate in order to follow the methodology.

First, we will look at the HTTP application-based anomalies. Remember that you should be able to identify the responses from the error-prone application if you are aware of the response code. As you know, HTTP is based on the request/response model, where a client requests for a certain resource to the server and the server responds with the valid resource if available; if not, then with a certain error code, which your browser is able to translate.

HTTP error codes are categorized into five sections of errors, where each error is based on certain logical parameters. To learn more about error code, visit `http://www.w3.org/Protocols/rfc2616/rfc2616-sec10.html`. For illustration purpose, I will explain the procedure so that you can figure out the most commonly seen error code, which is client errors.

The infrastructure I am going to use is pretty simple, easy, and similar to the one that we used earlier. The client is located at `192.168.10.196` and the gateway is located at `192.168.10.1`. I will try to make a few requests to the gateway and a few to any web server located in the wild (note that my intention is just to replicate error code that you can see in the list pane of Wireshark, and not to compromise any web server.)

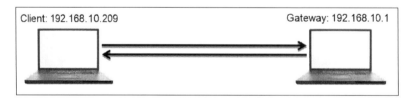

At first, we will try to generate some client error code. Follow the next steps to walk through this; otherwise, you can just read it once and then replicate the whole scenario:

1. Open your browser and visit the default home page of your gateway. Hopefully, it will present you with a login screen like the one shown here:

Figure 8.24: The gateway's Login panel

2. Open Wireshark, and let it run in the background while capturing all your activities.

3. Enter an incorrect password in the password field and click on **Login**. This will show you the **incorrect login name and password** message on the screen or something similar.

4. Next, visit any random website and click on any link. After the link is successfully opened, change the web extension of the web page visible in the address bar to anything such as `.foo`, `.abc`, and so on. Doing this will give you an error on the web page, such as **page not found**. Just ignore it for time being.

5. Now, come back to Wireshark and stop the packet capturing process that we started earlier.

6. You should be able to see a number of packets in the list pane, but our concern in this section is to look at error code messages and nothing else.

7. Now, click on the display filter box and apply the `http.response.code >= 400` filter. Then, click on **apply**. Refer to the following screenshot that illustrates this:

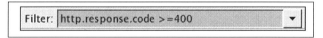

Figure 8.25: Display filter

8. Once the filter has been applied, you will be able to see only those packets that match the criteria. Refer to the following screenshot that illustrates this:

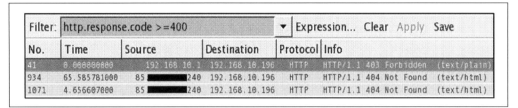

Figure 8.26: HTTP Response code >= 400

9. See, how easily you were able to identify error code from an enormous trace file.

10. You can also create a button for the same. Once you click on it, you will only be able to see relevant packets. You can colorize them for a better viewing experience.

11. We learnt about Coloring options in the earlier chapter. I want you to learn how to create a button for specific display filters this time.

12. Do not clear the current filter; just click on the **Save** button that is next to the **Apply** button in the display filter area.

Figure 8.27: The display filter toolbar

13. Once you click on **Save**, you will be presented with a dialog. To provide a name for the button, specify any name of your choice and click on **OK**. Refer to the following screenshot that illustrates this:

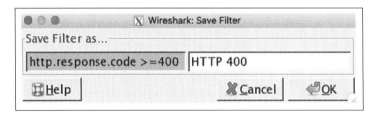

Figure 8.28: Creating a button

14. Once you click on **OK**, you will be able to see the button next to the **Save** button in the display filter toolbar area.

15. Now, whenever you want, you can create a similar display filter without typing it into the display filter box. You just need to click on the button that you created recently.

Figure 8.29: The newly added button

To make this more interesting, I would advise you to create a coloring rule for the **HTTP 404** error. This will definitely help you identify particular error types more conveniently.

Next, we will see another application protocol that is commonly used by various applications in order to translate a domain name to its IP address. Yes, I am referring to DNS. As we know, the DNS protocol runs over a UDP or TCP. There are various response code that relate to DNS errors that range from 0 to 21. The dissectors present in Wireshark do know about response code. Using this, Wireshark is able to show you messages relevant to the error code. To replicate an error, I will visit a website that does not exist on the Web; hence, I will receive an error. But my gateway does not know about this, so it will try to resolve the IP address associated with that name. In return, we will see a DNS response containing an error. The infrastructure is the same that we used in the preceding examples. The client is located at 192.168.10.209 and the gateway is at 192.168.10.1.

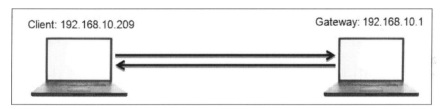

You can replicate the scenario step by step with me or do it later once you finish reading. Follow these steps to replicate the scenario:

1. Open Wireshark, and start capturing. Let it run in the background.

2. Open a terminal (Command Prompt) of whichever operating system you are using, type nslookup in it, and press *Enter*.

3. Now, you'll enter the interactive mode of the `nslookup` tool. If you are not aware of the tool, do read about it before you proceed. There are plenty of documents available for the tool. Refer to the following screenshot:

Figure 8.30: The NSLOOKUP tool

4. To generate DNS error response code, just type any domain name and press *Enter*. Before you specify a domain change the type of query to `A` by using the `set type=a` command and then give the domain you want.

```
Anonymous:~ NotFound$ nslookup
> set type=a
> google.com
Server:          192.168.10.1
Address:         192.168.10.1#53

Non-authoritative answer:
Name:    google.com
Address: 208.117.231.155
Name:    google.com
Address: 208.117.231.154
Name:    google.com
Address: 208.117.231.148
Name:    google.com
Address: 208.117.231.151
Name:    google.com
Address: 208.117.231.150
Name:    google.com
Address: 208.117.231.152
Name:    google.com
Address: 208.117.231.153
Name:    google.com
Address: 208.117.231.149
>
```

5. First, we can try the same for a domain that exists, such as `google.com`. Then, you can try it for the nonexistent domain. Refer to the *Figure 8.31* shown here.

6. The preceding screenshot shows the various IP addresses that are associated with the `google.com` domain. The domain already exists. That's why we are able to see the reply. What if you try a domain that doesn't exist. Refer to the following screenshot that illustrates this:

```
Anonymous:~ NotFound$ nslookup
> set type=a
> charitmishra.co.uk
Server:          192.168.10.1
Address:         192.168.10.1#53

** server can't find charitmishra.co.uk: NXDOMAIN
>
```

Figure 8.31: The nonexistent domain

7. I typed my name in place of the domain name and pressed *Enter*, and this is what I saw because there was no domain with that name. The DNS server was not able to resolve an IP address, hence resulting in the reply `server can't find`.

8. Now, you can go back to Wireshark and stop the capture process. We will now start analyzing error code.

9. The best option would be to segregate the DNS error response code from the normal frames in the trace file that we have. To achieve this, apply the `dns. flags.rcode == 3` display filter, which means that the shown DNS response frame with error code 3 is for nonexistent domains. For more information on DNS error code, visit `https://tools.ietf.org/html/rfc2929`.

10. Once you have applied the preceding display filter, you will only see relevant packets matching your filter expression.

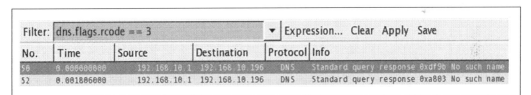

Figure 8.32: DNS error response

11. As you can see in the list pane, only packets that are related to error code 3 are visible.

12. If you want, you can save the filter expression in the form of a button for later use following the same approach we used earlier.

Troubleshooting application-based issues depends on how well you are aware of the error code. There might be a case that you can witness where you don't have the option of installing Wireshark for your assistance. You will be presented with error code for troubleshooting purposes. So I recommend that you at least know about the common error codes in the most popular application protocols that are normally used.

Summary

Troubleshooting is an art that comes with experience, and to become a master in it, you are required to practice things practically on your own.

There are various error recovery features that are provided by the TCP protocol that help us to recover from loss of packets that might happen commonly in a production environment.

TCP retransmission and duplicate ACKs are some of those techniques that are used by the TCP protocol in order to make the life of network administrators a bit more comfortable.

Slow network is one of those common problems that you have to face on a daily basis. Before you start solving these latency issues, you should know the basic methodology that you can follow, that is, to categorize your scenario in one of the latency categories: a wire, client, or server.

Solving bottleneck issues, such as packets getting queued up inside the sender buffer area and causing trouble, is quite important. The best approach in solving a bottleneck issue would be to take the help of IO graphs that you learned about in the earlier chapter to visualize a situation and get hold over it.

Applications use protocols such as HTTP and DNS. This is very common, but you must be aware of error codes these can present, and without using Wireshark, you should be able to identify the situation. I do not know every error code, even I can not do that. But the most common ones that you might witness.

Creating a baseline is one of the most convenient ways of dealing with issues in your network. When you have a trace file containing an optimized traffic pattern, then, by comparing the normal pattern with the deviated pattern, you can solve the issue in less time with few resources. Collect the network traces for your baseline from various locations in your network at least 2-3 times.

Practice questions

Q.1 Create a baseline from different positions of your network regarding various common protocols used in communication.

Q.2 Explain the various characteristics that TCP error recovery features have.

Q.3 Which protocols other than DNS and HTTP can be troublesome for you, and what approach will you follow in order to troubleshoot them?

Q.4 What do you understood by the term "bottleneck issues", and can they be ignored. If yes/no, why?

Q.5 Create a trace file for your own host and at least capture 10,000 packets. Then, analyze how many types of errors you are able to see for the HTTP protocols, and how many of them can you replicate.

Q.6 Using the baseline that you created earlier, try to match an unusual traffic pattern and observe what anomalies you can figure out by the comparison process.

Q.7 For the DNS protocol, replicate an error code other than 3 and capture traffic for the same.

Q.8 Prepare a checklist for the latency types we discussed and mention as many scenarios as you can think about in each category. Once you've prepared this, try using the same in a troubleshooting scenario. Does this speed up your overall process?

Q.9 Try creating coloring rules for error responses for various application protocols you want to and analyze what difference does it makes in the troubleshooting issue.

Introduction to Wireshark v2

9

This chapter will introduce you to the amazing features launched with the latest version of Wireshark. The following are some of the prominent changes that users will become aware of, and all the sample examples in this chapter are being using version 2:

- Comparison between Wireshark v2 (QT) and the Legacy framework (GTK)
- The intelligent scroll bar
- The Translation feature
- Graph improvements
- Newer TCP streams
- USBPcap
- Summary
- Practice questions

Wireshark has been there with us for approximately two decades now; there weren't any major updates that we witnessed during its lifecycle. However, there were minor updates introduced to make the application more convenient and robust during this long period. But this time, we have a newly branded Wireshark v2 with glazing arsenal. Yes, we are really lucky to witness this major update for the most popular and amazing tool in the protocol analysis industry.

I am really excited to discuss the different sets of tools introduced with the latest release, but, before that, it is necessary that you get acquainted with the background of the QT and GTK frameworks. You definitely have to Google these either now or maybe after reading this chapter. However, make sure that you note them.

For your convenience, I will give you a gist and some background of these frameworks; the reason why I am emphasizing the difference between the two is that the newly developed version 2 of our protocol analyzer is developed using the QT framework. QT and GTK are frameworks used for the development of GUI cross-platform utilities such as Wireshark. In general, from the end user's perspective, the difference would be based purely on graphical changes, but performance wise, GTK is more economical as compared to QT. For better understanding, these aren't just toolkits and frameworks; instead, these are sets of libraries used by developers to create better GUIs for end users. Basically, it's reusing the designs already made by others. The main advantage of reusing designs is that it allows the newly installed program to look more similar to the other already installed programs on your machine. For instance, let's see both the new and old version of the application parallelly; refer to the following screenshot for this:

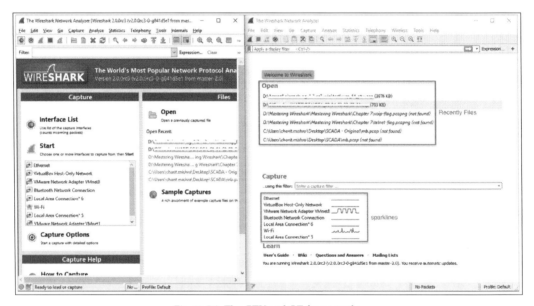

Figure 9.1: The GTK and QT frameworks

You must be wondering how you can get your machine installed with the latest version of Wireshark. It's really easy; you just have to visit `http://wireshark.org`, and then go to the download page. There, you will find the latest release. Download the one appropriate to your operating system. During installation, there is one important question that you will be asked, that is, whether you want to install the legacy version along with the newer release or you just want to install the newer version (note that only Windows users have this privilege; Mac and Linux users can just install the latest version of the application).

There is one more component that you will see being installed on your machine: USBpcap. I have dedicated a separate section in this chapter for this particular topic. For the sake of basic introduction, USBpcap facilitates users to capture data that moves back and forth from your machine's USB port. The tool has been available for Linux users for quite a long time, but luckily, Windows users can also utilize this now.

For starters, let's have a look at the main screen , which has a completely different feel from the previous version. Refer to the following screenshot to get a look:

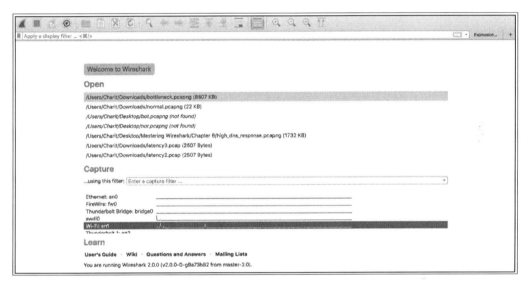

Figure 9.2: The main screen of Wireshark v2

I hope you feel the same way I do about the new, exciting look. Everything in this version looks so properly arranged and cleaner. Even a novice user who has no experience at all in protocol analysis can get a great head start just because this has now become a simple and attractive interface.

Just observe the toolbar area, for instance. In this version, it seems like the developers have filtered out the unwanted and less commonly used tools, which eventually makes the interface quite comfortable for the eyes. In this new version, we have quick access directly to a basic toolset, such as the start and stop capture buttons, the interface customization button, a button to save/open/close the current capture file, some navigational tools, and the auto scroll and coloring activate/deactivate button.

Just below the toolbar area, we have our good old friend, the **Display Filter** toolset, which is redesigned with great efforts. On the leftmost side of display filter text box, you will see a bookmark kind of icon (in blue — top-left corner) that will show you the default and manually created filter expressions. Refer to the following screenshot that shows an illustration:

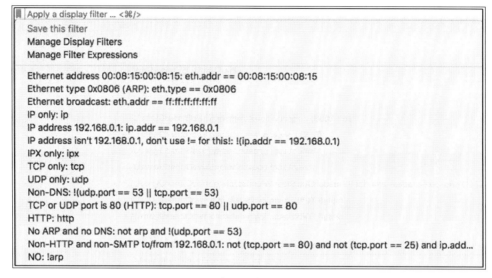

Figure 9.3: The Display Filter toolbar

As you can see, all the filters are listed, which you might have created, or are default ones. So now, it's a matter of just a click if you want to activate any one of them, instead of getting a pop-up window from where you choose and apply the filter, like in the older version. This definitely speeds up the process of analyzing and makes the life of IT professionals easier.

On the other end of the **Display Filter** toolbar, we have a few old tools that have been remodeled in a fresh look, along with some functionality improvements; refer to the following screenshot for an illustration:

Figure 9.4: The Display Filter toolset

To apply any display filter now, you just need to click on the arrow, and the dropdown next to it will give you access to frequently used filter expressions (history of last-used expressions). Then, you have the **Expression** button, which will help you access the dialog where you can get access to all possible filter expressions categorized on the basis of protocols. Next, on the rightmost side of the display filter textbox, you have the + sign; by clicking on this, you can create a filter button. Let me help you in creating one for yourself in the newer version to get started.

For example, I want to create a button to see only the ARP packets, so I will type `arp` in the display filter area and click on the + sign at the end of the toolbar. Then, you need to specify the name of the button you want:

Figure 9.5: Adding a custom display filter expression button

This will add a physical button next to the + sign. This technique will prove worthy and very effective when you have long display filter expressions, which you might need often. So, instead of typing the whole expression again, you can just activate them with a single click. As a result, you will see something like what is shown in the following screenshot. Now, you are just a single click away from applying **arp** as the display filter:

Figure 9.6: The display filter button created

Next, below the display filter toolbar, you can see the recently used files; just double-click on any file you want to open.

After the **Open** file section, we have the capture filter toolbar, and I don't think you need any explanation regarding what it is for and how you are going to use it for your perusal.

Now comes the major change that you will witness on the main screen, that is, the interface's name followed by an interactive graph. The graphs you will see are actually live, meaning you will see the fluctuations, that is, the lines going up and down. The miniature graph followed by the interface name represents the amount of traffic moving back and forth from the interfaces you have. The proper terminology for these miniature graphs is sparklines. In the older legacy version, we had the live statistics in numerical form.

Now, if you decide to capture traffic from a particular interface, just double-click on the graph area, and Wireshark will do the rest for you.

The intelligent scroll bar

This is one of the features launched in the latest release, and you might have already noticed some colored sections/lines in the scroll bar area. If not, then go back to any of the capture files you have, slowly scroll up and down, and observe the coloring pattern in the scroll bar area. Any guesses what difference it would make in the analysis process? Let's understand this with an example.

I will use a previously captured file for demonstration purpose, which has HTTP and HTTPS packets along with some retransmission and duplicate frames. There is no difference that you can figure out at first glance, but as soon as you start scrolling, the coloring pattern will be shown in the scroll bar area. This pattern is based on the coloring rules that you have in your application. For example, as per the default coloring rules, duplicate and retransmission packets are usually seen with a black background and a red foreground, and HTTP packets are shown with a green background and a black foreground. Now, let's verify this in the application itself. Refer to the following figure for the same:

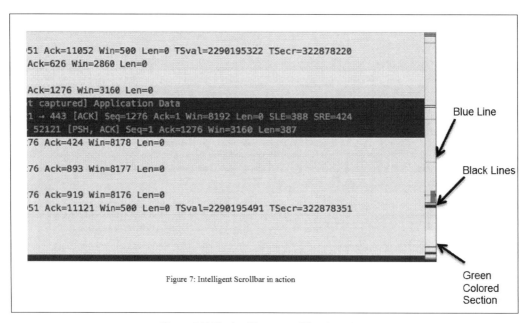

Figure 7: Intelligent Scrollbar in action

Figure 9.7: The intelligent scroll bar in action

The way packets in the list pane are shown in different colors is similar to the way the scroll bar represents the different sections of your list pane.

In the same way that the blue line indicates the selected packet, the black lines denote the duplicate ACKs and retransmissions, and the green-colored section indicates that at the bottom of the capture file, we have some HTTP packets listed. By just observing the coloring pattern in the scroll bar area, we can figure out what sort of packets we have ahead, and most importantly, navigating to a certain section of packets you are looking for is now much easier and faster.

We already discussed customizing the coloring rules in previous chapters; let's take one more example of the same capture file, and this time, I want to customize the HTTP packet coloring rule. We will change the green background color to yellow. Let's see what difference it would make in the scroll bar area in the following screenshot:

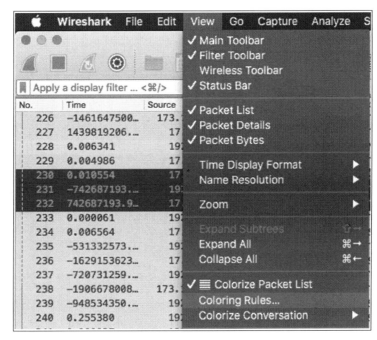

Figure 9.8: Accessing the coloring rules dialog

To access the coloring rules, you need to click on **View** from the menu bar and then choose **Coloring Rules** at the bottommost corner, which will show you the dialog where all coloring rules will be listed. Try changing the HTTP coloring rule to yellow. Once this has been done, close the dialog and reopen the capture file in order to see the change.

Now, try scrolling the same file, and I hope you will see the difference in the coloring pattern in the scroll bar and your list pane too, where all HTTP packets are colored with a yellow background. Refer to the following screenshot:

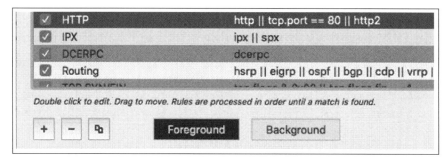

Figure 9.9: The HTTP coloring rule

Now, let's compare what difference it made when we tried scrolling up and down in the list pane after the new coloring rule was applied. Refer to the following screenshot to go through the illustration:

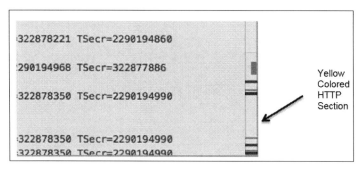

Figure 9.10 Effect of the HTTP coloring rule can be seen in the scroll bar

A good amount of cleanup has been done from the toolbar area where, for example, the **coloring rules** toolset has been removed, and now you can access it from the **view** menu. The + and – symbols at the bottom of the coloring rules window can facilitate you with the configuration of the rules.

Translation

I think this amazing and pretty cool feature is not able to gain limelight, so I want you to know that Wireshark offers you to change the language to any other language of your choice, for example, Spanish, Japanese, Chinese (Mandarin actually), Polish, French, and so on, and this feature has been there their since version 1.99.

Giving the privilege to users to change the default language of the application to their native language is all about personalizing user experience while working with the application. If users feel more connected and comfortable with the application, then they will definitelybecome more productive.

Let's see, with the help of an example, how we can change our system's default language to Japanese (launched with version 2.0). Follow the given steps to achieve the same:

1. Navigate to **Wireshark | Preferences** (Windows users need to navigate to **View | Edit | Preferences**):

2. Now, choose **Japanese** from the drop-down list at the bottom, and click on **OK**:

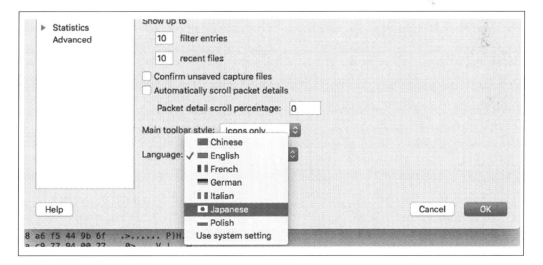

3. Now, you probably will see everything in Japanese, as shown in the following screenshot:

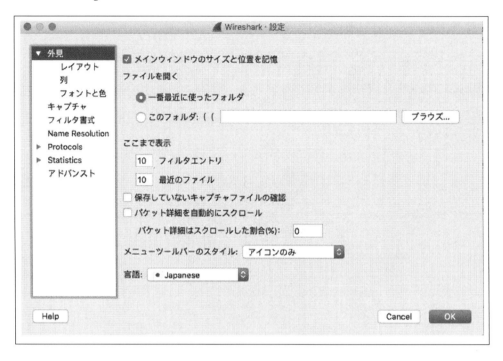

4. To revert it back to System Default, follow the same steps.

The most amazing thing about this is that you can also become part of the change; this means that if you want to help Wireshark's team in adding your native language, then you can get in touch with them.

From the help menu, you can list all the keyboard shortcuts, which can be used to make things work faster than usual. Even to make graphs, now you have a shortcut available.

Graph improvements

This is something that you will be really pleased to know about. Yes, Wireshark has made quite significant changes that will make your analytical tasks more comfortable. To understand the difference, the best option will be to go through an example.

We will try to create an IO graph in order to witness the changes that the new version has. I am using a capture file from the previous chapter, which has mixed packet types and mostly contains VoIP traffic. The sole purpose of this exercise is to see how graphs can be of better assistance in version 2 of Wireshark. Follow these steps to create an IO graph in Wireshark version 2.0:

1. Capture the normal traffic from your network or open any previously captured trace file that you have.

2. Click on **IO Graph** under **Statistics**. Once you do that, you will be directly presented with a graph without any further hassle:

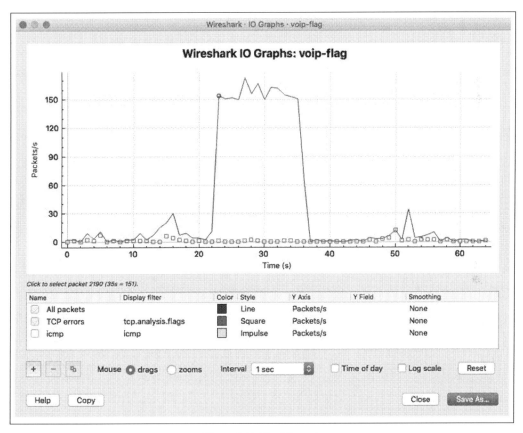

Figure 9.11: The IO graph

3. Now, if you want to modify and configure the graph, then you can use various configurable options given at the bottom of the dialog.

4. For instance, if I want to add any filter to the graph, I can click on the **+** symbol at the bottom and a new line will be shown, as in the following screenshot:

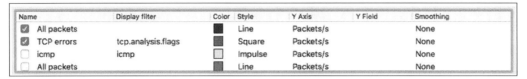

Name	Display filter	Color	Style	Y Axis	Y Field	Smoothing
☑ All packets		◼	Line	Packets/s		None
☑ TCP errors	tcp.analysis.flags	◼	Square	Packets/s		None
☐ icmp	icmp	☐	Impulse	Packets/s		None
☐ All packets		◼	Line	Packets/s		None

Figure 9.12: Adding a filter to a graph

5. Now, I want to see the traffic pattern for the ARP packets along with other traffic-related details. So, I would write `arp` as a filter expression in the display filter column and **ARP packets** in the name column. If you want to customize the look and feel too, you are most welcome to do so.

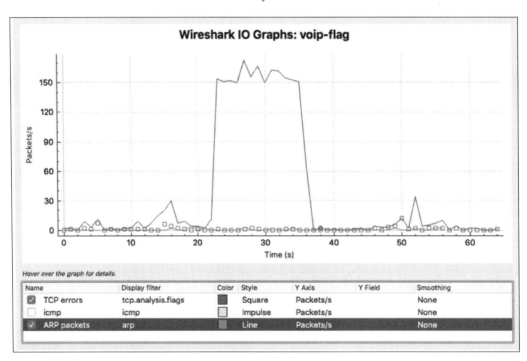

Figure 9.13: The ARP filter added in the IO graph

6. As you can see, our newly created filter is in effect, and we can observe the frequency of ARP packets appearing in our graph as well.

Using graphs is now much more convenient, as you are no longer required to pass any statistical information to the graph. Just choose whichever graph you want, and then the default version of the graph will be presented to you without any questions asked. Now, if you feel like changing the graph as per your need, then just use the toolset given at the end of the graph to custom configure it.

Now, after we have made an IO graph, you will see how clean it looks; there are lots of features that have been introduced. Using the default graph, most of the time you will be able to figure out the ups and downs in your trace file. The legends are shown at the bottom most in a separate section, along with other configurable options like changing colors, hiding or enabling a filter, and much more.

Additional features can be listed and explored in the graphs; all you need to do is right-click on the graph area. The graph can now be moved along with the **x** and **y** axis by just clicking and dragging. Adding new arguments to the graph couldn't be any easier than this. As you can see, so many new amazing features are waiting for you to discover them.

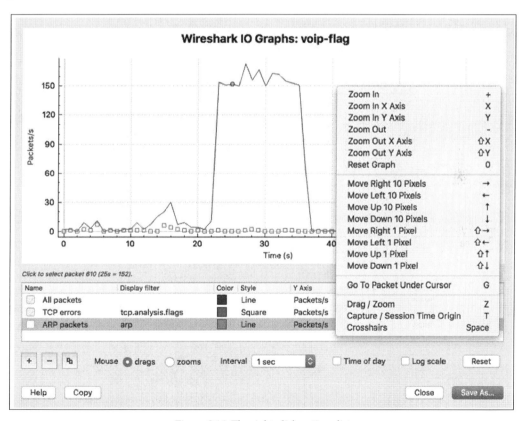

Figure 9.14: The right-click options list

Opening two graphs is now possible; and maybe someday, you will feel like comparing the traffic patterns in two trace files that you have. For example, I want to compare the normal VoIP traffic pattern and the malicious traffic pattern. Then, we can use two graphs to figure out the difference graphically, and it's really effective. Refer to the following screenshots:

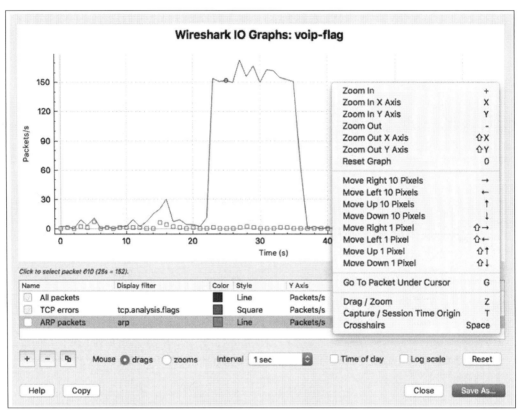

Figure 9.15: Comparing two graphs at a single instance

Similarly, you can create a flow graph that can be of great assistance while analyzing the TCP flow and to know how SYN and ACK coordinate with each other. I would highly recommend that you create the flow graph in the newer version of Wireshark.

To switch between the graphs, you have the drop-down list sitting at the bottom-left corner of the graph window, which can assist you in doing so, and you are no longer required to go the window in the background to switch between graphs.

Another useful feature that can be taken advantage of when you are trying to create reports for your client or maybe for your own reference purpose is to export the graphs in PDF formats. You might have done this before; if not, then let's do this together here. Follow the given steps to do so:

1. You need to click on the **Save as** icon at the bottom-right corner in the graph dialog window. Now, choose the location where you want to save the PDFs and click on **Save**.

2. Once this has been done, you can export the PDF to anywhere you want to. Refer to the following screenshot:

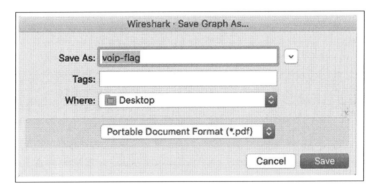

Figure 9.16: Exporting graphs to PDF format

Now, whenever you want to import it into your report, just add it like an image and the graph from the PDF you exported will be added to your document. Doing this is really this easy:

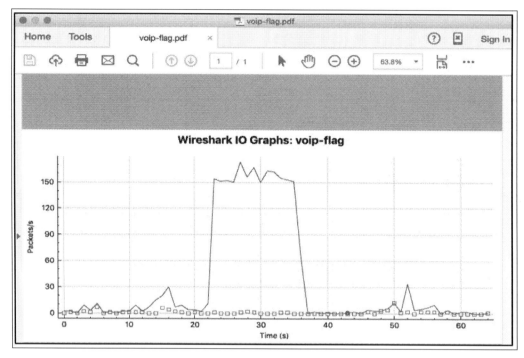

Figure 9.17: The graph exported as PDF

TCP streams

This is one of the features that you might have used very often so far, and I suppose the story will be same for all IT professionals using Wireshark as a utility. The gist of the tool definitely will remain the same in the next version, which is going to come in the future; however, there are some new things that I would like to emphasize. To view the TCP stream window, the process remains the same as usual. Right-click on the list pane area and choose **Follow** by hovering your mouse over it, which will the present available different streams. Then, click on **TCP Stream** options. Refer to the following screenshot to see these steps:

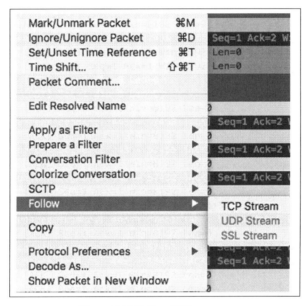

Figure 9.18: Follow TCP streams

Following this will present you with a usual-looking stream window similar to what we have seen in our previous chapters. However, we definitelyhave some new features to discuss, such as the flexibility of moving back and forth between the different TCP/UDP streams available, and the **find** utility that lets you search in the stream window for any text.

First, we will see how you can traverse in between the different streams available in your trace file. Then, we will try to search some text through the follow streams window. Refer to the following **Stream** option screenshot that can be used to traverse between various TCP streams available:

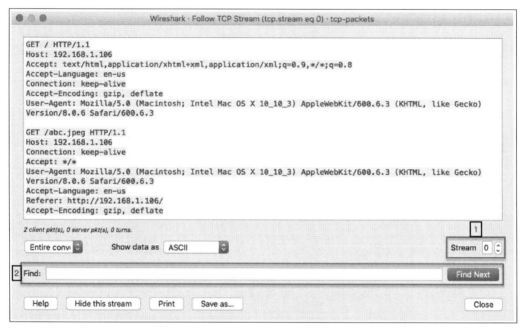

Figure 9.19: Follow the TCP Stream dialog

The stream option labeled (**1**) at the bottom-right corner of the preceding dialog gives you the flexibility to move back and forth between the different streams available. You have two choices here: you can specify the number of the stream you want to look at or you can traverse up or down by clicking on the up/down arrow followed by the textbox. So now, if you are looking for a different stream, you don't have to close and reopen the dialog, like we did while working with the earlier version of the application. Refer to the following screenshot:

Figure 20: The Stream option

The part labeled (**2**) gives you the facility to find any ASCII text inside the Follow stream dialog, which definitely gives an extra mile advantage for every person actively using this beautiful application. Most of the time, when we are using the stream dialog, it is for analytical purpose, and with these new features, our job becomes more easy and interesting. Refer to the following screenshots for reference regarding both the newly introduced options:

Figure 9.21: The Find utility in the Follow TCP stream dialog

For example, if you want to search for the text abc in the current stream, then just type the search string in the find textbox and press *Enter* or click on **Find Next**.

Figure 9.22: The Find utility in the Follow TCP stream dialog

USBPcap

USBPcap has been there from a long time with Linux and Mac users, but for Windows, this is the first time that users will be able to sniff the activity over USB interfaces. So, let's quickly walk through this latest feature and try to understand how to work with it with the help of an example. Follow the given steps to replicate the scenario:

1. After the successful installation of Wireshark on your Windows machine, it is highly recommended that you restart your machine because USBPcap might give you some trouble.

2. After your PC has restarted, open Command Prompt and change your current directory to the USBpcap installation directory that should be located at C:\Program Files\USBPcap\.

3. Now, perform a directory listing using the dir command to check whether USBPcapCMD.exe is present in the directory. Refer to the following screenshot that represents this step:

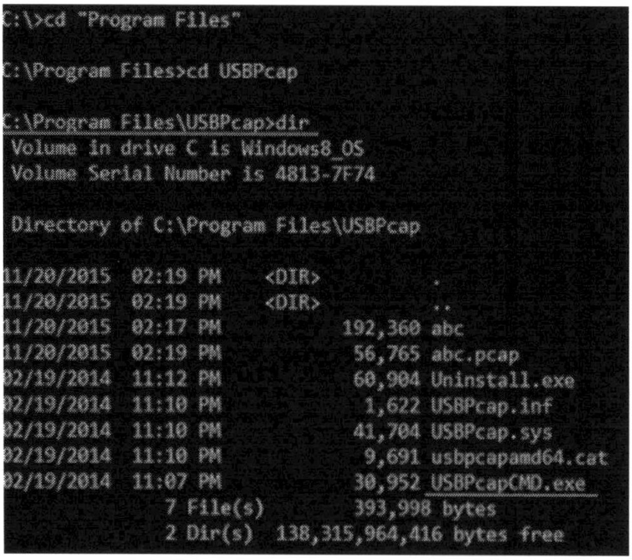

Figure 9.23: The USBPcap installation directory

4. Type USBPcapCMD.exe in the Command Prompt to launch the sniffing application.

5. As soon as it has been launched successfully, you will be asked to choose a root hub over which you want to sniff the traffic and the name of the trace file where you want to redirect the output. Refer to following screenshot that illustrates this:

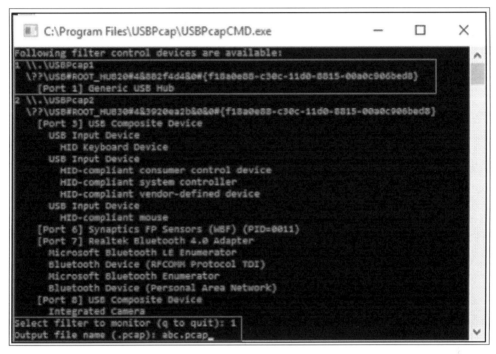

6. Now, as instructed, the application will initiate the sniffing process over root hub 1 and will dump any activity captured over the USB interfaces to the abc.pcap file.

7. Now, try to copy something from your PC to the USB drive or vice versa. You probably won't be able to see any live activity over the Command Prompt, but in the background, it is actually running.

8. Whenever you want to stop the sniffing process, you can press *Ctrl + C*.

9. Now, it's time to open the abc.pcap file using Wireshark to see what we have in the trace file. Refer to the following screenshot that illustrates this:

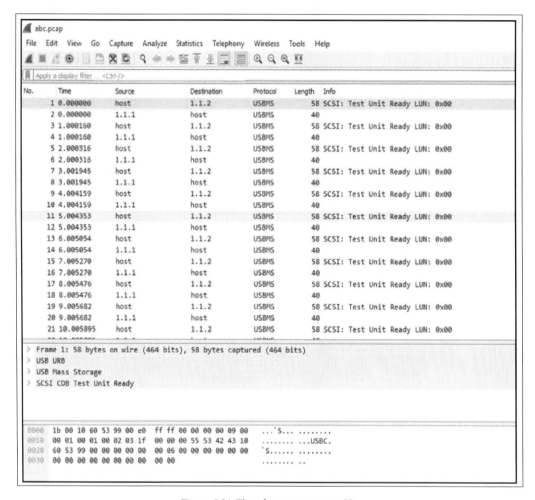

Figure 9.24: The abc.pcap trace file

As you can see, we have an activity, which got captured; it all looks similar to what we saw with network packets. We have all the familiar columns that list out various details such as time, source, destination, and so on. So we were able to successfully dump the activity over available USB interfaces without any technical hassle and I hope you will do some research to get a better understanding about USBPcap.

Summary

The newer version of Wireshark has adopted a new framework that gives us a new and totally amazing GUI. The older version was built upon the GTK framework, and since now we have the QT framework, from the perspective of a normal user, the differences are mostly concerned with its look and feel.

Scrolling is definitely one of the tools that we all have seen in all major applications, but hats off to the developers who came up with such a creative idea of showing the coloring pattern of your trace file inside the scroll bar while you are trying to look for something specific. It does give an extra advantage.

The Translation feature makes Wireshark more international and close to every user in terms of personalization. As many Wireshark users might not comfortable with the English language, now they have the facility to change the language to their native language, which would make the analytical process for a professional more effective.

Graphs are one of the features using which differences between normal and abnormal conditions can be figured out, and are used very often. Now, creating and customizing graphs is easier than ever, and the look and feel has drastically improved as well.

The following protocol-specific streams dialog is introduced with some of the new features that let you find an ASCII string, and it lets you move easily between the streams available too; you don't have to close and reopen the dialog to move to a different stream.

USBPcap has been there with us for quite a long time, and most Linux and Mac users are probably aware of this fact. The way your NIC card lets you listen over the wired/wireless channel is similar to the way the USBpcap option would let you listen over the USB ports that you have. This means that now, Wireshark can also trace the activities happening over a USB interface.

Practice questions

Q.1 Try to find out the major differences between the GTK and QT frameworks. And which one do you think is better?

Q.2 Try out the Translation feature by changing the system default language in Wireshark to any other language of your choice.

Q.3 Create a Flow graph using the newer version and the legacy version, and observe how many differences you can figure out between the graphs.

Q.4 Open any previous capture file you have, and try to figure out how many TCP streams there are in it.

Q.5 Figure out a way to remove the display filter button for the ARP protocol that we created earlier in this chapter.

Q.6 Try changing coloring rules for ARP packets, and check whether you can observe the difference in the intelligent scroll bar area.

Q.7 After installing the newer version of Wireshark on a Windows machine, try to launch USBPcap. Then, copy and paste from your PC to the sub device or vice versa (dump all the activities in the `test.pcap` file).

Q.8 Open the recently captured `test.pcap` trace file for the USB interface activity in Wireshark, and try to figure out what the packets listed in the list pane state. Specifically, try to analyze the values shown in the source and destination columns.

Index

A

ACK packets 170
Address Resolution Protocol (ARP)
  about 4
  poisoning 12-14, 194
advantages, Wireshark
  cost 16
  filters 15
  platform independent 15
  robustness 15
  support 16
  user friendly 15
application-based issues
  troubleshooting 253-259
association request/response 169

B

Base Service Set Identifier (BSSID) 156
bottleneck issues
  troubleshooting 250-253
BPF syntax
  identifiers 33
  qualifiers 34
brute force attacks
  malicious traffic, inspecting 209-216
  real-world CTF challenges,
    solving 216-228

C

capture filters
  example 35
  using, techniques 33, 34
  with protocol header values 37

capturing methodologies
  about 10
  ARP poisoning 12-14
  first capture, starting 20-24
  hub-based networks 10
  passing, through routers 14, 15
  switched environment 10, 11
Carrier Sense Multiple Access and Collision
    Avoidance protocol (CSMA/CA) 155
client-side latency issues 244-250
Command Line-fu 80-86
comparison operators 40
control frame
  about 163
  Acknowledgement (ACK) 163
  Clear-to-send (CTS) 163
  Request-to-send (RTS) 163
conversations 58-60
cyclic redundancy check (CRC) 166

D

deauthentication packet 178
disassociation packet 178
display filters
  about 38-40
  retaining, for later use 41, 42
distribution system (DS) 165
Domain Name Service (DNS)
  about 9, 92
  error code, URL 259
  packet, dissecting 92-94
  packet, fields 92, 93
  query/response, dissecting 94-96
  unusual DNS traffic 96, 97

Dynamic Host Configuration Protocol (DHCP) 145, 146

E

encrypted traffic (SSL/TLS)
decrypting 122-124
endpoints 60-63
Expert Info dialog
about 74-79
Chat section 76
details 78
error section 78
Note section 77
Packet Comments 78
warning messages 77
Extended passive (ESPV) mode 98
Extended Port (EPRT) 100

F

fields, domain name system (DNS) packet
about 92-94
checksum 130
data 130
options 130
urgent pointer 130
window size 130
File Transfer Protocol (FTP)
about 3, 97
communications, dissecting 98
packets, dissecting 100-102
unusual FTP 103
filters
display filters 38
Find dialog
used, for searching for packets 42, 43
flags, TCP
ACK (acknowledgement) 129
CWR (congestion window reduced) 129
FIN (finish) 129
PSH (push) 129
RST (reset) 129
SYN (synchronize) 129
URG (urgent) 129
flow control mechanism 237-239

flow graphs 66, 67
FTP communications
active mode 99, 100
dissecting 98
passive mode 98, 99
FTP packets
dissecting 100

G

Google
reference link 94
graph improvements 272-278

H

half-open scan (SYN)
closed state 191
filtered state 191
open state 191
performing 190, 192
header fields, TCP
acknowledgement number 129
data offset 129
destination port 129
sequence number 129
source port 128
header types, IEEE 802.11 packet structure
control frames 163
data frames 163
management frames 162
HUB 10
hub-based networks 10
hubbing out 11
Hyper Text Transfer Protocol (HTTP)
about 3, 104
request 105-107
response 108
unusual HTTP traffic 109-111
working 105

I

IEEE 802.11
about 154
basic service set (BSS) 155

distribution system (DS) 155
extended service set (ESS) 155
independent basic service set (IBSS) 155
packet structure 161
standards 154, 155
station (STA) 155
wireless access point (AP) 155
wireless communications, modes 155
information gathering
about 188, 189
half-open scan (SYN), performing 190-192
OS fingerprinting 192-194
PING sweep, performing 189, 190
Initial Sequence Numbers (ISN) 132
Institute of Electrical and Electronics
        Engineer 802.11. *See* **IEEE 802.11**
Internet Protocol (IP) 9
IO graph
about 64, 65
creating 273-278
working with 63

L

layers, TCP/IP model
about 2
Application Layer 3
Internet layer 4
Link Layer 4
Transport Layer 3
logical operators 40

M

malicious traffic
inspecting 209-216
management frames
about 162
associate response frame 162
association request frame 162
authentication frame 162
beacon frame 162
deauthentication frame 162
disassociation frame 162
probe request frame 162
probe response frame 163
reassociation (request/response) frame 163

maximum segment size (MSS) 130
Message Integrity Check (MIC) 173
MetaGeek
reference link 158
modes, wireless communications
about 155
Ad Hoc mode 156
infrastructure/managed mode 156
master mode 157
monitor mode 157
strength 158-161
wireless interference 158-161
Multiple-Input Multiple-output
        (MIMO) 155

N

Network Interface Card (NIC) 4, 60
network latencies
troubleshooting 239-243
Nmap
reference link 190
Null Function packets 170

O

Orthogonal Frequency Division
        Multiplexing (OFDM) 154
OS fingerprinting
about 192
active fingerprinting 192
passive fingerprinting 192

P

packet analysis, Wireshark used
about 5-7
aspects 6
performing 7
packets
searching, Find dialog used 42, 43
structure, in IEEE 802.11 161-166
traffic colorization 44-48
Pairwise Transient Key (PTK) 174
password-based key derivation function
        (PBKDF2) 183

ping sweep attack
  performing 189, 190
Point to Point (PPP) 4
port mirroring 10
Pre Shared Key (PSK) 174
processes, protocol analyzer
  analyze 9
  collect 9
  convert 9
Protocol data unit (PDU) 4
Protocol Hierarchy 57, 58

Q

QOS data packet 170
qualifiers
  direction 34
  proto 34
  type 34

R

Radio Frequency Monitor Mode
  (RFMON) 157
Radio Frequency (RF) 158
Read filter 84
Real-time Transport Protocol (RTP) 116
real-world CTF challenges
  solving 216, 217
receive sequence counter (RSC) 174
recovery features
  application-based issues,
    troubleshooting 253-259
  bottleneck issues, troubleshooting 250-253
  client-side latency issues 243-250
  flow control mechanism 237-239
  network latencies, troubleshooting 239-242
  server-side latency issues 243-250
  slow Internet, troubleshooting 239-242
request-to-send (RTS) frame 166
routers
  passing through 14, 15

S

Secure File Transfer Protocol (SFTP) 102
server-side latency issues 243-250

Service Set Identifier (SSID) 156
Session Initiation Protocol (SIP) 116-118
Simple Mail Transfer Protocol (SMTP)
  about 3, 112
  encrypted traffic (SSL/TLS),
    decrypting 122-124
  Session Initiation Protocol (SIP) 116-118
  unusual traffic patterns 121
  usual, versus unusual SMTP traffic 112-115
  Voice Over Internet Protocol
    (VOIP) 116-118
  Voice Over Internet Protocol (VOIP)
    traffic, analyzing 118, 119
Simple Network Management Protocol
  (SNMP) 3
slow Internet
  troubleshooting 239-243
standards, IEEE 802.11 154, 155
Statistics menu
  about 54
  Protocol Hierarchy 57, 58
  using 54, 56
switched environment 10

T

TCP
  about 4, 9, 128
  analysis flags, checking in Wireshark 142
  communicating 130
  flags 128
  graceful termination 133, 134
  header 128
  relative, verses absolute numbers 135-139
  RST (reset) packets 134
  unusual TCP traffic 140, 141
  working 131-133
TCP/IP model
  layers 2-4
  overview 2
TCP sliding window mechanism 237
TCP stream graphs
  about 68
  Round-trip time (RTT) 68, 69
  Throughput graphs 69
  Time-Sequence graph (tcptrace) 70-72

TCP streams
  about 279-281
  following 72-74
Temporal Key Integrity Protocol (TKIP) 172
three-way handshake 128
translation 270-272
Transmission Control Protocol. *See* **TCP**
Trivial File Transfer Protocol
      (TFTP) 146, 147

U

UDP
  about 4, 143
  Dynamic Host Configuration
      Protocol (DHCP) 145, 146
  header 144
  Trivial File Transfer Protocol
      (TFTP) 146, 147
  unusual traffic 148, 149
  working 144, 145
UDP header
  about 144
  checksum field 144
  destination port field 144
  packet length field 144
  source port field 144
Uniform Resource Locator (URL) 105
unusual FTP 103
USBPcap 282-284
User Datagram Protocol. *See* **UDP**
usual SMTP traffic
  versus unusual SMTP traffic 112-115

V

VirusTotal
  reference link 214
Voice Over Internet Protocol (VOIP)
  about 116-118
  packets, resembling for playback 120
  traffic, analyzing 118, 119

VOIP traffic
  analyzing 118, 119
  packets, reassembling for playback 120, 121

W

WEP
  about 167, 168
  open key 167-169
  personal 172-176
  shared key 167-172
  traffic, decrypting 179-181
Wi-Fi Protected Access (WPA)
  about 172
  enterprise 177-179
  traffic, decrypting 179-181
Wired Equivalent Privacy. *See* **WEP**
Wireshark
  about 7, 8
  advantages 15
  analysis flags, checking 142, 143
  packet analysis 5
  profiles, creating 48, 49
  reference link 7, 15, 24
  Statistics menu 54
  working 8, 9
Wireshark GUI
  about 16
  installation process 16-20
Wireshark v2
  graph improvements 272
  TCP streams 279
  translation 270
  USBPcap 282

Z

Zero window notification 238

Manufactured by Amazon.ca
Bolton, ON